Gregor M. Hörzer
Understanding Physicalism

Epistemic Studies

Philosophy of Science, Cognition and Mind

Edited by
Michael Esfeld, Stephan Hartmann, Albert Newen

Editorial Advisory Board:
Katalin Balog, Claus Beisbart, Craig Callender, Tim Crane, Katja Crone,
Ophelia Deroy, Mauro Dorato, Alison Fernandes, Jens Harbecke,
Vera Hoffmann-Kolss, Max Kistler, Beate Krickel, Anna Marmodoro, Alyssa Ney,
Hans Rott, Wolfgang Spohn, Gottfried Vosgerau

Volume 43

Gregor M. Hörzer
Understanding Physicalism

—

DE GRUYTER

ISBN 978-3-11-112500-8
e-ISBN (PDF) 978-3-11-068842-9
e-ISBN (EPUB) 978-3-11-068846-7
ISSN 2512-5168

Library of Congress Control Number: 2020936598

Bibliographic information published by the Deutsche Nationalbibliothek
The Deutsche Nationalbibliothek lists this publication in the Deutsche Nationalbibliografie;
detailed bibliographic data are available on the Internet at http://dnb.dnb.de.

© 2022 Walter de Gruyter GmbH, Berlin/Boston
This volume is text- and page-identical with the hardback published in 2020.
Printing and binding: CPI books GmbH, Leck

www.degruyter.com

Contents

Preface —— IX

List of abbreviations —— XIII

1 Introduction —— 1
1.1 The general aim of this book —— 1
1.2 The line of argument in broad brushstrokes —— 3

2 "I want it all" —— 10
2.1 Substances, individuals, and other particulars —— 10
2.1.1 Early modern materialism and its appeal to substances —— 10
2.1.2 From substances to particulars: token physicalism —— 14
2.1.3 Numbers, deities, and other necessary beings —— 19
2.2 Moving on to properties —— 21
2.2.1 Wholly physical beings: type physicalism —— 21
2.2.2 Narrowly and broadly physical properties, fundamentality and dependence —— 22
2.2.3 Necessarily instantiated properties —— 32
2.2.4 Haecceitistic properties —— 33
2.2.5 Positive and negative properties —— 38
2.2.6 Relations —— 40
2.2.7 Relativizing to worlds —— 42
2.3 Summary —— 43

3 "Physical" —— 44
3.1 Physical properties: a catalogue of constraints —— 46
3.2 *A posteriori* accounts of the physical —— 51
3.2.1 Hempel's dilemma: trouble for currentists and futurists —— 51
3.2.2 How (not) to be a currentist: Andrew Melnyk's account of the physical —— 56
3.2.3 How (not) to be a futurist: Jeffrey Poland's and Janice Dowell's accounts of the physical —— 64
3.3 *A priori* accounts of the physical —— 73
3.3.1 It is none of that stuff: the '*via negativa*' —— 73
3.3.2 Jessica Wilson's mixed view of the physical —— 86
3.3.3 Should physicalism be incompatible with panpsychism? —— 88
3.3.4 Robert Howell's neo-Cartesian account —— 91

3.4	A way out: reference-fixing accounts of the physical —— 99	
3.4.1	Frank Jackson's object-based reference-fixing account —— 99	
3.4.2	Appeal to the common nature of physical properties: a property-based reference fixing account —— 101	
3.5	Summary —— 107	
4	**"The bare necessities" —— 108**	
4.1	Necessitation —— 109	
4.1.1	Why necessitation is necessary for metaphysical dependence —— 110	
4.1.2	Propositional necessitation and the contingency of physicalism —— 111	
4.1.3	Property necessitation —— 113	
4.2	Supervenience —— 115	
4.2.1	Individual supervenience —— 116	
4.2.2	Multiple domain supervenience —— 120	
4.2.3	Global supervenience —— 121	
4.3	Which supervenience claim is necessary for physicalism? —— 127	
4.3.1	The contingency of physicalism, epiphenomenal ectoplasm and other extras —— 127	
4.4	Can physicalism be fully characterized in purely modal terms? —— 138	
4.4.1	The problem of blockers —— 138	
4.4.2	Can supervenience be a metaphysical dependence relation? Considerations on formal characteristics —— 143	
4.4.3	Necessitation without metaphysical dependence? Fine's challenge to supervenience-based accounts of physicalism —— 146	
4.4.4	Necessitation dualism and the supervenience of emergent properties —— 148	
4.4.5	Explanation to the rescue of an ontological stalemate? —— 152	
4.4.6	Necessitation dualism and Hume's dictum —— 155	
4.5	Summary —— 162	
5	**"Higher Ground" —— 163**	
5.1	The characteristics of Grounding: Taking stock —— 165	
5.2	Grounding and the zoo of 'small-g' grounding relations —— 170	
5.2.1	Is Grounding the only game in town? —— 170	
5.2.2	The higher-order property realization relation —— 172	
5.2.3	The powers-based realization relation —— 176	
5.2.4	The determinable-determinate relation —— 180	

5.3	No work for Grounding? —— **184**	
5.3.1	Grounding as a replacement for 'small-g' grounding relations —— **185**	
5.3.2	Full Grounding, partial Grounding, and the strong emergentist view —— **187**	
5.3.3	The priority argument: Grounding as a priority-fixing relation —— **193**	
5.3.4	The unity argument: Grounding as a unifier of 'small-g' grounding relations —— **203**	
5.4	Grounding Grounding —— **213**	
5.4.1	What Grounds Grounding? —— **214**	
5.4.2	Grounding Grounding in the natures of the relata —— **215**	
5.4.3	Lessons from the debate about Grounding Grounding —— **221**	
5.5	Summary —— **224**	
6	**Conclusion** —— **225**	

Bibliography —— **228**

Index of names —— **238**

Index of subjects —— **240**

Preface

This book is a revised version of my doctoral dissertation, which I successfully defended in August 2018 at Osnabrück University, Germany. When I started this project, I knew that I wanted to work on metaphysical questions concerning physicalism, but it took a while until it began to dawn on me that I did not really know what the thesis of physicalism is in the first place, and this was not due to not knowing the literature on the topic well enough. I thus investigated this question in more detail, singled out further questions I needed to address in order to come closer to an answer, and tried to answer them in a reasonable way. The outcome of the process of thinking hard about these issues for a few years is the book at hand.

The thesis of *physicalism* is the contemporary descendant of early modern materialism, as prominently defended by Thomas Hobbes, combined with some aspects of the positivist views about the priority of physics over the other sciences put forward by Rudolf Carnap and Otto Neurath, who first introduced the term 'physicalism' in the early 1930s. Many different variants of physicalism have been proposed by advocates of the view, and rejected by their pluralist rivals. However, not only is it difficult to frame a watertight argument for or against the view, it also turns out to be notoriously difficult to formulate what exactly the thesis of physicalism is in the first place. There are, of course, some rough-and-ready formulations virtually everybody agrees to, which I use as a starting point for my inquiry. One can say either that physicalism is the thesis that (i) *everything is physical*, or that it is the claim that (ii) *there is nothing over and above the physical*. In order to transform these very crude formulations into a substantial one, I address three questions: *First*, drawing on formulation (i), I clarify what it means to say that *everything* is physical. What entities is physicalism concerned with, and what kinds of entities do we have to explicitly ascribe *being physical* to? I suggest that we need to focus on properties of individuals. *Second*, again drawing on formulation (i), I address what it means to say that everything is *physical*, and more specifically, what it means for a property to be a physical property. I consider the options available in the literature, reject the standard views, and develop an alternative account based on the idea that physical properties share a common nature. *Third*, drawing on formulation (ii), I analyze what it means to say that a property is *nothing over and above* certain other properties. Formulation (i) might suggest that the relation in question is identity, but I argue that although identity can indeed account for nothing-over-and-above-ness, a weaker notion of *metaphysical dependence* also suffices to capture the relevant idea of nothing-over-and-above-ness and enables us to properly draw the boundary between physicalist views and their pluralist rivals. However, the required notion of metaphysical dependence goes beyond the purely modal notions of necessitation and supervenience, and more closely resembles the notion of Grounding that has recently taken center stage in the metaphysics literature. In sum, the answers to these three questions provided in this book combine into a comprehensive picture that helps us to better understand physicalism.

A number of people have contributed in different ways to make this project possible, and I am very grateful for their support. Sven Walter has been an excellent advisor. He left me with enough freedom to work on a topic that is somewhat untypical for a dissertation at a cognitive science department, and provided me with many insights and helpful comments, not only regarding the content of this book. Most importantly, he showed me how encouraging and fruitful the relationship between a professor and a doctoral student can be. I am very happy to have him as my *Doktorvater*.

My current and former colleagues at the cognitive science department as well as the philosophy department at Osnabrück University contributed to the warm and friendly working environment I find myself in. Without them, my time in Osnabrück would not have been the same: Benjamin Angerer, Diego Azevedo Leite, Lasse Bergmann, Frieder Bögner, Susanne Boshammer, Samuel Cosper, Armin Egger, Sascha Fink, André Grahle, Nikola Kompa, Charles Lowe, Imke von Maur, Uwe Meyer, Jumana Yahya (Morciglio), Anna Nuspliger, Asena Paskaleva-Yankova, Andrea Robitzsch, Sebastian Schmoranzer, Stefan Schneider, Kathrin Schuster, Achim Stephan, Jennifer Wagner, Sven Walter, and Carlos Zednik.

I learned a lot about metaphysical dependence from Jessica Wilson during the summer course she taught at the University of Hamburg in 2017. Frances Egan and Brian McLaughlin made possible my research stay at Rutgers University in New Brunswick, NJ, USA, in early 2018, funded by the DAAD. I made a lot of progress writing this book during that time. Brian McLaughlin also agreed to join Sven Walter and Achim Stephan in taking up the laborious task of thoroughly reading the dissertation manuscript and writing a referee report. Uwe Meyer and Kai-Uwe Kühnberger joined the defense committee. Malte Achenbach helped me a lot in setting up the index at the end of this book.

A few more people made substantial contributions along the way. Michael Seitlinger, a fellow student at the University of Technology in Graz, Austria, encouraged me to take my very first philosophy class at the University of Graz back in 2004. At the time, I did not even have a clear conception of what philosophy is, but it did not take long before I was hooked. Martina Fürst established the contact to Sven Walter in 2012. Without her, I would probably never have come to Osnabrück. Last, but not least, thanks to Hannes Fraissler, with whom I had many insightful philosophical discussions over the years since I got to know him as a fellow student at the University of Graz.

On a more personal note, I would like to thank Sabine Weißenberg and her family for their ongoing support since the time I first came to Osnabrück as a visiting student in 2012, and for enduring all my enthusiastic monologues about philosophical issues. Finally, I am deeply grateful to my family for the unconditional support and encouragement they have provided to me throughout my life. This applies in particular to my siblings Markus and Michael, my mother Friederike, as well as my father Josef Hörzer, who sadly did not live to see this project finished. Thanks for everything!

Gregor M. Hörzer
Osnabrück, February 2020

List of abbreviations

GN	Global necessitation
IN	Individual necessitation
MP	Moderate physicalism
MSS	Strong multiple domain supervenience
MWS	Weak multiple domain supervenience
NFM	Non-fundamental mentality
NP	Nonphysical properties
PM	Priority monists
PP	Priority pluralists
RMP	Reasonably moderate physicalism
RR	Relevant Rival
SD	Shamik Dasgupta
SI	Système international (d'unités) – International system of units
SP	Strong physicalism
SR	Scientific Realist
TDS	Trans-world disposition set
WP	Weak physicalism

1 Introduction

1.1 The general aim of this book

This book is in a certain respect different from many other philosophical works. In most cases, the aim of a philosophical project is to argue for, or sometimes against, a particular thesis. This is not what I aim for here, at least not with regard to the main thesis under consideration: *physicalism*. Rather than trying to argue that physicalism is true, or that physicalism is false, I take a step back and focus on the question of how to best understand the thesis. The thesis is easy to express very roughly. Physicalism is the claim that *everything is physical*, or maybe more accurately, that *there is nothing over and above the physical*. However, spelling out the thesis in a more exact and rigorous manner is more difficult than one might expect.

Among contemporary philosophers, physicalism is one of the most widely accepted views in the philosophy of mind and metaphysics. According to a recent survey of Bourget and Chalmers (2014), the majority of philosophers accept or at least lean towards the view.[1] Some (Gillett and Loewer 2001: ix) even take physicalism to be the *Weltanschauung* of much of contemporary philosophy. Moreover, most scientists, while not in general acquainted with the vast amount of philosophical literature and debates concerning the topic, would likely agree to something like the core idea because it is closely intertwined with our scientific worldview.

Given the pervasiveness of physicalism, one might think that it is perfectly clear, at least within the philosophical community, what exactly the thesis of physicalism amounts to. After all, it seems reasonable to assume that we need to understand the thesis we are concerned with in order to argue for or against its truth. It is thus somewhat surprising to note the great number and diversity of characterizations of the thesis proposed by authors writing on the topic, provided they offer a characterization at all. The question of how to best formulate the thesis of physicalism is all but settled. In fact, given the wide variety of characterizations, it may even seem that there is no single thesis of physicalism at all.

---

[1] Here are the details: Among 931 academic philosophers who participated in the survey, 56.6 percent responded that they accept (34.6%) or lean toward (21.9%) physicalism, whereas only 27.1 percent accept (14.2%) or lean toward (12.9%) non-physicalism. The rest is undecided/agnostic (2.5%), claim to accept an intermediate view (2.4%), or considers the question too unclear to answer (6.3%). Note also that the question is aimed at physicalism about the mental (Bourget and Chalmers 2014: 496).

Still, it is at least plausible that there is something like a minimal set of characteristics that different physicalist views have in common and that make up the core of what we might call 'minimal physicalism'. Different physicalist views add further commitments to this core thesis of minimal physicalism. As we will see, there are also some views that are not to be considered proper physicalist views by our contemporary standards even though they are traditionally so-called.

In this book, I focus on how we should interpret the thesis of minimal physicalism in a way that enables us to distinguish the view from its traditional rivals, respects the current state of the relevant debates, and takes into account the intellectual ancestry of contemporary physicalist views. These views have two main origins: the metaphysical views of early modern materialists like Thomas Hobbes, who opposed their dualist and idealist rivals like René Descartes and Bishop George Berkeley, on the one hand, and the views regarding the privileged status of physics in the hierarchical picture of the sciences in the works of positivist thinkers like Rudolf Carnap (1931; 1932) and Otto Neurath (1931), who first introduced the term 'physicalism' into the philosophical landscape, on the other hand. Interestingly, while physicalism, as understood today, is a metaphysical thesis, Carnap and Neurath had an outspoken anti-metaphysical stance, so the conception associated with the term 'physicalism' shifted during the 20th century. Nevertheless, there is still a component in the understanding of contemporary physicalism that pays tribute to its ancestry.

The term 'physicalism' is often more narrowly understood to express a thesis about the mental domain only. However, I focus on a characterization of physicalism as a general thesis, or physicalism *simpliciter*. Nevertheless, the mental domain plays a major role in the case of the more general thesis as well, because it is arguably the domain that leads to the most substantial troubles when arguing for the truth of the thesis. As already mentioned, there are two rough-and-ready formulations of physicalism that can serve as a starting point for further inquiry into the question of how to spell out the thesis more precisely. We can either say that (i) physicalism is the thesis that *everything is physical*, or that (ii) physicalism is the thesis that *there is nothing over and above the physical*. On the basis of these two formulations, I distinguish and address three questions that need to be answered in order to fully understand the thesis of physicalism. *First*, drawing on formulation (i), I focus on the question of what it means to say that *everything* is physical, or, what entities physicalism is concerned with. Do physicalists really want to claim that everything whatsoever is physical, or is the claim restricted to certain categories of entities? A closely related question is what categories we need to explicitly quantify over in formulating the thesis of physicalism. I evaluate and adapt various candidate phrasings in order to develop one I consider suitable to capture what physicalism intuitively is concerned with. *Second*, again drawing on formulation (i), I move on to clarify what it means that everything is *physical*. In other words, having settled on a conception of what categories the thesis quantifies over and which entities it attributes *being physical* to, I provide an account of what it means for entities from these categories to be *physical* entities. This question has only relatively recently begun to receive the attention it deserves. I discuss the options available in the literature, reject the whole range of standard views, and develop an alternative account. *Third*, drawing on formulation (ii), I clarify what it means for an entity to be *nothing over and above* some other entity. Formulation (i) might suggest that the relation in question is identity, but it is widely accepted that a relation weaker than identity suffices for physicalism to be true. What is needed is a relation of *metaphysical dependence* that can plausibly serve to capture nothing-over-and-above-ness in a way that enables us to draw the boundary between physicalism and its pluralist rivals.

1.2 The line of argument in broad brushstrokes

With regard to the question of which entities physicalism is concerned with, I argue in chapter two ("I want it all") that in order for physicalism to be true, the entities that must be physical are particulars like objects, for which I also use the term 'individuals', and maybe also events and facts. There are however some particulars physicalism is arguably not concerned with – those that are neither contingent nor causal entities. This restriction makes physicalism compatible with certain realist views about numbers, which, even if non-physical, are not to be considered a challenge for physicalism (cf. Melnyk 2003). I distinguish between different ways in which we attribute *being physical* to particulars, and argue that the way such entities are required to be physical derives from the relation between the property types these entities instantiate and physical property types. A mere claim of identity or metaphysical dependence of token instances of properties on instances of physical properties, at least without further commitments, is arguably not sufficient to capture the views of contemporary physicalists. While such a view rules out substance dualism, property dualists can also adopt it.

Physicalism rather requires that every property *type* instantiated by an individual is either a physical property type or metaphysically depends on physical property types, unless it is a property type that is necessarily instantiated by any individual whatsoever. I add the latter constraint to ensure that properties like *being self-identical* or *being such that 2+2=4* need not be physical properties or metaphysically depend on physical properties in order for physicalism to be true. I further address different notions of fundamentality and their viability as alternatives to the notion of metaphysical dependence for characterizing physicalism, as considered by Wilson (2018), and their connection to Schaffer's (2003) view according to which we have no clear evidence that there is a fundamental level. Moreover, I consider whether physicalism is to be considered compatible with the instantiation of haecceitistic properties, i.e. properties the instantiation of which requires the existence of a specific particular. Some explicitly exclude such properties from their framework in the first place (e.g. Chalmers 1996: 367), others claim that physicalism is incompatible with them (e.g. Hofweber 2005). I side with Chalmers in these regards, and argue that we do not need to worry much about haecceitistic properties in a physicalist framework. Furthermore, I discuss a much neglected aspect of physicalist claims, which is usually either completely neglected or brushed aside in a footnote: the explicit treatment of relations among individuals as an element of the physicalist thesis. Finally, I relativize the physicalist thesis to worlds. After all, we do not always want to only evaluate whether physicalism is true of our world. A physicalist thesis that is relativized to possible worlds enables us to address whether physicalism would be true if certain things were different than they actually are.

In chapter three ("Physical"), I discuss the question of how to understand the notion of a *physical* property. The most common view is to claim that physical properties are just those properties that are picked out by predicates of physics. This understanding immediately gives rise to a dilemma, however, first considered by Hempel (1980). Which physics is the relevant one: current or future physics? If it is current physics, then physicalism is very likely false, because current physics is probably incomplete and additional properties are going to be needed in the dependence base that would not count as physical on such a view. Melnyk (1997; 2003) tries to blunt this horn of the dilemma and accepts that physicalism as he construes it is likely false, but his arguments are unconvincing. One important reason, among others, is that if physicalism were indeed quite obviously false due to the incompleteness of physics, it cannot be the thesis that is most frequently challenged by using complex conceivability arguments like the zombie argument (Chalmers 1996; 2010) and the knowledge argument (Jackson 1982). If the relevant physics is future (or final, ideal) physics, then the thesis of physicalism lacks content because we do not know what future physics will be concerned with. We should also avoid defining 'future physics' as "the fundamental theory of everything". Tying physicalism to that notion of future physics would make physicalism a trivially true thesis. Moreover, some have considered a situation in which future physicists incorporate predicates like '… is an immaterial soul' into their theories. It seems odd to think that physicalism in such a case would turn out to be compatible with the existence of immaterial souls after all (see Montero 1999: 192, who attributes the worry to Chomsky 1993; 1995). Poland (1994) and Dowell (2006b) bite the bullet, but their criteria for an acceptable incorporation of entities into physical theories are too weak. Furthermore, as long as we tie the notion of a physical property too tightly to any *actual* physical theory, we cannot account for the idea of *alien* physical properties, i.e. properties we would clearly count as physical if they were instantiated, but which are in fact never instantiated and thus not addressed by any actual world physics (Stoljar 2010: ch. 4). Thus, notions of the physical tied to some particular actual world physics would at most allow us to characterize physicalism for the actual world, rather than for arbitrary possible worlds.

An alternative account of the physical that has gained some popularity in recent years because it completely avoids Hempel's dilemma is a view sometimes called the '*via negativa*' (e.g. Montero 1999; Spurrett and Papineau 1999; Crook and Gillett 2001; Montero and Papineau 2005). The basic idea is to provide a negative characterization of the physical as the non-mental. However, defenders of such a view must be careful to avoid understanding the term 'non-mental' in a way that trivially rules out views that take mental properties to be identical to physical properties. Even if this concern can be accounted for, however, such an account makes it difficult to distinguish between a domain-specific physicalism about the mental and a general, non-domain-specific physicalism, because it is overly inclusive with regard to what counts as physical.

There are also some accounts which mix aspects of the different views discussed so far, conjoining a clause that ties the notion of the physical to one or another physical theory with a clause that rules out as physical certain entities, especially mental ones, on *a priori* grounds (e.g. Wilson 2006). In turn, such a view renders certain live panpsychist accounts conceptually incoherent, which is unacceptable. In fact, we should not rule out the identity of mental and physical entities at all, the only thing we should make sure is that we do not trivially include them by including mental predicates into our physical theories. Following Lewis (1983: 362–363), I even consider some versions of panpsychism (e.g. those that are a version of the identity theory) to be compatible with physicalism, so we need to be careful not to rule out too much. Furthermore, I discuss Howell's (2013) neo-Cartesian account and Jackson's (1998) account that tries to fix the reference by pointing at paradigmatic physical objects. However, I find both accounts wanting, because they also rule out certain views as false or even incoherent that cannot be so easily dismissed.

Instead, I argue for an often-overlooked account that draws to some extent on Jackson's account, but does not run into the same problems. According to this view, physical properties are those which, broadly speaking, resemble paradigmatic properties of current physics in a certain respect, where the resemblance relation in question is a *sameness-in-kind* relation (for related views, see Nimtz and Schütte 2003: 419; Díaz-León 2008: 99). The underlying idea is closely connected to Strawson's claim that "'[p]hysical' is a natural-kind term – it is the ultimate natural-kind term" (2008 [2003]: 20). This view of the physical is not susceptible to the first horn of Hempel's dilemma because the ties to current physics are weak enough to be able to account for some as-of-yet unknown properties of future physics as well as physical properties alien to our world. Moreover, it is not susceptible to the second horn of Hempel's dilemma either, because the connection to paradigmatic properties from current physics gives the theory the required content, and the account does not allow for dualism to sneak in through the back door. Finally, the view accounts for the intuition that physics is concerned with the entities it is concerned with *because they are physical* rather than that those entities are physical *because physics is concerned with them*.

In chapters four ("The bare necessities") and five ("Higher Ground"), I address the last of the three questions, namely how to appropriately spell out *nothing-over-and-above-ness* or *metaphysical dependence* in the characterization of physicalism. In accordance with a view of metaphysics that focuses on questions regarding *structure* instead of merely on questions regarding *existence* (e.g. Schaffer 2009; Sider 2011), we need to address how everything else is linked to the physical in order to understand the thesis of physicalism. In chapter four, I focus on attempts to spell out metaphysical dependence in purely modal terms, and discuss the modal commitments physicalism comes along with. After the (at least partial) demise of traditional type identity theory (Place 1956; Smart 1959) due to arguments from multiple realizability (Putnam 1975b [1967]) as well as due to modal considerations (Kripke 1980: 148–155), the candidate relation that has dominated the literature for almost the last half century is the relation of supervenience (e.g. Kim 1993d [1984]; 1993e [1987]; McLaughlin 1995) and the related necessitation relation. Supervenience relations feature prominently in many attempts to formulate physicalism, either explicitly or implicitly (e.g. Lewis 1983; Chalmers 1996; Jackson 1998). However, in order to preserve the contingency of physicalism, the ties between metaphysical dependence and supervenience have to be weaker than one might initially expect. Nevertheless, physicalism clearly entails some supervenience claim. After all, the central arguments against the view are all based on the idea that such an entailment holds, and thinking otherwise does not properly respect one of the basic presumptions that virtually all advocates and adversaries of the thesis agree upon.

Over the years, philosophers have started to realize that supervenience and necessitation, being purely modal notions, fail to account for the idea that metaphysical dependence is more than mere necessary co-variation of property instantiation. Rather, it requires that the dependent properties are instantiated *because* the properties they depend upon are instantiated. In order to account for this difference between physicalism and its pluralist rivals, some have considered adding an explanatory component to the notion of supervenience, resulting in what Horgan (1993) calls '*superdupervenience*'. However, depending on how we understand the notion of *being explanatory*, this may bring in an unwanted epistemic component into a so far purely metaphysical thesis. I discuss a variety of different lines of argument for the claim that purely supervenience-based notions of are too coarse-grained, and are thus unable to distinguish between cases of dependence and cases of mere modal co-variation. Relatedly, purely modal accounts fail to distinguish physicalism from some nonstandard versions of dualism, including certain versions of emergentism. I elaborate on the question whether such views are coherent. These considerations are closely tied to a metaphysical principle called 'Hume's dictum': the claim that there are no necessary connections between distinct entities. The coherency of the views in question depends on what notion of *distinctness* is expressed. I draw on the discussion of notions of distinctness by Stoljar (2007; 2010) and Wilson (2010), and argue that the notion of distinctness involved is best understood as a notion of metaphysical independence or failure of metaphysical dependence. So understood, the views in question are most likely coherent, and a purely modal account of physicalism fails, as already indicated by a number of independent considerations.

In chapter five, I focus on more fine-grained accounts of metaphysical dependence that go beyond the purely modal realm. Recently, metaphysicians have begun to focus on the relation of *Grounding* to account for metaphysical dependence (Fine 2001; 2012; Correia 2005; Schaffer 2009), and a number of authors (e.g. Schaffer 2009; Dasgupta 2014) have proposed that it is the relation of dependence required for physicalism, while others remain skeptical (Melnyk 2016; Wilson 2018). Grounding is supposed to be a generic relation of metaphysical dependence that accounts for metaphysical structure and priority in a wide variety of different cases. Facts are usually taken to be the proper relata of the Grounding relation, although other sorts of entities have been considered as well (e.g. Schaffer 2009). Moreover, advocates of Grounding typically consider it to be an 'explanatory' relation (Fine 2001: 15), but the kind of explanation these authors seem to have in mind has little to do with how we usually understand the term. Finally, the notion of Grounding is often claimed to be primitive, which means that it cannot be analyzed in other terms (Fine 2001; 2012; Schaffer 2009), although some have considered doing so (Correia 2013).

I discuss the relation of Grounding, or at least a close cousin that relates properties, and investigate how Grounding is linked to other even more fine-grained relations that have been proposed as alternatives to supervenience in the literature. In particular, some have suggested that the relation of metaphysical dependence most well-suited to the task of formulating the thesis of physicalism is the *realization* relation. Melnyk (2003) has proposed a detailed account of physicalism employing a version of the realization relation based on the notion of a higher-order property. Wilson (1999; 2011) and Shoemaker (2007) have provided an alternative account of physical realization that is based on a set-subset relation between causal powers. Moreover, some have claimed that we can understand metaphysical dependence in terms of the determinable-determinate relation. Specifically, Yablo (1992) has considered this relation as a candidate for metaphysical dependence with regard to the mental domain. I argue that while such relations are indeed sufficient for metaphysical dependence, they fail to be necessary for it, and we need a more general notion of metaphysical dependence that subsumes these fine-grained relations as members of a broader family of relations of metaphysical dependence, roughly along the lines of what Wilson calls 'small-g' grounding relations (2014; 2018) and Bennett (2017) calls 'building relations'.

I then turn to criticism against a Grounding-based account of physicalism. I argue that Wilson (2014; 2018) correctly claims that Grounding is not able to replace the more fine-grained relations of dependence. Nevertheless, unlike Wilson, I think there is reason to believe that we cannot do without it. Two lines of reasoning are central here. First, one potential job for Grounding is fixing the order of priority between the relata of the 'small-g' grounding relations, if one thinks that the 'small-g' relations are unable to do that on their own. I argue that Wilson's alternative fundamentality-based account leads to more problems than Wilson expects, and thus is unable to replace appeal to Grounding to fix the order of priority. Moreover, even if we do not need a generic Grounding relation to fix the order of priority between the relata of 'small-g' relations, we still need at least a generic *concept* of Grounding or metaphysical dependence to unify at least those 'small-g' relations that allow us to account for the nothing-over-and-above-ness of non-physical over physical properties. The generic concept of metaphysical dependence builds on features these 'small-g' relations have in common. My view in this regard is somewhat similar to Bennett's (2017) view regarding her notion of 'building'. The relevant metaphysical dependence relations are strict partial ordering relations, entail certain necessitating links between the dependent properties and their dependence base, and are what Bennett calls 'productive' or 'generative' relations. Drawing on considerations of Dasgupta (2014), Melnyk (2018) and Goff (2017), I argue that we can further illuminate how the latter feature is established by investigating the essential natures of the properties in question. These natures illuminate why it is that a particular 'small-g' grounding relation holds between the properties in question, and the way this works is common to all 'small-g' relations.

The considerations put forth in this book provide us with a better understanding of the thesis of minimal physicalism. Particular variants of the view have of course a more detailed story to tell with regard to certain parts of the thesis, and further questions to resolve to come up with each fully fleshed out physicalist picture of what the world is like. My in this regard somewhat more moderate aim here is to provide a general framework that unifies these accounts. Now, without further ado, let us delve into the details of answering the central question: "What is physicalism?"

2 "I want it all"

As discussed in the introduction, we can divide the question how a minimal definition of physicalism is to be spelled out in detail into three similar sounding but in fact very different sub-questions. *First*, what do we mean when we say that *everything* is physical? *Second*, what do we mean when we say that everything is *physical*? *Third*, what do we mean when we say that everything *is* physical? In this chapter, I will focus on answering the first of the three questions, and thereby provide the basis for answering the other two.

With respect to this question, the first thing that comes to mind is what categories we quantify over when we say that *everything* is physical. Do we mean entities from any category whatsoever that is part of one's ontology, be it objects, events, facts, laws, properties, tropes, sets, propositions, and what have you, so that the domain of quantification is completely unrestricted, or do we need to make some restrictions with respect to the domain of quantification relevant to physicalism? To take an analogy (see also Stoljar 2010: 29), some might think that the 'everything' in 'everything is physical' is similar to the 'everything' in 'everything is self-identical', which seems to be the prototypical case of an unrestricted quantification if anything is. But even regarding the latter statement, philosophers have debated whether it is really a case of unrestricted quantification, and whether unrestricted quantification makes sense at all (see e.g. Williamson 2003; Rayo and Uzquiano 2006). Instead of asking whether unrestricted quantification is adequate for the case of physicalism, I want to start at the other end with an ancestor thesis that arguably restricts the domain of quantification too much for the purpose of today's debate: early modern materialism.

2.1 Substances, individuals, and other particulars

2.1.1 Early modern materialism and its appeal to substances

The early modern debate between materialists and dualists, probably most prominently represented by Thomas Hobbes and René Descartes, respectively, focused on the question whether every *substance* is material, and is thus a case where the domain of quantification is restricted to such entities. Since materialism is one of the two main ancestor theories of contemporary physicalism,[2]

---

[2] The other ancestor of contemporary physicalism I have in mind is the 'physicalism' of Rudolf Carnap (1931; 1932) and Otto Neurath (1931). Neurath and Carnap were members of the so-called

this is an adequate starting point for the inquiry about physicalism. This does not mean that a restriction to substances is adequate for drawing the distinction between contemporary physicalism and its rivals, but starting from there and adapting the thesis according to the further requirements is helpful to find a thesis that is adequate and does not get us into the kind of trouble that comes along with an unrestricted domain of quantification.

Throughout the book, as is typical for the debate (e.g. Stoljar 2010: 39), I assume a broadly realist picture of the kinds of entities quantified over. That is, when I quantify over individuals or properties, I presuppose that such entities exist without adding an explicit clause to the thesis that says so. So for example, if we take my final formulation (P) at the end of this chapter as it is, somebody with strict nominalist inclinations who claims that there are no properties whatsoever is committed to believing that physicalism is true, for the trivial logical reason that a universally quantified statement is true if there is nothing to be quantified over.[3] However, it is strange to think that all nominalists are committed to believing that physicalism is true. In order to avoid this, we can implicitly assume that a further conjunct is added to each formulation that says that the kinds of entities in question exist, which amounts to a broadly realist background assumption without any further commitments as to what the exact nature of the kinds of entities is.

If we were to ask early modern materialist thinkers like Thomas Hobbes, one of the intellectual ancestors of contemporary physicalists, who opposed the dualist view which we today most strongly associate with René Descartes, the answer to the question what materialism amounts to would be that every *substance* is material. How exactly the term 'substance' is to be understood by early modern thinkers is a matter of debate, and we do not need to go into too much detail. For the purpose at hand, it suffices to get a rough idea of what they had in mind.

'Vienna Circle', a group of philosophers and philosophically inclined scientists around the physicist and philosopher Moritz Schlick with a strongly anti-metaphysical tenor, and first used the term 'physicalism' in their writings. Their views were arguably somewhat different from each other, but what is sometimes (e.g. Hempel 1949) attributed to them (which is arguably closer to Carnap's than to Neurath's view) is that their 'physicalism' is a semantic thesis about the synonymy of special science statements and statements of physics, so that any meaningful special science statement (especially including first-person psychology) is translatable into a statement of physics (see also Stoljar 2010: 21–23). I put scare quotes around the term 'physicalism' in their use because it is certainly not the metaphysical thesis that we are concerned with today, which they would consider meaningless. Nevertheless, the conviction of contemporary physicalists that physics has a certain priority with respect to other sciences has remained.

3 I would like to thank an anonymous reviewer for pointing this out to me.

In his "Leviathan", Hobbes takes the terms 'substance' and 'body' to be coextensive, and takes 'body' to pick out entities that fill or occupy space (1998 [1651]: 261 [xxxiv.2]):

> The word *body* [...] signifieth that which filleth, or occupieth some certain room, or imagined place; and dependeth not on the imagination, but is a real part of that we call the *universe*. [...] The same also, because bodies are subject to change, that is to say, to variety of appearance to the sense of living creatures, is called *substance*, that is to say, *subject*, to various accidents; as sometimes to be moved; sometimes to stand still; and to seem to our senses sometimes hot, sometimes cold, sometimes of one colour, smell, taste, or sound, sometimes of another. And this diversity of seeming, (produced by the diversity of the operation of bodies on the organs of our sense) we attribute to alterations of the bodies that operate, and call them *accidents* of those bodies. And according to this acceptation of the word, *substance* and *body* signify the same thing; and therefore *substance incorporeal* are words, which when they are joined together, destroy one another, as if a man should say, an *incorporeal body*.

Entities that fill or occupy space clearly need to be *spatially* (or maybe *spatiotemporally*) *extended* entities. This is also how Descartes characterizes material substances in his "Meditations on First Philosophy". There, he opposes material substances to mental substances, which he characterizes as non-extended and thinking (Descartes 2008 [1641]: 32 [iii.44]):

> For when I think that a stone is a substance, that is to say, a thing capable of existing by itself, and likewise that I am myself a substance, then although I conceive myself to be a thinking and not an extended thing, and the stone, on the other hand, to be an extended and not a thinking thing, so that there is a very great difference between the two concepts, they seem, however, to have this in common: they both represent a substance.

Descartes' use of a stone as an example of an extended substance arguably indicates that early modern thinkers' use of substance might be close to our ordinary understanding of 'object', or 'thing'.

In his "Principles of Philosophy", Descartes spells out more clearly his use of the term 'substance'. He says that "[b]y '*substance*', we can understand nothing other than a thing which exists in such a way that it needs no other thing in order to exist" (Descartes 1982 [1644]: 23 [I.51]), and immediately adds that strictly speaking, this applies only to God. Nevertheless, there is a derived use of 'substance' in the sense of being a thing the existence of which requires only the existence of God. Each substance has "only one principal property which constitutes its nature or essence, and to which all the other properties are related" (Descartes 1982 [1644]: 23 [I.53]). So substances are entities that have exactly one property that constitutes their nature, and their existence depends on nothing else than the existence of God. Even setting aside the dependence on the existence of God, it remains at least debatable whether our usage of the term 'object' fits the requirement that the existence of the entities picked out by the term does not depend on the existence of any other entity, but the details need not concern us here. The important thing is that for Descartes, the constitutive property of material substances, the property that makes the substance a material one, is extendedness.

John Locke, in his "Essay concerning Human Understanding" adds a further characteristic to Descartes' extendedness. For Locke, *solidity* (which presupposes extendedness) is what characterizes matter (Locke 1975 [1690]: 123 [II.iv.1]):

> That which thus hinders the approach of two Bodies, when they are moving one towards another, I call *Solidity*. [...] [I]f any one think it better to call it *Impenetrability*, he has my Consent. Only I have thought the Term *Solidity*, the more proper to express this *Idea*, not only because of its vulgar use in that Sense, but also because it carries something more of positive in it, than *Impenetrability*, which is negative, and is, perhaps, more a consequence of *Solidity*, than *Solidity* it self. This of all other, seems the Idea most intimately connected with, and essential to Body, so as no where else to be found or imagin'd, but only in matter[.]

Provided with these considerations, we are set to state what might be the thesis of materialism, i.e. the claim that everything is material, on the conception of early modern thinkers:

(M) Materialism is true *iff* every substance is material, i.e. extended (and solid).

To a first approximation, one might think that we can understand physicalism in a similar way. Let us substitute the early modern notion of a substance with that of an ordinary object, which is close to taking 'everything' to just be 'every thing', where 'thing' is understood in more or less the ordinary way. Moreover, let us take the criteria for a thing to be physical to be the same as the criteria for a substance to be material:

(P1) Physicalism is true *iff* every individual[4] is physical, i.e. extended (and solid).

---

4 Note that what is universally quantified over here and in later formulations are entities that exist in the world considered. We do not want to include merely possible entities. Since physicalism is usually considered to be a contingent thesis, the mere metaphysical possibility of a Cartesian soul or of ectoplasm should not make physicalism false.

I use the notion of an individual here because the term 'object' has certain connotations that I would rather like to avoid, but one might replace my 'individual' with 'ordinary object' if one takes it to be sufficiently broad to not only extend to middle-sized objects like books, oak trees, cats and people, but to objects on all levels of the mereological hierarchy. Thus, smaller scale things like particles, H₂O molecules, cells and bacteria, as well as larger scale things like planets and galaxies are to be counted as ordinary objects, or individuals, as well.

2.1.2 From substances to particulars: token physicalism

Since the days of early modern materialist thinkers, our scientific notion of matter has changed. Thus, the notion of the physical as understood in (P1) arguably does not fit today's scientific worldview, even if we restrict ourselves to focusing on objects. Extendedness and solidity are properties that are not even shared by all objects physics is explicitly concerned with. At least within contemporary physical theory, particles like quarks and leptons are understood as point-like entities that are not extended and thus do not fill space. Similar considerations hold for solidity. While '... is solid' is still a predicate of contemporary physics, it does not have much to do with solidity in Locke's sense, and physical entities need not have the corresponding property. Still, we want to say that such entities are physical. Thus, these properties are inadequate, given our contemporary physical theories, to capture what a physical object is.

In the contemporary debates in the philosophy of mind and metaphysics that focus on questions around physicalism, the received view is that that objects are physical only in a derived sense. Instead of focusing on what first-order properties all and only physical objects have in common, what they have in common is only a second-order property.[5] An individual, or object, is typically considered

---

5 There are several uses of the notion of properties of different orders. One common use is to take first-order properties to be properties of particulars, second-order properties to be properties of first-order properties, and so forth with higher-order properties. An example of a second-order property, according to this use, is the property of *being a color*, which is a property of the property of *being red*. The use I have in mind here, however, is to take both first- and second-order properties to be properties of particulars. Second-order properties are properties a particular has in virtue of having some first-order property that satisfies certain constraints. An example of a second-order property, according to this use, is the property of *being a mousetrap*, which is characterized in terms of a certain functional role. A certain particular has that property in virtue of having some first-order property that satisfies the functional role. This is the usage that prominently features in functionalist views in the philosophy of mind, and functionalist accounts of physicalism more generally (e. g. Melnyk 2003). Similarly, the property of *being colored*

physical *iff* it has *at least one* physical property. Thus, what all physical objects have in common is the second-order property of having at least one physical property.⁶ Accordingly, the debate has shifted towards the question what makes a property a physical property, rather than focusing on what makes an object a physical object.⁷ I will address the former question in detail in the next chapter.

With regard to the relevant categories of particulars, the debate about physicalism has shifted (or rather broadened) in focus as well. For example, many physicalists claim that in addition to objects, there are further categories we need to consider. Besides objects and properties, two further categories are frequently taken into account: events and facts. Entities from these categories need to be physical as well in order for physicalism to be true. In order to also account for entities like events and facts, which are not encompassed by our notion of an individual (or of an ordinary object), one can adapt proposal (P1) by substituting 'individual' with the broader 'particular', and to understand a particular's being physical in the derived sense(s) just discussed:

(P2)   Physicalism is true *iff* every *particular* is physical.

Definition (P2) is what some call 'token physicalism' (e.g. Stoljar 2015: section 6).⁸ The term 'particular' is to be understood as contrastive to 'universal'. I do not want to enter into the debate about how to make that distinction precise, not only because it turns out difficult to do so, but mainly because this debate is orthogonal to the debate about physicalism. A simple way to make the distinc-

---

is a property certain particulars have due to having some other property, e.g. the property of *being red*.

6 Analogously, an individual is non-physical if it has at least one property that is not physical. Hence, it is perfectly consistent to claim that an individual is both physical and non-physical, even though on first glance, this might seem otherwise.

7 Ned Markosian (2000) defends the view that the defining property of physical objects is spatial location. Since that does not entail that they are spatially extended, the point particle can still count as physical on such a view – although there might still be worries regarding the question whether particles, according to particular interpretations of quantum physics, always have a spatial location. In any case, I do not find Markosian's view compelling, because I do not see a non-question-begging reason to rule out by definition that Cartesian souls or ectoplasm, which obviously should not come out as physical objects, might have a spatial location as well. Of course, there might be applications of such a view, but not in the context of spelling out the thesis of physicalism.

8 It is worth noting that many token physicalists claim more than that. Along the lines of Donald Davidson's Anomalous Monism (2001d [1970]: 214), they add a supervenience claim (see chapter 4) to what is claimed by (P2).

tion sufficiently clear for our purposes appeals to the relation of instantiation: Particulars can instantiate property types and kinds (which are often conceived of as universals, but might also be conceived of as tropes, for example), but cannot themselves be instantiated by anything. If universals exist, they can be instantiated, but also instantiate other universals.[9] I take ordinary objects, facts and events to be particulars, but this list is not meant not be exhaustive. For example, states, or processes might be further candidates. Property types or kinds, however, are not to be considered particulars.[10] Importantly, the expression '... is physical' is not to be understood in terms of extendedness and solidity, as in (P1). Nevertheless, I did not replace the predicate '... is physical' by '... has at least one physical property' to accommodate the idea that certain kinds of particulars are not physical in virtue of having a physical property, but in virtue of having physical properties as constituents or parts, along the lines of the views of events and facts discussed below.

Two main reasons for thinking that we need to add events to our ontology have been put forward by Donald Davidson (2001a [1967]; 2001b [1969]; see also Loux 2006: 149). Both have a somewhat Quinean touch along the lines of the slogan "to be is to be the value of a [bound] variable" (Quine 1953 [1948]: 15). One reason is that we need them to account for causal talk, especially in causal explanations. According to a widely received view, events are the entities that stand in causal relations. They are the entities quantified over in expressions like 'For all x (of kind P), there is a y (of kind Q) such that y causes x'. Furthermore, Davidson takes sentences like "The water boiled quickly in the kitchen this morning" (Loux' example) to have the logical form of an existential quantification: "There is an x such that x is quickly and x is in the kitchen and x is this morning", and the water's boiling, an event, is what is claimed to exist according to the statement. Yet another reason that Davidson (2001b [1969]: 165) attributes to Kim (1966) is that the identity theory in the philosophy of mind identifies mental and physical events, which presupposes that there are such entities. This can of course be no independent reason to add events to the relevant categories for our

---

[9] For example, if universals exist, every universal instantiates the universal of *being a universal*, if that is one.

[10] Note that trope theorists might not be happy with what I say here. While tropes, strictly speaking, are considered to be particulars as well, they are supposed to play the roles played by universals in other theories (see e.g. Maurin 2013 for an overview of trope theory). Thus, it does not seem to make much sense to say that the tropes are physical in a derived sense. While I certainly do not want to exclude trope theorists from playing the physicalist game, I do not bother to adapt the definition accordingly. Nevertheless, it is easy enough to see how one might do so.

purposes, but it at least shows the relevance of such entities in the debates around physicalism.

With regard to facts, the main argument for believing that we need to add them to our ontology is that we need them in order to account for the truth and falsity of propositions. Take the true proposition that Aristotle is a philosopher. What makes this proposition true? The existence of both Aristotle and the property of *being a philosopher* do not suffice. Even the existence of the relation of instantiation in addition to the other two entities does arguably not suffice. Friends of facts claim that what is required in order to account for the truth of the proposition that Aristotle is a philosopher is the existence of the fact that Aristotle exemplifies the property of *being a philosopher*, which ties those elements together (cf. Loux 2006: 143).

Some formulate physicalism only in terms of facts, so that for the truth of physicalism it is required that all facts are physical facts. Still, since facts are closely tied to the other categories just discussed, these categories are arguably considered implicitly by such a formulation as well. However, I prefer to frame things in terms of properties, because similar to the case of objects, I think that entities that belong to the categories of events and facts are physical only in a derived sense, insofar as their *being physical* is derived from certain properties' *being physical*. How exactly this works depends on what one's particular metaphysical views are regarding what entities of such categories are like, and I think that the thesis of physicalism needs to remain as neutral as possible regarding such views. Nevertheless, I would like to provide some examples what *being physical* in a derived sense might amount to for such entities.

On Davidson's (2001c [1970]) account, physical events are those that have a physical description. One might think that an event's being physical is in this case analogous to the case of an object: Physical events are those that have a physical description, or can be described using a physical predicate. Combined with the view that a predicate can be truly applied to (or is satisfied by) an entity *iff* the entity has the property the predicate designates (or expresses), we might think that an event is physical *iff* it has (or instantiates) at least one physical property.[11] But I think this is misguided. Take the event of the water's boiling. What the physicalist is interested in is the property of *being boiling*, which is a property of the water rather than the event. The event's own properties are of little interest for the physicalist.

---

[11] Note that Davidson himself did not like to move from metaphysically neutral predicate talk to talk about properties.

The idea that what is at issue with regard to events are still the properties of individuals is even more prominent in Kim's (1993b [1973]; 1993c [1976]) property exemplification account of events. On this view, events are structured complexes constituted by an object (Kim uses the term 'particular object' in his 1993b [1973] and 'substance' in his 1993c [1976]), a property type and a time.[12] An event is considered physical *iff* that event's constitutive property is a physical property.[13] In such a case, in terms of properties the event has (i.e. instantiates), one might say that the event is physical insofar as it has the property of *having some physical property as its constitutive property*.[14] The constitutive property itself is had, or instantiated, by the constitutive object of the event. This is important, because if an event is considered physical as soon as it has a physical property as a constitutive property, we need not explicitly quantify over events in order to account for their *being physical* because the properties that are constitutive of the event are properties instantiated by objects, and so are considered anyway as soon as we quantify over the objects.[15]

Similarly, if one holds a view of facts according to which facts are complex entities that have properties as parts, or constituents, then a fact's *being physical* derives from the properties' *being physical* that are its parts, or constituents. For example, the fact that a certain rock has a mass of 1 kg is physical if *having a mass of 1 kg* is a physical property. If there is more than one property involved, there is a stronger and a weaker sense in which facts, so conceived, can be physical. Either, one could say that a fact is physical if it has at least one physical property as a part, or one could say that it is physical if all the properties it has as parts are physical. The properties had as parts by the fact are typically had (i.e., instantiated) by particulars (which are also parts of the fact). On

---

12 Strictly speaking, an event is constituted by an n-tuple of particulars, an n-adic relation and a time (Kim 1993c [1976]: 34).
13 It does not suffice to say that an event is physical if it has a physical object as its constituent particular. This would make the event [Paul, pain, t] physical in case Paul has some physical property unrelated to the event in question, even if the property of *being in pain* is not a physical property.
14 At this point, we need to be careful. The relation of *having as a constitutive property* is not the same as the relation of *having* (or *instantiating*), as in the case of Paul having the property of *being in pain*. The event does not instantiate its constitutive property. Rather, what instantiates the constitutive property is the constitutive object of the event. (Kim 1993c [1976]: 43) A related property the event instantiates is the (first-order!) property of *having some physical property as its constitutive property*.
15 This holds at least if events do not have other events as their constitutive 'object', i.e. there are no events of the following form: [[o, P, t], Q, t], i.e., the event of *the event of o's having P at t's having Q at t*.

such a view, facts have a quite similar structure to events as conceived by Kim. Insofar as the relevant properties are already accounted for by quantifying over objects (individuals), we need not quantify over facts in addition.

If we need not quantify over events and facts explicitly, a variant of (P2) may be that we use (P2') instead:

(P2') Physicalism is true *iff* every *individual* is physical.

If one would like to stick with talk about particulars, it is important to note that when it comes to such things as events or facts, '... is physical' needs to be interpreted in terms of constitutive properties rather than properties instantiated by those entities, as already mentioned above. However, the explicit inclusion of events and facts as entities quantified over does not come without further problems. These problems only become apparent later in this book (see section 4.3). All things considered, I am inclined to think that we can, and should, in the end do without quantifying over events and facts explicitly because what physicalism is concerned with is the constitutive properties of events and facts, which are properties instantiated by individuals. I will thus use the notion of an *individual* rather than that of a *particular* in my further definitions.

2.1.3 Numbers, deities, and other necessary beings

One problem of both (P2) and (P2') is that the notions of a particular and an individual also include mathematical entities like numbers (and maybe sets). Many philosophers consider numbers to be Platonic entities: abstract objects that exist 'outside' of space and time. Moreover, they are often thought to exist necessarily, no matter what a possible world is like in other respects.[16] If numbers are such entities, physicalists do not and should not care at all about them (cf. Melnyk 2003: 11; Wilson 2005: 454 [fn1]). If physicalism would be a claim about such entities as well, the following argument would be a perfectly legitimate and probably devastating argument against the view:
(1) There are Platonic numbers.
(2) Platonic numbers do not have physical properties.
(3) If there are Platonic numbers, and Platonic numbers do not have physical properties, then physicalism is false.
∴ Physicalism is false.

---

16 Similar views exist with regard to propositions (e.g. Merricks 2015: 192–193).

I have never seen any such argument in the literature, and I am sure that this is because everybody agrees that (3) is false.

However, the falsity of (3) is hard to argue for by somebody who takes physicalism to be expressed by (P2) or (P2'), and so physicalism as defined in (P2) and (P2') comes out false if Platonic numbers exist and do not have physical properties.[17] One might account for that by trying to make the notion of a physical property permissive enough to make sure that even numbers have physical properties, but that most likely goes along with unwanted side effects. Another approach could be to exclude *abstract* entities from the scope of the physicalist thesis, but the distinction between abstract and concrete entities is not very well understood and should thus be avoided. Another reason against excluding abstract entities is that trope theories take tropes to be abstract particulars, but it would be odd if a trope theorist with physicalist inclinations would not need to make sure that their tropes are physical entities. What about restricting physicalism to spatio-temporal particulars or individuals? There, my worry is that physicalism should rule out the existence of a deity, at least if deities are understood as something like spiritual entities. Even if such an entity exists 'outside' of space and time, physicalism should still come out false.

The better option is to add to the definition that the individuals physicalism is concerned with are those that only exist contingently (cf. Melnyk 2003: 10–11):

(P3)   Physicalism is true *iff* every individual *that exists contingently* is physical.

This makes sure that if one takes numbers to be necessary existents, physicalism is not concerned with them. However, by adding this additional constraint, physicalism is made compatible with a necessarily existing deity, even if it is a spiritual entity, and that is bad news because physicalism intuitively should not be compatible with such entities. In order to circumvent this problem, Melnyk (2003: 10–11) proposes that physicalism is not concerned with entities that are neither contingent nor causal, which applies to Platonic numbers, but not a deity, at least if the deity under consideration is thought to be the *causa prima* or otherwise interacts causally with other entities:

(P4)   Physicalism is true *iff* every individual that exists contingently *or is causal* is physical.

---

[17] This would become an even more pressing issue in (P5) and later definitions, where *all* properties of numbers would have to be physical if we would not make the corresponding exception.

While this seems to me a bit like a workaround rather than a substantial solution,[18] I have no better suggestion, so I adopt Melnyk's proposal.

What exactly does it mean for an individual to be causal? Most contemporary philosophers think that the relata of the causal relation expressed by the predicate '... causes ...' are events. Some think that facts are suitable candidates to stand in the causal relation, either in addition to or instead of events. But only very few contemporary philosophers defend a more Aristotelian conception of causation that allows for objects, or individuals, to cause something, literally speaking. Nevertheless, it is reasonable to think that objects (and facts) are at least causal entities in some derived sense, even if they do not cause anything themselves. Again, I want to leave open here how this is to be done, because the thesis of physicalism should not presuppose any particular view regarding causation.

2.2 Moving on to properties

2.2.1 Wholly physical beings: type physicalism

Numbers and deities are not the biggest issues for token physicalism as construed in the definitions above. The most pressing problem is that token physicalism is unable to rule out an important contemporary form of dualism. While a dualism of individuals (e.g. Cartesian substance dualism) is ruled out, the most prevalent contemporary form of dualism, which is a dualism of property types (e.g. Chalmers 1996), remains compatible with these definitions. Property dualists are happy to agree with what the right-hand side of the definitions we just considered states. What they deny is that this entails that physicalism is true. On their view, besides having physical properties, at least some individuals also have non-physical properties that are completely independent of, or something over and above, the physical properties. The most hotly debated candidates for such properties are phenomenal properties like *being in pain*. Normative properties are further candidates that are likely to trouble the physicalist. What contemporary physicalists claim thus needs to be stronger than the theses

---

[18] The problem is that it still does not rule out a deity, understood as a spiritual entity, which exists necessarily but does not have any causal impact whatsoever. Intuitively, it seems that physicalism should be false in such a case, but I do not know what to say to rule it out. In any case, I think that this is certainly not the biggest problem for defining physicalism, so I will just set this concern aside.

above. What comes much closer to their claim is that the individuals in question are not only physical, but that they are *wholly* physical.

The notion of a wholly physical individual needs explication. The most immediate proposal that comes to mind certainly is that all properties had by the relevant individuals are physical properties:

> (P5) Physicalism is true *iff every property had by* any individual that exists contingently or is causal *is a physical property.*

This definition, while still quantifying over individuals, also quantifies over property types. Thus, let me call a physicalism defined along these lines 'type physicalism'. A bit more formally, (P5) says that physicalism is true just in case for every property P, if there is an individual x such that x is contingent or causal and Px, then P is physical. In many cases, definitions of type physicalism do not explicitly mention individuals. A typical such statement is that physicalism is true *iff* every instantiated property type is a physical property type (see e.g. Stoljar 2015: section 6). One might add that what is meant is first-order property types only, i.e. properties of individuals, rather than properties of other properties. This however makes it difficult to include the constraints that enable us to account for the issues regarding numbers and deities. Thus, it is more accurate to explicitly quantify over individuals as well to be able to restrict the thesis to those individuals that are intuitively relevant to the physicalist.

2.2.2 Narrowly and broadly physical properties, fundamentality and dependence

There are two ways we might understand the expression 'is a physical property' that we need to distinguish. The first, which makes use of the notion of a *narrowly* physical property, is the following:

> (P6) Physicalism is true *iff* every property had by any individual that exists contingently or is causal is a *narrowly* physical property.

The expression 'narrowly physical property' has been used in different ways in the literature. Barbara Montero uses it to denote the properties "posited by the physical sciences" (2013: 96). David Chalmers uses it to denote "microphysical role properties, such as the dispositional property associated with having a certain mass", which he opposes to "properties that realize the relevant roles: categorical bases for the mass dispositions" (2017 [2015]: 27). Chalmers calls the combination of both kinds of properties "broadly physical properties" (2017 [2015]: 27). Andrew Bailey and Joshua Rasmussen use the term 'narrowly physical properties' to denote "those nonmental properties that figure in fundamental physics" (2016: 340 [fn5]). I do not use the expression in any of these ways, but in a way that is more similar to Melnyk's (2016: 251) usage:

> [A] formulation of physicalism must indisputably do at least the following two things. First, it must characterize a relatively narrow class of physical entities that are, as it were, physical in their own right; it might characterize them, for example, as those entities expressible in the proprietary vocabulary of physics [...]. Call these entities *narrowly* physical. Second, it must specify a relation R such that, necessarily, if an entity which isn't narrowly physical (e.g., a chair or a zebra) stands in R to an entity which is narrowly physical, then the former entity is nothing over and above the narrowly physical entity in the intuitive sense required for physicalism. Call such an entity *broadly* physical.

As will become clear in the next chapter, I do not agree with Melnyk's view about the proper characterization of physical entities. Still, the distinction between narrowly and broadly physical properties I make is along the same lines, although on my usage of the terms, the set of narrowly physical properties is a subset of the broadly physical ones. A more elaborate characterization of the narrowly physical must wait until the next chapter. For the moment, it must suffice to say that I take the narrowly physical properties to be those properties that are picked out by the predicate '... is a physical property' in the restricted sense developed in the next chapter, and the broadly physical properties are the narrowly physical properties conjoined with those properties that *metaphysically depend* on the narrowly physical ones.

I take (P6) to be indeed a variant of physicalism, on the assumption that we plug in an adequate definition of 'physical property'. There are two different physicalist views that are in line with this definition. If one holds (P6), one can either be a *type identity physicalist* or be a *radical eliminativist physicalist*.[19] Both claim that every instantiated property is a member of the set of properties picked out by the predicate '... is a physical property'. So with respect to the entities that exist in the world, they agree with each other. The difference is with

---

[19] These views are not to be confused with the type identity theorist and the eliminativist from debates in the philosophy of mind, which focus on domain-specific questions about the mental. The properties the identity theorist in such debates identifies mental properties with are usually special science properties. The typical example from the literature is the (also empirically doubtful) type identification of pain with C-fiber firing (cf. Kripke 1980: 144). This leaves open the question how special science properties relate to narrowly physical properties. The eliminativist in such debates is often concerned with folk psychological predicates only (cf. Churchland 1981).

respect to the extension of special science predicates (amongst others). While the type identity physicalist claims that predicates like '... is in pain' pick out a property that is in the extension of '... is a physical property', the radical eliminativist physicalist claims that '... is in pain' picks out no property at all.

Even if (P6) is a variant of physicalism, it is arguably not a *minimal* physicalist thesis. That is, the truth of the right-hand side claim of (P6) is a sufficient, but not a necessary condition for the truth of physicalism. Many physicalists claim that certain properties they think are in fact instantiated cannot be strictly type-identified with narrowly physical properties. Most notably, functional properties, like *being a heart*, *being a mousetrap* or *being a table*, are thought to be *multiply realizable*. The notion of multiple realizability was introduced by Hilary Putnam (1975b [1967]) and notably developed by Jerry Fodor (1974). How the notion of realization is to be defined is a matter of debate (e.g. Gillett 2003; Polger 2004: ch. 1; Bickle 2013: section 1.1; see also section 5.2 below), but what different views regarding multiple realizability have in common is that the instantiation of the realized property type is guaranteed given the instantiation of any one of several numerically distinct physical (and maybe also non-physical) property types (or configurations thereof), the potential realizers (which need not be, and normally are not, co-instantiated). Hence, the instantiation of neither one of the potential realizer properties is necessary for the instantiation of the multiply realizable property. Therefore, the multiply realizable property type cannot be identical to any one of the realizer types. Still, we would like to say that the existence of multiply realizable functional properties, although they are not identical to narrowly physical properties, does not render physicalism false.

One way to try to account for this issue is to add a further restriction to the properties that are quantified over:

(P7)   Physicalism is true *iff* every *fundamental* property had by any individual that exists contingently or is causal is a narrowly physical property.

This seems to be a move into the right direction – after all, properties like the functional ones mentioned above, at least intuitively, are not to be taken as fundamental. Still, the definition is arguably not very illuminating if we do not properly understand the notion of fundamentality, and we thus cannot tell what the conditions are for a property to be fundamental. What we obviously cannot say is that a property is fundamental *iff* it is narrowly physical, because then we would just say that every narrowly physical property is a narrowly physical property, which is trivial, and would make physicalism an analytic truth (cf. Stoljar 2010: 34).

Some have argued that the notion of fundamentality is primitive, i.e., it cannot be defined in other terms. Jessica Wilson draws an analogy between fundamental entities and the axioms in a theory. According to her, "they are basic, they are 'all God had to do, or create'. As such[, ...] the fundamental should not be metaphysically defined in any other terms, whether these be positive or negative" (Wilson 2014: 560).[20] Moreover, according to Karen Bennett (2017: 113), Kit Fine has something similar in mind when he claims that "there is a primitive metaphysical concept of reality, one that cannot be understood in fundamentally different terms" (Fine 2001: 1). Others have argued that the notion of fundamentality can be characterized via a notion of metaphysical dependence (see below), which is in turn taken to be primitive by some (e.g. Schaffer 2009; 2016). Defenders of such views will likely prefer to express the thesis of physicalism in terms of metaphysical dependence instead of fundamentality.

A further worry with regard to a definition of physicalism that appeals to a notion of (absolute) fundamentality is that physicalism intuitively is compatible with a case in which the world in question has no fundamental level, such that for each level in an infinitely descending hierarchy, there is always a further level one step down. After all, it is arguably even an open question whether the world we live in has a fundamental level (Schaffer 2003), and a negative answer to that question should not be sufficient to render physicalism false. Stoljar (2010: 35) thinks that such considerations make a definition along the lines of (P7) unfavorable.[21] Regarding this worry, I think we have to be careful not to conflate different kinds of fundamentality (and uses of the term 'level', for that matter).

---

20 Wilson's phrasing suggests that notion of metaphysical definition is mainly concerned with properties and the question what it is that makes a property a fundamental property, or with the nature of the property of fundamentality (as instantiated by certain properties). This is different to the question how the predicate '... is fundamental' is to be defined, or how the concept of fundamentality is to be analyzed. Her notion of metaphysical definition thus seems to be closely related to Fine's (1994) notion of a *real definition*, which is supposed to state *what an entity is*, rather than to provide the meaning of a term. While Fine originally focuses on particular objects, Rosen (2015) discusses the application of real definitions to properties as well. I think there is some room for debate whether or not Wilson's claim that a metaphysical definition of the *property* of fundamentality in terms of other properties has to be rejected entails that our *notion* (or *concept*) of fundamentality is primitive. Since she puts forward her considerations as a reply to claims of others who explicitly state that the notion of a fundamental entity can be defined negatively in terms of the notion of grounding (Wilson cites Schaffer 2003: 87), I take her to think that there is such an entailment. For more on these issues, see section 5.3 below.
21 The definition Stoljar explicitly addresses is that "[p]hysicalism is true if and only if every instantiated fundamental property is physical" (2010: 35).

As Schaffer (2003: 500) indicates, the main understanding of the term 'level' concerns mereology. Typically, entities on different levels are conceived of as related via the mereological part-whole relation.[22] Such a notion focuses on individuals rather than properties. We can distinguish between a notion of *absolute fundamentality* and a notion of *relative fundamentality* here. An individual is absolutely fundamental in this sense *iff* it cannot be further divided into parts, and an individual is relatively fundamental to another individual *iff* the former exists at a lower level of the mereological hierarchy than the latter.[23] The question whether or not there is a fundamental level, as discussed by Schaffer, is most tightly connected to the notion of absolute fundamentality in the above sense.

This cannot be the notion of fundamentality present in definition (P7), however, because (P7) makes use of a notion of fundamentality that is applied to properties rather than individuals. While it might sometimes appear more reasonable to talk of the fundamentality of property tokens (and thus of individuals, or at least of particulars), this cannot be appropriate here. First, the "had by" indicates that the thesis concerns property types rather than property tokens. But more importantly, if (P7) would be a claim about property tokens, it would suffer from the same problems as token physicalism, which we dismissed above as insufficient for physicalism. At least if we allow that one and the same token can be an instance of several distinct types, it does not rule out property pluralism.

As with the notion of fundamentality of individuals above, the notion most relevant for Stoljar's concern is one of absolute rather than relative fundamentality. We can distinguish several notions of fundamentality with regard to properties. *First*, we can consider a notion of fundamentality of properties that derives solely from the fundamentality of individuals. In this sense, an absolutely fundamental property is a property that is instantiated by an absolutely fundamental individual in the above sense. According to such an account of the fundamentality of properties, if there is a fundamental mereological level, then all properties had by individuals on that level count as fundamental. Importantly, as long as we remain talking about types, this may include also properties that are instantiated *as well* by individuals on higher levels of the mereological hierarchy. An example for such a property might be the property of *having mass*. It is reasonable to think that this property is instantiated by individuals on dif-

---

22 This of course is not to say that any two entities on different levels stand in the part-whole relation to each other.

23 Philosophers who advocate a priority monist view (Schaffer 2010), which takes wholes to be metaphysically prior to their parts, alternatively claim that an individual is absolutely fundamental *iff* there exists no individual of which it is a proper part. My formulation of relative fundamentality is supposed to be compatible with priority monism as well.

ferent levels of the mereological hierarchy. If it is also instantiated by individuals on the fundamental level (given that there is such a level), it counts as fundamental in the sense under consideration. It is not required that it is *only* instantiated by fundamental individuals.

There might be property types that are indeed only instantiated by mereologically fundamental individuals. Maybe *being a particle* is such a property if particles don't have further parts. We can further restrict our notion of a fundamental property to properties that are instantiated *only* by absolutely fundamental individuals. On such a view, having mass is not a fundamental property if it is also instantiated by non-fundamental individuals. If one of these conceptions of a fundamental property would be applied in (P7), then Stoljar's worry would indeed be pertinent. However, I don't think that this is what we mean in the case of (P7). While *having mass* may well be one of the narrowly physical properties we have in mind, I don't think that what we mean when we say that a property is fundamental is that it is instantiated by mereologically fundamental individuals, *amongst others*, nor do I think that all properties had by fundamental individuals are to be counted as fundamental in the relevant sense. After all, a physicalism along the lines of (P7) that uses such a notion of a fundamental property would come out false if certain functional properties of the fundamental individuals, which would count as fundamental given this account of the fundamentality of properties, are not type-identical to physical properties. Furthermore, such an account would not rule out property pluralism. If mental properties are not instantiated by fundamental individuals, physicalism so construed turns out not to be concerned with them at all.

Second, we can consider a sense of fundamentality of properties that is closely linked to a notion of metaphysical dependence. Again, as in the case of individuals, we can distinguish between notions of absolute fundamentality and relative fundamentality of properties. On such a conception, a property is relatively fundamental to some other property *if(f)*[24] the latter metaphysically depends on the former, and absolutely fundamental *iff* it does not metaphysically depend on any other property (cf. Schaffer 2009; 2016). Further restrictions might be made with respect to which other properties are considered. One might only

---

[24] The brackets around the second 'f' should indicate that the left-to-right direction (i.e. the 'only if' direction) seems to be plausible at most if what we have in mind is partial rather than full dependence. Intuitively, we are inclined to say that *being red* is more fundamental than *being red and round*, even though *being red* only provides a partial dependence base for *being red and round*. What we are most interested in, however, is full dependence, rather than partial dependence. One reason for this is that partial dependence does not come with the required modal commitments (for more on this, see section 5.3 below).

consider those properties instantiated (i) by the same individual, (ii by individuals on the same mereological level, (iii) by individuals on the same and lower mereological levels, or (iv) by any individual whatsoever.

Cases (i) and (ii) are concerned only with an *intra-level* hierarchy of properties, while cases (iii) and (iv) are not limited to an intra-level hierarchy. Following Kim (1998: 83), we might call this intra-level hierarchy a hierarchy of *orders*[25] to distinguish it from the hierarchy of mereological levels. A typical example of relative fundamentality of properties of the same individual is the case of the relation between the property of *being red* and the property of *being crimson*, which stand in a determinable-determinate relation to each other. Any individual that instantiates the property of *being crimson* simultaneously must instantiate the property of *being red*, and we are inclined to say that the individual instantiates *being red because* it instantiates *being crimson*, which indicates that *being red* metaphysically depends on *being crimson*. The property *being red* is thus of higher order than *being crimson*, but the two properties are same-level properties because both properties are had by the same individuals. Thus, *being crimson* in this sense is more fundamental than *being red*. A similar story can be told with regard to functional properties like *being a mousetrap* and *being a heart* and their corresponding realizer properties, where the functional properties are higher order with respect to their realizers. If this hierarchy of orders bottoms out at some point, then we might say that the properties at the bottom of orders are absolutely fundamental properties. In the case of the hierarchy of determinables and determinates, maximally specific determinate properties might be thought of as absolutely fundamental in this sense.

Cases (iii) and (iv) also consider relations between properties instantiated by individuals across the *inter-level* hierarchy. Sometimes, we might want to say that certain properties of a whole's parts are more fundamental than the properties of the whole and have in mind more than the sense of fundamentality of properties that derives solely from the fundamentality of individuals.[26] This seems to be the case in a variant of physicalism we can call 'microphysicalism' (for the distinction, cf. Hüttemann 2004; Hüttemann and Papineau 2005; Papineau 2008). Some physicalists want to claim that there is a hierarchy of metaphysical dependencies among properties that bottoms out at those properties instantiated by the entities at the microphysical level. Papineau (2008: 127) tries to spell out the distinction between physicalism and microphysicalism in terms of

---

25 This notion of orders should not be confused with the notion of orders appealed to when discussing properties of properties.
26 Again, the priority monist will claim that a reverse dependency holds, i.e. that the properties of the whole are more fundamental than the properties of the whole's parts.

two theses: (1) that "[a]ll facts metaphysically supervene on the physical facts" and (2) that "[a]ll physical facts metaphysically supervene on the microphysical facts". According to Papineau, physicalism consists in thesis (1) only, while microphysicalism is the conjunction of (1) and (2). He notes that even some contemporary dualists like David Chalmers might agree that (2) is true, but they certainly reject (1). Moreover, since he considers himself a physicalist, but not a microphysicalist, he only commits to (1), but not to (2) (2008: 128–129). Setting aside that Papineau's formulation quantifies over facts rather than properties, and that he frames the relation in terms of metaphysical supervenience rather than in terms of metaphysical dependence, the relative fundamentality in question in cases (iii) and (iv) is also implicitly present in Papineau's thesis (2).[27]

As long as we do not take physicalism to be microphysicalism,[28] it is not clear that Stoljar's worry regarding infinite descent as introduced by Schaffer applies with regard to the notion of fundamentality in (P7). If the notion of fundamentality as applied in (P7) only concerns an *intra-level* (in the mereological sense) hierarchy of properties, we need not worry about infinite descent on the mereological hierarchy. Nevertheless, if an analogous infinite descent with regard to the intra-level hierarchy of properties of different orders is possible, an analogous concern as the one regarding mereological levels applies, since physicalism intuitively seems to be compatible with cases of infinite descent. Other than in the mereological case, however, it is much less clear whether or not an intra-level infinite descent is possible. For example, take the determinable-determinate relation again. An infinite descent would mean in this case that for every determinate of a determinable, there is a further determinate relative to which the original determinate is a determinable. At least with regard to examples like colors, at least *prima facie*, it does not seem to make sense to claim that a specific color like International Klein Blue has a further determinate it is a determinable of.

In any case, what these considerations show is that it would be better to avoid a notion of *absolute* fundamentality, both with regard to individuals and with regard to properties, when formulating physicalism. Still, a notion of *relative* fundamentality might remain useful, but cannot simply be plugged into

---

[27] I take it that the microphysical facts are a subset of the physical facts. Otherwise, the case in which some fact metaphysically supervenes on the microphysical facts directly would need to be handled separately because such a case should not make physicalism false.

[28] Aside from microphysicalism, similar considerations hold for a notion of fundamentality along the lines of the priority monist view if we take into account the possibility of a never-ending hierarchy of more and more encompassing wholes (Schaffer (2010) uses the term 'junk', inspired by Lewis' (1991: 20) term 'gunk' for atomless wholes).

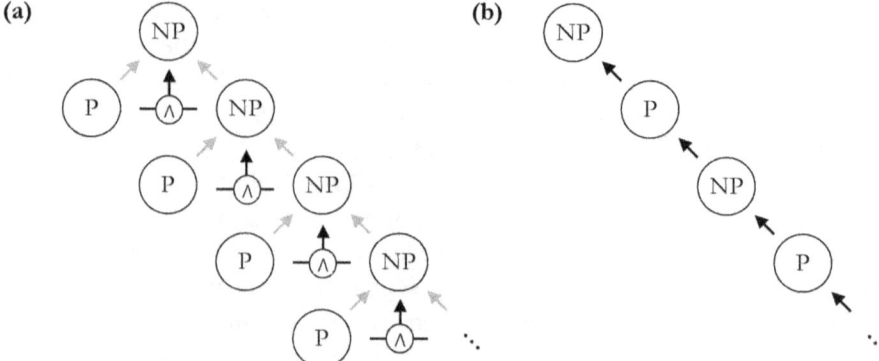

Figure 1: Infinitely descending chains of more and more fundamental properties. Circles labeled 'P' indicate narrowly physical properties, circles labeled 'NP' indicate nonphysical properties. Gray arrows indicate mere partial dependence, and black arrows indicate full dependence. The dots indicate that the pattern continues infinitely.

(P7) by adding the term 'relative'. Instead, a more appropriate formulation of physicalism that makes use of a notion of relative fundamentality might be something like the following:

(P8) Physicalism is true *iff* for every property Q had by any individual that exists contingently or is causal there is a narrowly physical property P^{29} such that either (i) P is identical to Q or (ii) P is more fundamental than Q.

Here, the notion of relative fundamentality is expressed by the predicate '... is more fundamental than ...'. Such a formulation of physicalism clearly is compatible with cases of infinite descent. There are some cases of infinite descent that some might find troubling for a formulation of physicalism along the lines of (P8). Such cases involve possible worlds that include somewhat odd chains of relatively fundamental properties, such as chains where narrowly physical properties alternate with properties that are not narrowly physical themselves (see Figure 1 (b); cf. Montero 2006). Such cases similarly concern formulations of physicalism that make use of a notion of metaphysical dependence, as discussed in chapter 5.

As I noted above, the notion of relative fundamentality of properties just considered seems to be closely tied to the notion of metaphysical dependence.

---

29 P can be a complex property composed of other properties by conjunction.

However, it is tied more closely to what we might call 'partial dependence' rather than 'full dependence'. Consider the case of a conjunctive property, like *being red and round*. This property partially depends on *being red*, and partially depends on *being round*, but does not fully depend on any of them, because *being red and round* is something over and above each of its conjuncts, taken separately. Nevertheless, we would like to say that the conjuncts are more fundamental than the conjunctive property. This leads to another potentially problematic case for (P8), as illustrated by a chain of dependencies as depicted in Figure 1 (a). If one thinks that in the case depicted physicalism should come out false, then (P8) is not appropriate, because on definition (P8), physicalism comes out true if we take each of the conjuncts to be more fundamental than the dependent property. After all, in every case, one of the conjuncts is a narrowly physical property. Since it is debatable what the correct intuition regarding the truth and falsity of physicalism is supposed to be in the cases depicted in Figure 1 (a) and (b), i.e. since it is debatable whether physicalism should be true in a world in which there is such a chain of dependence between the instantiated properties,[30] I will set them aside.

Instead of restricting the thesis to fundamental properties to be able to stick with the notion of a narrowly physical property, we can return to adapting (P5) by appeal to the notion of a *broadly* physical property instead:

(P9*) Physicalism is true *iff* every property had by any individual that exists contingently or is causal is a *broadly* physical property.

The set of broadly physical properties encompasses (i) narrowly physical properties and (ii) properties that *metaphysically depend* on narrowly physical properties. We can make this explicit in our definition of physicalism by rephrasing (P9*) accordingly:

(P9) Physicalism is true iff every property had by any individual that exists contingently or is causal either (i) is a narrowly physical property or (ii) metaphysically depends on narrowly physical properties.

---

[30] Even if one thinks that physicalism is false in such a case, it is far from clear that it is a case of dualism, or pluralism, either. I am not even sure whether I can properly conceive of such worlds.

What exactly metaphysical dependence amounts to will be addressed in chapters 4 and 5, where I discuss different candidate relations of nothing-over-and-above-ness.

2.2.3 Necessarily instantiated properties

There are certain properties that physicalists need not worry about at all, but that are instantiated by contingently existing individuals. Consider, for example, the property of *being self-identical*, the property of *being such that 2+2=4*, or the property of *being a philosopher or not a philosopher*. On the assumption that these are respectable properties in the first place, it seems reasonable to think that they are properties every individual has necessarily (that is, in all worlds in which the respective individual exists), and which are instantiated by some individual in every possible world (assuming that there is no possible world in which there is no individual at all). Is it part of the commitments of the physicalist that such properties need to be broadly physical as well? I do not think so.

On the formulation of the physicalist thesis above, physicalism comes out false if the properties just considered are neither physical nor metaphysically depend on physical properties. Thus, a further modification is required. Let me consider three potential alternative cases:

(P10a) Physicalism is true *iff* every property had by any individual that exists contingently or is causal either (i) is a narrowly physical property or (ii) metaphysically depends on narrowly physical properties *or* (iii) *is a property that is necessarily had by that individual.*

(P10b) Physicalism is true *iff* every property had by any individual that exists contingently or is causal either (i) is a narrowly physical property or (ii) metaphysically depends on narrowly physical properties *or* (iii) *is a property that is necessarily had by some individual.*

(P10c) Physicalism is true *iff* every property had by any individual that exists contingently or is causal either (i) is a narrowly physical property or (ii) metaphysically depends on narrowly physical properties *or* (iii) *is a property that is necessarily had by every individual.*

We can immediately rule out modification (P10a) as adequate. First, note that the new clause in (P10a) captures even properties that are not instantiated in every possible world (unless we think that every individual exists necessarily, which seems unreasonable). The idea is rather that the property is instantiated by the individual in question in every world *in which the individual exists*.

What makes (P10a) inadequate is the following: Consider for example the property of *being human*. This is a property that is arguably had by you and me, not only contingently, but necessarily. After all, *being human* seems to be essential to us, and this entails that we have this property necessarily, i.e. in every possible world in which we exist (cf. Kripke 1980). Now, suppose that being human neither is a physical property nor metaphysically depends on physical properties. In such a case, physicalism should intuitively come out false. But it does not, according to (P10a), because of the new clause (iii). Thus, (P10a) is too liberal, has to be rejected.

What about (P10b) and (P10c)? In order to account for the example properties of *being self-identical*, *being such that 2+2=4*, and *being a philosopher or not a philosopher*, the more restrictive (P10c) suffices. There are some properties, like *being prime*, which are arguably necessarily instantiated by some, but not all individuals, and which the physicalist should not be concerned about either. But as long as such properties are only instantiated by individuals that are neither contingent nor causal, as is the case with *being prime*, which is instantiated only by certain numbers, they are not considered anyway, so we need not move to (P10b) to account for them. There is further reason to favor (P10c) over (P10b). Suppose that there is a deity that exists necessarily, and thus instantiates the property of *being a deity* in every possible world. In such a case, physicalism should come out false if *being a deity* is neither a physical property nor metaphysically dependent on the physical properties, so (P10b) should not be adopted. This leaves us with (P10c).

2.2.4 Haecceitistic properties

There is another controversial set of properties that might trouble our definition of physicalism: haecceities and, more generally, haecceitistic properties. Examples of the former properties are the property of *being identical to Socrates* and the property of *being the number Two*. Other terms for such properties include 'thisnesses' and 'individual essences' (Cowling 2016: section 2). Examples of the latter properties include haecceities as well as further properties like *being Saul Kripke's father* and *being at three meters distance from Dan Dennett*. For haecceities like the property of *being (identical to) Socrates* to be instantiated, the existence of the individual in question, in this case of Socrates, is both necessary and sufficient, and only that individual can have this property. The property of *being at three meters distance from Dan Dennett* likewise requires the existence of the individual in question, Dan Dennett, but it can be instantiated by other individuals than Dan Dennett, and the existence of Dan Dennett is not sufficient for it to be instantiated. In the actual world, it is likely that we always find something that has that property, but consider a possible world in which poor Dan Dennett is the only entity in the whole universe.[31] In such a world, although Dan Dennett exists, no individual has the property in question.

One important reason for introducing haecceities is that we arguably need them to account for cases that extend the one Max Black (1952: 156) considers as a counterexample against the principle of the identity of indiscernibles:

> Isn't it logically possible that the universe should have contained nothing but two exactly similar spheres? We might suppose that each was made of chemically pure iron, had a diameter of one mile, that they had the same temperature, colour, and so on, and that nothing else existed. Then every quality and relational characteristic of the one would also be a property of the other.

Take the world under consideration, and consider a world very similar to this one, with one difference: The two spheres have switched their places. If you think that the worlds just considered are indeed two different worlds rather than one and the same, the question is: What is the difference between these two worlds? Since the two worlds are qualitatively[32] exactly similar, what is it that accounts for the alleged difference between the worlds? The friend of haecceities has a simple solution. The two worlds differ with respect to the distribution of the haecceitistic properties *being identical to this sphere* and *being identical to that sphere* (cf. Cowling 2016: section 4.1).

The connection between haecceities, haecceitistic properties more generally, and physicalism is controversial. Take the property of *being identical to Socrates* again, and suppose that Socrates, an individual, indeed instantiates this property. Physicalism on our current definition (P10c) requires that this property is either (i) a physical property, or (ii) a property that metaphysically depends on physical properties, or (iii) a property that is necessarily instantiated by every individual whatsoever. We can obviously rule out (iii), since only Socrates can have this property, so there are only two remaining options. Either, the property of

---

31 If you don't believe that there is such a possible world, replace Dan Dennett in the example with some individual you think could also exist in an otherwise empty universe (maybe some fundamental particle) and call it, say, "Fred". Then, the relevant haecceitistic property is *being at three meters distance from Fred*.
32 I do not want to delve into the details of how to define what a qualitative property is. The notion of a qualitative property is one of those philosophical notions that turn out to be notoriously difficult to define without relying on other notions that are similarly difficult to define. For an overview over the various accounts, see Cowling (2015), who finally settles for the view that the notion is primitive.

being identical to Socrates is a physical property, or it metaphysically depends on physical properties. Now, if metaphysical dependence entails necessitation, so that the instantiation of the dependent property is guaranteed given the instantiation of the dependence base properties, it is clear that the haecceitistic properties do not metaphysically depend on any qualitative properties. To see this, consider the two spheres again: They do not differ qualitatively, but differ with respect to their haecceities. If all physical properties are qualitative properties, then the two remaining options (i) and (ii) are ruled out as well. So, in order for physicalism in the form of (P10c) to be compatible with haecceitistic properties, we need to assume that there are non-qualitative physical properties. In this case, haecceitistic properties either would need to be physical properties themselves or would need to metaphysically depend on physical properties, including non-qualitative ones. Whether or not physical properties can be non-qualitative depends on what is meant by a physical property. My account (see section 3.4.2) does not rule out such a situation, but does not suggest it either.[33]

Sam Cowling (2015: 280–281), who assumes that physical properties are all qualitative, argues that we should not draw the conclusion that physicalism is incompatible with haecceitistic properties. Rather, we should restrict the physicalist thesis to qualitative properties only. David Chalmers (1996: 367) makes a similar claim:

> I will always be considering worlds 'qualitatively,' and abstracting away from question of 'haecceity.' That is, I will count two worlds that are qualitatively identical as identical and will not be concerned with questions about whether individuals in those worlds might have different 'identities.'

Thus, in accordance with what Chalmers and Cowling claim, we can reformulate physicalism as follows:

(P11) Physicalism is true *iff* every *qualitative* property had by any individual that exists contingently or is causal either (i) is a narrowly physical property or (ii) metaphysically depends on narrowly physical properties or (iii) is a property that is necessarily had by every individual.

---

33 If one thinks, other than I have suggested, that identity properties like *being (identical to) Socrates* are instantiated qualitative properties, then, on my view, one is committed to the claim that such properties are either physical or metaphysically dependent on physical properties if one wants to be a physicalist. Thanks to an anonymous reviewer for pointing that out to me.

Brian McLaughlin (2007a: 201) takes things somewhat differently than Cowling and Chalmers. He claims that physicalists agree on certain assumptions, including the assumption that haecceitism is false:

> [There are] certain (not entirely uncontroversial) assumptions that are common ground to a priori and a posteriori physicalists. One such assumption is that haecceitism is false, where haecceitism is understood to be the doctrine that two worlds can differ either only in what objects they contain or only in which objects have which complete qualitative profiles. It will be assumed here that all truths globally supervene on qualitative truths, and so that haecceitism is false.

This is not yet the claim that physicalism is incompatible with haecceitism. If it is just that physicalists agree on the claim that haecceitism is false, then one might think that all that is claimed is that at least with regard to the actual world, the adaptation introduced in (P11) is unnecessary since all instantiated properties in the actual world are qualitative anyway.

Thomas Hofweber (2005) advocates the stronger view that physicalism and haecceitism are indeed incompatible. More generally, he argues that physicalism is incompatible with the instantiation of object-dependent properties, and furthermore with the direct reference theory for proper names, since the truth of direct reference theory allegedly entails the instantiation of object-dependent properties. According to him, "the supervenience of the nonphysical properties of physical objects on their physical properties is generally believed to be a necessary condition for a satisfactory physicalistic world view, and an acceptable version of physicalism" (2005: 5). Thus, it seems that on his view, (P11) would be too weak because it explicitly leaves out non-qualitative properties. However, he does not argue for this claim, but presupposes it for his argument against the compatibility of physicalism with the instantiation of object-dependent properties, and thus haecceitistic properties.

Hofweber also claims that there are no object-dependent properties that are physical. He starts out outlining in broad brushstrokes what he conceives to be the basic idea behind physicalism (2005: 18):

> To see which properties are the physical ones we have to look at what motivated the idea of physicalism, the idea that the physical determines the rest. The idea, again simply put, was that all physical objects are made up from smallest stuff, and this smallest stuff has basic properties and relations which together are sufficient to determine its behavior. In addition, the properties that count as physical are only the ones that are necessary in the determination of the behavior of the smallest stuff. If one class of properties is sufficient to determine the behavior then any class that contains it will be sufficient as well, but this larger class will contain nonphysical properties. The physical properties are thus the smallest class of properties that are sufficient to determine the behavior of the smallest stuff. The idea of

physicalism is that since everything is built up from this smallest stuff these properties are sufficient to determine the rest.

What Hofweber describes here is clearly a form of microphysicalism, a thesis that is stronger than the minimal physicalism I have in mind. What I find more interesting, however, is that he starts out with the claim that the underlying idea of physicalism is that the physical properties are sufficient to determine the *behavior* of the smallest stuff, but then goes on to claim that physicalism entails that these properties are sufficient to determine the rest (instead of *the behavior of* the rest). If the claim were the latter, then object-dependent properties would not be an issue if they do not play a role in the behavior of any entity. On the basis of these considerations about the characteristics of physical properties, Hofweber (2005: 18) goes on to argue that there are no object-dependent physical properties:

> Thus the question whether or not some physical properties are object-dependent properties is not whether or not some physical objects have object-dependent properties, but whether or not these properties are part of the smallest class of properties that are jointly sufficient to determine the behavior of the stuff that all physical objects are made of. And it is here that the strangeness and irrelevance of object-dependent properties becomes apparent at the physical level. Even if the smallest stuff has object-dependent properties, these properties are completely irrelevant for their behavior.

So according to Hofweber, since object-dependent properties do not contribute to the behavior of the entities in question, but physical properties do, object-dependent properties are not physical.

Daly and Liggins (2010) challenge Hofweber's argument. They consider the propery of *having a certain space-time location*, which seems to be a good candidate for a prototypical physical property that plays a certain role in how the things that have it behave, and argue that Hofweber does not provide any good reason to think that this property is not an object-dependent property. This strategy seems to be close to the strategy I considered earlier – that is to claim that some physical properties might be non-qualitative, so that other non-qualitative properties, although not being necessitated by the qualitative physical properties, might be necessitated by the physical properties if we take into account both qualitative and non-qualitative ones. Similarly, Almotohari and Rochford (2012) argue that given the way Hofweber envisages things, it is no wonder he thinks that physicalism is incompatible with the existence of object-dependent properties. However, the friend of object-dependent properties can resist Hofweber's claim that object-dependent properties do not play any role in bringing about the behavior of objects, and thus also Hofweber's conclusion that they are non-physical.

Given that I understand the notion of a physical property quite differently to Hofweber, as will become clear in the next chapter, I agree with his critics' suggestion that it remains open to the physicalist to claim that haecceitistic properties are physical. Moreover, what has been said so far does not provide us with a good reason to think that we should not restrict physicalism to qualitative properties, which would save us from all these worries in the first place. Since (P11) is the less restrictive thesis, it seems that we can take up (P11) as our candidate physicalist thesis, unless there are further concerns that have not been addressed yet. In case it later turns out that there are other problems with (P11) that do not affect (P10c), we can still take a step back and avoid the adaptation in (P11). Even in this case, there remain options for the friends of haecceities to account for them in a physicalist framework, even though these options come with certain commitments with regard to the nature of physical properties that some may not like.

2.2.5 Positive and negative properties

There is a final set of properties that we have not addressed yet that physicalists intuitively need not be worried about, but that require adaptation of our definition. These are properties like *being such that there are no ghosts*, a property that everything instantiates contingently if it is instantiated at all, and properties like *being the tallest building*, a superlative property contingently instantiated by a physical individual only on the assumption that there are no taller buildings made of ectoplasm. Whether or not, and if so, where, these properties are instantiated seems to depend at least in part on the *absence* of certain property instances. It does not intuitively seem that physicalism would be false even if those properties would turn out to neither be physical properties nor metaphysically depend on the physical properties. We will later get back to these properties when considering some of the problems of supervenience-based characterizations of physicalism (section 4.4.1). For now, what is important is how we accommodate for the exclusion of these properties in our definition. Following Chalmers (1996), let us call the set of such properties the set of 'negative properties', and the set of all properties that do not belong to this set the set of 'positive properties'. We can then adapt our definition as follows:

(P12) Physicalism is true *iff* every *positive* qualitative property had by any individual that exists contingently or is causal either (i) is a narrowly physical property or (ii) metaphysically depends on narrowly physical properties or (iii) is a property that is necessarily had by every individual.

There are a couple of ways that one might try to get a better grip on how positive and negative properties are distinguished from each other. One way, considered by Daniel Stoljar, is to say that "a positive property is a property whose canonical expression does not involve negation" (Stoljar 2010: 135), and likewise to take a negative property to be one whose canonical expression does. This intuitively seems to capture properties like *being such that there are no ghosts* or *being such that there is no ectoplasm*. But it also requires that the canonical description of the property of *being the tallest building* is something along the lines of *being a building that is such that there is no taller building*, which seems a little bit off as a canonical description.

David Chalmers (1996: 40) provides an alternative account of the notion of a positive property:

> [A] positive property is one that if instantiated in a world *W*, is also instantiated by the corresponding individual in all worlds that contain *W* as a proper part.

The idea behind this definition is simple. Suppose you have a world that is just like the actual world, which we assume to include no ghosts, but in addition to all the entities in our world, there are some ghosts in that world. Since the property of *being such that there are no ghosts* is not instantiated by anything in that world, while it is instantiated by everything in our world, this property is to be considered a negative property. Likewise considerations apply to the property of *being the tallest building*. A world that in addition to everything in our world includes an ectoplasmic building that is taller than any physical building will be such that *being the tallest building* is instantiated by something else than in our world, and so this property is to be considered a negative property.

Such a definition of a positive property requires that we can make sense of the notion of correspondence of individuals in different possible worlds, and the conditions under which one world is a proper part of another world. One way to deal with the correspondence of individuals is in terms of the instantiation of haecceities. According to such an account, an individual in a world w corresponds to another individual in world w^* *iff* the individuals instantiate the same haecceity or individual essence. However, it is very controversial whether there are haecceities in the first place, and whether inhabitants of different worlds can instantiate the same haecceity. This is an issue that is closely connected to questions regarding of trans-world identity of individuals. An alternative way to account for the issue of correspondence of individuals across worlds is in terms of a resemblance-based counterpart theory (e. g. Lewis 1986) that does not require trans-world identity. Such accounts are similarly controversial.

Similar issues arise with regard to the idea of one world being a proper part of another. Depending on one's views about what a possible world is, this might be spelled out in different ways. A full-fledged modal realist like David Lewis (1986), who thinks that other possible worlds are concrete entities just like the actual world, might tell a different story than somebody who thinks that possible worlds are abstract entities like maximal consistent sets of propositions (e. g. Adams 1974) or complete possible states of affairs (Platinga 1974; 1976). Chalmers takes the notion of one world being a proper part of another, or what he calls the 'containment relation', to be primitive, as he indicates in a footnote (Chalmers 1996: 363 [fn14]):

> For the purposes of this definition, the containment relation between worlds can be taken as primitive. [...] Something needs to be taken as primitive, and the containment relation seems to be as clear as any.

Again, I do not think that the truth of physicalism should presuppose the truth of any of these views regarding the nature of possible worlds, the possibility of trans-world identity and the like, and thus leave it to defenders of particular physicalist views to spell out how these notions are to be understood in detail.

2.2.6 Relations

Typically, physicalism is formulated in terms of properties, and it is quietly assumed that this is understood broadly to also capture relations (see e. g. Stoljar 2010: 40). In order to make this explicit, we can reformulate our thesis of physicalism as follows:

(P12) Physicalism is true *iff*
    (a) every positive qualitative property had by any individual that exists contingently or is causal either
        (i) is a narrowly physical property or
        (ii) metaphysically depends on narrowly physical properties *and relations* or
        (iii) is a property that is necessarily had by every individual, *and*
    (b) *every positive qualitative relation had by any plurality that exists contingently or is causal either*

(i) *is a narrowly physical relation or*
(ii) *metaphysically depends on narrowly physical properties and relations or*
(iii) *is a relation that is necessarily had by every plurality formed of the same number of individuals.*

In principle, one could also reformulate the statement by quantifying over any number of individuals and any relation between that number of individuals, but this becomes complicated very quickly, so I use the notion of a plurality to make it easier to talk about relations between individuals. A plurality is taken to be formed of the individuals that stand in the relation in question, and it is structured or ordered in a similar way as tuples are, so that the plurality formed of Paul and Mary, in that order, may instantiate the relation *being the brother of*, whereas the plurality formed of Mary and Paul does not instantiate this relation. I take it that it is the plurality that instantiates the relation in question, but the notion of a plurality is supposed to come with as little ontological baggage as possible. It is just whatever is needed to make sense of statements like 'There is an x such that x instantiates relation R', and the existence of a plurality is supposed to require nothing more than that the corresponding individuals exist and stand in relation R. If one thinks for example that the entities instantiating the relations are tuples of individuals, and so that pluralities are just tuples, I am fine with that. I avoid using the notion of a tuple here because it might lead to the confusion that we are talking about abstract entities.

Note also that we need not consider pluralities formed of individuals that inhabit different worlds. In order for clause (iii) to be satisfied, what is required is that every plurality formed of individuals from the same world stand in the relation in question. So for example, the relation expressed by the predicate '... inhabits the same world as ...' falls into the set of properties that satisfy (iii), even though it is not satisfied by pairs of individuals that inhabit different worlds. If we would require such inter-worldly pluralities to stand in the respective relations in order for (iii) to be satisfied, then a physicalist would have to account for relations like the one just considered in terms of clauses (i) and (ii), but intuitively, no one would expect the physicalist to be required to do so.

Having formulated the thesis to include relations in this chapter explicitly, I will in the further chapters for the most part follow the habit of others to speak about properties more loosely to also include relations. This makes it easier to express things, and as far as I can see, nothing I say later requires that we restrict ourselves to properties *proper* (as opposed to properties understood in the broader sense that includes relations).

2.2.7 Relativizing to worlds

So far, the definitions only considered criteria for physicalism to be true, and this is typically understood as 'true of the actual world'. While physicalism is typically considered with regard to the actual world, we can also ask whether physicalism is true of some other possible world we want to consider. Thus, in order to relativize to arbitrary worlds, we need to restate the thesis as follows:

(P)   Physicalism is true *of world w iff*
   (a) every positive qualitative property had by any individual *at w* that exists contingently or is causal either
      (i) is a narrowly physical property *instantiated at w* or
      (ii) metaphysically depends on narrowly physical properties and relations *instantiated at w* or
      (iii) is a property that is necessarily had by every individual, and
   (b) every positive qualitative relation had by any plurality *at w* that exists contingently or is causal either
      (i) is a narrowly physical relation *instantiated at w* or
      (ii) metaphysically depends on narrowly physical properties and relations *instantiated at w* or
      (iii) is a relation that is necessarily had by every plurality formed of the same number of individuals.

While the first 'instantiated at *w*' in both clauses is somewhat redundant because the identity relation between the narrowly physical property/relation in question and the property/relation had by an individual at *w* already makes sure that the property/relation is instantiated, the second 'instantiated at *w*' plays a more important role, since it secures that the physical properties and relations other properties/relations metaphysically depend upon are indeed instantiated in the world in question. This becomes relevant in the case in which a property/relation has multiple dependence bases. Consider the example of color properties again: Let us assume that the property of *being red* metaphysically depends on the property of *being crimson*, but also on the property of *being scarlet*. Now consider the thesis that at world *w*, determinable colors metaphysically depend on determinate colors. It does not help that *being red* also metaphysically depends on *being scarlet* if we consider a world in which the only instantiated shade of red is *being crimson*.

In general, the definition we have now arrived at seems to be a very good candidate for an appropriate definition of physicalism, and will serve as the basis for the further investigations in the rest of the book.

2.3 Summary

Starting out from one of the historical ancestors of physicalism, early modern materialism, and adapting the phrasing to account for various challenges, including challenges that are well-known, as well as some that do not typically receive the required attention in the literature, I have developed a more rigorous formulation of physicalism that can provide the basis for the work in the further chapters. I have made clear that physicalism is to be understood primarily as a claim about property types instantiated by individuals. This does not mean, however, that it is not also a claim about objects (individuals), events, facts and the like. It is only that such particulars are physical only derivatively, in virtue of only having properties that are closely tied to the physical properties, or by being constituted by properties by such properties. What physical properties are, and how other properties need to be tied to the physical properties, that is, how the notion of metaphysical dependence is to be spelled out, will be addressed in the remaining chapters.

3 "Physical"

In the previous chapter, I have arrived at a definition of physicalism of the following form:

(P) Physicalism is true of world w *iff*
    (a) every positive qualitative property had by any individual at w that exists contingently or is causal either
        (i) is a narrowly physical property instantiated at w or
        (ii) metaphysically depends on narrowly physical properties and relations instantiated at w or
        (iii) is a property that is necessarily had by every individual, and
    (b) every positive qualitative relation had by any plurality at w that exists contingently or is causal either
        (i) is a narrowly physical relation instantiated at w or
        (ii) metaphysically depends on narrowly physical properties and relations instantiated at w or
        (iii) is a relation that is necessarily had by every plurality formed of the same number of individuals.

In this chapter, I will move on to address the question what is meant by a narrowly physical property. I however omit the qualifier 'narrowly' from now on, and take it as understood that whenever I talk about a physical property without further qualification, what I mean is a narrowly physical property. The subsequent chapters will then address the question of what exactly metaphysical dependence is.

Philosophers are often concerned with trying to provide conceptual analyses of terms within ordinary language. For example, the long-lasting debate regarding the notion of knowledge, initiated by the seminal two and a half page paper "Is justified true belief knowledge?" by Edmund Gettier (1963), has revolved around the question of finding an adequate definition of the term 'knowledge' that fits our intuitions regarding all kinds of specific cases, which are arguably driven by ordinary language use. For the present purposes, however, we do not need a conceptual analysis of 'physical property' that fits all cases in ordinary language, and I think that this would be a Sisyphean task anyway. Rather, we need a definition that is suitable for a particular thesis as debated by philosophers: *physicalism*. Thus, we do not need to shy away from providing a *stipulative* definition of the term 'physical'.

Nevertheless, similar to the case of a definition of 'knowledge', we can test definitions of the term 'physical', or definitions of physicalism, by using the *method of cases*. That is, we can take a suggestion for a definition of 'physical property', plug it into a definition of physicalism, and ask whether physicalism, so defined, is true of worlds we (that is, in this case, philosophers who are well-acquainted with the corresponding debates) would intuitively consider paradigmatic cases of physicalist worlds, and false of worlds we would consider paradigmatic cases of non-physicalist worlds. For example, if an alleged definition of physicalism is such that it is true of a world that is as Descartes thought our world is, and thus populated by immaterial souls, we are strongly inclined – and rightly so – to think that there is something wrong with the definition. In such a case, there are at least two options to try to fix the problem. Either, we can try to adapt our definition of physicalism while keeping fixed our characterization of the physical, or we can try to keep fixed the definition of physicalism and adapt our characterization of the physical. In this chapter, I will investigate the latter route.

The question how to characterize the notion of the physical has not been considered problematic by all philosophers concerned with how to define the thesis of physicalism. On the very first page of her 1978 book entitled "Physicalism", Kathleen Vaughan Wilkes writes the following (1978: 1–2):

> For our present purposes the scope of the term 'physical' is relatively unproblematic. All we need to say about it at the moment is that the expression 'the physical' picks out all and only the items, processes, concepts, laws, hypotheses, theories, or theoretical postulates used essentially by physical scientists. Any concept, therefore, which plays a significant role in a theory belonging to the physical sciences is *eo ipso* a physical concept. [...] [The philosopher] must accept as 'physical' whatever the physical scientist says is such.

In this short passage, Wilkes might be taken to make three important claims.[34] *First*, she seems to claim that the notion of the physical is quite unproblematic in the context of defining physicalism. I find this claim very surprising. As we will see shortly, finding a proper account of the physical, even if we restrict ourselves to properties, turns out to be more problematic than Wilkes seems to expect.

Second, she claims that the notion of the physical is tied to what physical scientists are concerned with. She mentions a couple of different categories of entities, but it seems to me that the most important one for her is the category of physical theories. After all, it is the *theories* of physical scientists that make

---

[34] Whether this interpretation is the one she intended is of no concern for our purposes.

use of predicates that pick out entities from the other categories she mentions. It is not quite clear from the quotation, however, which physical theory exactly she has in mind. Some might think that it is *current* physics, but with very few exceptions (mainly Melnyk 1997; 2003), philosophers who participate in the debate disagree. Some suggest that rather than current physical theory, what is appealed to is a complete or ideal *future* physics (e.g. Poland 1994; Dowell 2006a; 2006b). This distinction between current and future physics plays a prominent role in what has been called 'Hempel's Dilemma'[35] (Hempel 1969; Hellman 1985; Melnyk 1997), which I will address in section 3.2.1 below.

Third, Wilkes claims that philosophers (*qua* being philosophers) are not qualified to tell what counts as physical. Rather, the physical scientists have to decide about that. This seems to be correct if she means that once we have decided that the notion of the physical is tied to physics, the philosopher cannot deny that a certain concept used essentially by physical scientists to outline their theories is a physical concept, and the properties picked out by such concepts are physical properties. However, since physicalism is a metaphysical doctrine and thus belongs to the domain of philosophy, the question how the notion of the physical *as used in the definition of physicalism* is to be understood seems to be a genuinely philosophical question. Several options have been addressed in the debate, and while many of them indeed tie 'the physical' to the notion of a physical theory, or to physics, not all of them do. I will address some such views in section 3.3 and 3.4.

3.1 Physical properties: a catalogue of constraints

Before moving on to the critical evaluation of different accounts from the literature, I would like to assemble something like a 'wish-list' with constraints that, from my point of view, a proper definition of '… is a physical property' as used within a definition of physicalism is supposed to fulfill:[36]

- *Truth-Aptness Constraint:* Physicalism is to be defined in a way that makes physicalism a truth-apt thesis. While some have denied that physicalism is truth-apt at all and claim instead that physicalism is an attitude or an oath towards science (e.g. Ney 2008a), the 'physicalism' that is based on such an account of the physical cannot be what is debated using the typical

---

[35] While Hellman already states that Hempel's concern poses a dilemma, Melnyk (1997) first introduces the name 'Hempel's Dilemma'.
[36] Some of these criteria are similar to those proposed by Poland (1994: 123–124) and Dowell (2006b: 28–30).

arguments that are put forward against the view – most notably Jackson's (1982) knowledge argument and Chalmers' (1996; 2010) conceivability argument. Since my focus of interest here is the thesis that underlies these debates, accounts that do not satisfy this constraint cannot be what is at issue.

- *Nontrivial Truth Constraint:* The predicate '... is a physical property' has to be defined in a way that does not make physicalism a thesis that is trivially true, that is, true by definition, of the actual world, or even of all possible worlds (see also Dowell 2006b: 28). If, say, we would claim that a property is physical *iff* it is instantiated in the actual world, then physicalism would come out trivially true of our world, whether or not our world is inhabited by all sorts of entities like Cartesian souls, ghosts and ectoplasm with all their corresponding properties, whatever they might be. So this cannot be what we want. Similarly, we should not say that a property is physical *iff* it does not metaphysically depend on any other properties instantiated at w, or that a property is physical *iff* it is an absolutely fundamental property at w. According to such a definition, physicalism would come out true of all possible worlds in which metaphysically independent or absolutely fundamental properties are instantiated, respectively, but only for the uninteresting reason that we defined it in that way. Another obvious dead end is a view that takes physical properties to be the properties physics is concerned with, and takes physics to be *the true theory of everything*, not in the sense of an *a posteriori* empirical hypothesis, but in the sense of a definition. Of course, if physicalism is true, physics might serve this purpose. But we should not *define* physics in this way in order to avoid triviality.
- *Nontrivial Falsity Constraint:* Likewise, the predicate '... is a physical property' has to be defined in a way that does not make physicalism trivially or otherwise obviously false, given our current understanding of what the world is like. To make physicalism trivially false is to define it in a way that entails a contradiction, and this is obviously not a good idea. Definitions that make physicalism 'otherwise obviously' false do not involve a contradiction, but are still such that such a definition of the physical plugged into a definition of physicalism would clearly render physicalism false of the actual world. For example, if we would say that a property is physical *iff* it is picked out by a predicate of 19th-century physics, physicalism so construed would be clearly false of the actual world. As we will see in the next section, similar considerations apply if we use current physics instead of 19th-century physics in such a way. One important reason why we should not define the notion of a physical property in a way that makes physicalism come out obviously false is that such a definition of physicalism cannot be the one in question in the central debates about whether or not physicalism is true, which are most-

ly driven by complex conceivability arguments. If physicalism were a thesis that is obviously false, why would philosophers like David Chalmers (1996; 2010) bother to put forward more and more complex arguments based on the alleged conceivability of zombies and the like?

- *Contingent A Posteriori Thesis Constraint:* In general, a definition of physicalism that enables us to decide on *a priori* grounds whether physicalism is true or false does not seem to be appropriate. Rather, physicalism is supposed to be a substantial contingent *a posteriori* thesis about what the world under consideration is like, that is, its truth or falsity should depend on the properties that are instantiated in the world under consideration, including the contingently instantiated ones. This criterion is linked to the *Nontrivial Truth Constraint*, as almost all of the unacceptable example definitions of '... is a physical property' provided above are such that we could know on *a priori* grounds that physicalism is true.
- *Progress of Physics Constraint:* The predicate '... is a physical property' is not to be defined in a way that entails that almost *any* substantial further progress in physics, like the introduction of a further kind of fundamental particle, would render physicalism false. The reason to think that this constraint should be respected is the same as the one I have provided above for the *Nontrivial Falsity Constraint*. If we would only need to show that physics will likely introduce further kinds of fundamental entities (and thus further properties) to show that physicalism is likely false, why would anyone bother providing such complex arguments as the conceivability argument for the falsity of physicalism?
- *Traditional Rivals Constraint:* The predicate '... is a physical property' is to be defined in a way that does not rule out a proper distinction of physicalism from its traditional rivals, *dualism*, and more generally *pluralism*, as well as monist rivals such as *idealism*[37] and what I would like to call '*ectoplasmism*'. The latter view is formulated analogously to physicalism, but instead of '... is a physical property', we plug '... is an ectoplasmic property' into the definition. Here, ectoplasmic properties are supposed to be of a nature very different to the nature of the properties instantiated in our world. Ectoplasmism only becomes important once we do not restrict our focus to the actual world, but consider the truth of physicalism in other possible worlds,

---

[37] There is a special case in which idealism and physicalism coincide. This is due to the liberal account of minimal physicalism I develop here, which I take to be compatible with some forms of panpsychism. The case I have in mind is one in which every single instantiated property turns out to be both mental and physical, so that both idealism and physicalism are true at the same time.

because physicalism should intuitively not be true of a world in which the properties on which everything else depends are very different in nature from those instantiated in our world.

- *Nontrivial Inclusion of Special Science Properties Constraint:* As indicated earlier, I take physicalism to have two main historical ancestors: early modern materialism and the neo-positivist doctrine of semantic 'physicalism' of Carnap (1931; 1932) and Neurath (1931). The latter view takes physics to have a special role within the sciences, insofar as every meaningful statement, including those of the special sciences, is synonymous with a statement that only includes terms of physics and topic-neutral terms. In some sense, this ancestry needs to be reflected in our definition of the physical. Accordingly, a physicalism *simpliciter* that takes the properties of the special sciences, such as chemical, biological, or even psychological (i.e., mental), social or economic properties to be physical by definition is not acceptable. Such an account is too inclusive and makes the thesis of physicalism a rather weak thesis (cf. Poland 1994: 114–115).[38] It might turn out that some of the special science properties are indeed identical to physical properties, but if this is so, it is a matter of *a posteriori* identity rather than a matter of definition.

- *Alien Physical Properties Constraint:* An alien physical property[39] is a physical property that is not instantiated in our world. What I have in mind here is e.g. the property of *being such-and-such kind of particle*, where there are no such particles at our world, but they are only slightly different from the particles we have in our world. There seems to be nothing wrong with such a property, and if it would exist, we would have no concerns to include it into our physics. Still, any definition of a physical property that is closely tied to actual world physics, regardless of whether it is current or future physics, will not allow for such properties. Thus, if we do not want to rule out the possibility of alien physical properties, we need to make sure to define the predicate '... is a physical property' in a way that is liberal enough to capture these properties. Like the issue of ectoplasmic properties, this is only

---

[38] Another way to see this is the following: Suppose somebody claims that mental properties need to metaphysically depend on biological properties, say, because otherwise they would be very spooky. Furthermore, this person claims that biological, chemical, etc. properties do not metaphysically depend on the physical properties. Rather, they are all fundamental properties that show no dependency structure whatsoever, but according to this person, there is nothing spooky about that. A notion of the physical that includes all special science properties by definition would be compatible with such a view, but it is a view I find very strange.

[39] The notion of an alien property is due to David Lewis (1983).

relevant for a definition of physicalism that is applicable to arbitrary possible worlds, rather than just the actual world. Since the former is what I attempt here, the account of the physical needs to be liberal enough to capture cases of alien physical properties (see also Daly 1998: 202).
- *Direction of Priority Constraint:* As mentioned earlier, there are different versions of physicalism with regard to the metaphysical dependence relations across the mereological hierarchy. I take physicalism to be different from microphysicalism, which is a version of physicalism that takes the entities at the micro-level to be mereologically prior to or mereologically more fundamental than the entities composed of them. Since I think that minimal physicalism should be compatible with priority monism (Schaffer 2010; Goff 2017), which claims that wholes are mereologically prior to their parts, so that the universe as a whole is the mereologically most fundamental entity, the notion of the physical should not presume a particular order of priority with respect to the mereological hierarchy.
- *Non-Physic_sal-Properties Constraint:* According to advocates of an idea that can be traced back to Bertrand Russell (1927), physics, and natural science more generally, only tells us what entities do, rather than what they are, or what their nature is. In other words, physics talks about the properties it is concerned with in purely dispositional terms. Galen Strawson (2008 [2003]) calls dispositional properties pertinent to physics 'physic_sal properties', as opposed to 'physical properties', which he understands more broadly as also encompassing the categorical bases of dispositional properties.[40] The notion of a physical property should not rule out *a priori* that categorical base properties of dispositional properties are physical.[41]

---

40 While Strawson's distinction is in general associated with a family of pan(proto)psychist views labeled 'Russellian monism' that has gained much attention in the recent years (for an overview, see e.g. Alter and Nagasawa 2012), I take this constraint to be neutral with respect to the relation between the categorical properties which underlie the dispositional properties physics is concerned with on the one hand, and (proto)phenomenal properties on the other.
41 Whether or not we should count *any* categorical base property of a dispositional property pertinent to physics as physical depends on at least two factors. On the one hand, it depends on the way the semantics of natural science predicates works. If those predicates pick out categorical base properties, categorical properties should clearly count as physical; if they pick out dispositions, it is less clear what we should say. Second, it depends on the role of laws of nature in establishing the link between categorical properties and dispositions. In case the connection between the two is only established by a law of nature, one might think that both the disposition and its categorical base are on a par with regard to metaphysical priority (cf. Chalmers 2015: 264).

3.2 *A posteriori* accounts of the physical

After considering the constraints that a definition of the physical is supposed to meet, we can now move on to discuss the views that are on the table and critically evaluate them with regard to their ability to satisfy these constraints. Some of the views advocated in the literature tie the notion of the physical to a specific theory of physics. Since such accounts largely leave the question of what counts as physical to the physicists, just as Wilkes does in the quote at the beginning of this chapter, they are considered to be *a posteriori* accounts of the physical. Such views are opposed to *a priori* accounts of the physical, which, somewhat in the tradition of classical materialist views that stipulatively defined the physical in terms of spatio-temporal extendedness and solidity, do not want to leave it to the physicists to tell us what counts as a physical property. Moreover, there are mixed views that combine aspects of both extremes. While advocates of *a posteriori* views of the physical agree that it is the job of the physicists to tell us what properties are physical, they may disagree on which particular physics the notion of a physical property needs to be tied to. The debate among *a posteriori* physicalists has mostly focused on the question whether we should appeal to *current physics* or rather to *future physics* to define our notion of a physical property. Along with Crook and Gillett (2001: 335), I call those who think that the notion of a physical property should be tied to current physics *currentists*, and those who go for future physics *futurists*.

3.2.1 Hempel's dilemma: trouble for currentists and futurists

In a 1980 commentary to Nelson Goodman's book "Ways of World Making", Carl Gustav Hempel raises a substantial problem for physicalists who want to tie the notion of the physical to a particular physical theory. His original worry is directed at Otto Neurath's semantic 'physicalism' (Neurath 1931), which I have pointed to above as one of the historical ancestors of physicalism, which is not a metaphysical thesis but one about the primacy of the language of physics as the unitary language of science. Nevertheless, an analogous worry can be directed at advocates of the metaphysical thesis of physicalism that I am concerned with here.

Geoffrey Hellman wrote the probably most often cited passage that articulates Hempel's dilemma (1985: 609):

> Perhaps the most serious objection to all efforts to articulate physicalism is that raised by Carl Hempel: current physics is surely incomplete (even in its ontology) as well as inaccu-

rate (in its laws). This poses a dilemma: either physicalist principles are based on current physics, in which case there is every reason to think they are false; or else they are not, in which case it is, at best, difficult to interpret them, since they are based on a "physics" that does not exist – yet we lack any general criterion of "physical object, property, or law" framed independently of existing physical theory.

On the currentist's horn of the dilemma, physical properties are considered to be the properties current physics is concerned with:

> *Currentism:* F is a physical property *iff* F is expressed by a predicate of current physics.

One question that immediately arises with respect to currentism is what exactly current physics is supposed to encompass. For example, should we include those parts of physics that are still debated among physicists? Melnyk (2003: 15–16), in his defense of a currentist account of the physical, argues that we should only include those theories the physicist community agrees upon, and set aside those theories that are still debated. This seems reasonable, especially given that for those physical theories that are still debated, there exist rival accounts, and such rival theories are very likely mutually inconsistent. Including all of them leaves us with an inconsistent body of theories, which is not only unlikely to be true but obviously false, and it is difficult to make a choice among them that does not seem arbitrary or *ad hoc*. Thus, it seems reasonable to leave out such theories from the start. However, this does not seem to solve the problem. There are major parts of current physical theory which are highly effective in making correct predictions and certainly count as well established and commonly agreed upon – yet, they are mutually incompatible. The probably most prominent case is the mutual incompatibility of the theory of general relativity and quantum field theory (see e.g. Wilson 2006: 65), which are two of the major theories of current physics. Both theories are well established among physicists and supported by the available empirical evidence, but cannot both be true.

The upshot of these considerations is that given the collected evidence from the history of science, which shows that physics, along with the other sciences, has been subject to substantial revision throughout the centuries, together with the observation that current physics is arguably still incomplete or even inconsistent,[42] it is very likely that the currentist version of physicalism is false.

---

[42] Daniel Stoljar (2010: 94) suggests that we should think of the distinction between current physics and future physics in terms of the distinction between the physical theory *that we cur-*

As I have already indicated in my list of constraints on a definition of the physical, one should in general be skeptical of a definition of physicalism that would allow physicalism to be rendered false by *any* further substantial progress in physics,[43] e.g. by a revised physics that postulates a new kind of fundamental particle to account for certain empirical observations (see also Crook and Gillett 2001: 342). This is expressed by my *Progress of Physics Constraint*, and closely linked to my *Nontrivial Falsity Constraint*. Reference to current physics (or any other physical theory subject to revision in the process of progressing scientific inquiry) ties the content of physicalism to a specific physical theory. Thus, within a currentist framework, any property expressed by a predicate that is introduced by a revised descendant of that physical theory, as well as properties that have been expressed by predicates of former physical theories but have since then dropped out of the picture fail to be physical according to such a definition. This does not mean however that there is anything 'spooky' about all these properties. So why should the introduction of such properties render physicalism false? These considerations indicate that a too close connection of the notion of a physical property to current physical theory restricts the applicability of the notion of the physical too much.

---

rently believe to be true, where 'we' is probably most charitably understood as 'the (majority of) physicists', and the physical theory *that is in fact true*. While this seems intuitively appealing, there is a worry here regarding the characterization of current physics: Do physicists really believe that current physical theory is true, or do they merely believe that it is the best theory we have so far, even if we know that it is false? Current physical theory provides us with fairly accurate and thus useful predictions, even if it is strictly speaking false. If physicists would believe that current physical theory is true, it seems that attempts to make further adaptations would be unintelligible – but it certainly does not seem like physicists have already come to an end in their project of inquiry. Maybe, one might think, after having singled out those parts of physical theory that are well established or commonly agreed upon, we have at hand the part of physical theory that is indeed believed to be true by physicists, but there are some parts missing that still need attention. However, I think this is implausible, given the considerations regarding the inconsistency of general relativity theory and quantum field theory. Since physicists are well aware of this inconsistency of different parts of physics, they will at most believe that one of the two theories is true, and so it is hard to see how current physical theory is the one that we currently believe to be true.

43 This is not to say that the truth of physicalism should be independent of any progress in physical theory. Of course, as will become clear in the discussion of the futurist account, not any kind of entity might be introduced due to progress within physics without influencing the truth of physicalism. For example, the introduction of immaterial souls into the theory of the fundamental furniture of physical reality, even if proposed by future physicists, indeed seems to render physicalism false.

To avoid this worry, some seek refuge by advocating an account of the physical in terms of *future* physics. Others consider *final* physics, *complete* physics, or *ideal* physics. If things are framed in terms of 'future physics' or 'final physics', the following concern arises: Suppose that due to some very unfortunate coincidence, the universe ends much sooner than we expected, so that the future or final physics is not a physical theory that has much progressed from current physics (cf. Stoljar 2010: 95). In such a case, the final physics would suffer from similar problems as current physics, so this cannot be the reading of 'future physics' or 'final physics' that the futurist has in mind.

Janice Dowell discusses a related concern for a futurist account that defines the notion of future physics in terms of whatever theory will be "ultimately developed in what we call 'physics departments'" (2006b: 37). Such a definition is subject to the worry that the content of the theory becomes indeterminate, and Dowell provides an illustrative case in point (2006b: 37):

> To sharpen the objection, suppose that future physicists, perhaps in a series of tragic lab accidents, will go off their collective rockers and take to channeling the dead. This possible scenario highlights just how unconstrained the notion of 'whatever future people we'll call 'physicists' will study' really is. Thus, consideration of this scenario illustrates just how indeterminate the indeterminacy of the content of the present formulation really is.

Dowell correctly claims that we certainly do not want to say that physical properties might well be just those properties posited by whatever theory these people come up with on the basis of their séances.

In order to avoid these worries, one might appeal to 'complete physics' or 'ideal physics'. However, this might bring up the worry that the notion of a 'complete' or 'ideal theory' is subject to certain epistemic limits due to our cognitive limitations as human beings. In order to avoid having to introduce the notion of something like Laplace's demon, devoid of any cognitive limitations, to spell out what complete or ideal physics is supposed to be, or to introduce an additional principle that ties these notions to the notion of truth, appealing to '*true* physics' right away seems to be the best alternative (see also Stoljar 2010: 95–96). In any case, the latter formulation seems to best catch the spirit of the view in the sense that it tries to avoid appeal to a false or incomplete theory.

Thus, on the futurist's horn of the dilemma, it is supposed that physical properties are the properties the true physical theory we hope to obtain in the future postulates:

Futurism: F is a physical property *iff* F is expressed by a predicate of the true physics.

This suggestion is not subject to the problem that revision of physics may render physicalism false, because it is defined in a way that makes further revision unintelligible.[44] However, according to the second horn of Hempel's dilemma, physical theory might be revised so substantially that resemblance with current physics becomes rather weak. The content of 'the physical', and thus of 'physicalism', becomes indeterminate if we allow such substantial revisions. This leaves us with a view the truth of which we are unable to evaluate, because we are unable to determine the content of the thesis in the first place – at least for now. But it is even worse. Without further restrictions, future physics might be concerned with all kinds of things, so that physicalism, so construed, might be rendered trivially true. As an illustrative example, consider a scenario in which future physicists start postulating immaterial souls and include the corresponding predicates into their theories. In such a case, immaterial souls (or rather: the property of *being an immaterial soul*) would come out as physical.[45]

It is clear that something must have gone wrong in such a case. After all, such a permissive notion of the physical seems no better than a notion of the physical tied to physical theory defined simply as the true theory of everything, which would make physicalism an analytic truth. If physicalism is construed in a way that makes it even compatible with Cartesian substance dualism, what remains of the original idea? Indeed, physics is often thought to be the theory that fully accounts for fundamental reality, that is, fundamental objects and all of their fundamental properties, and all the laws that obtain between them. However, it is no good to *define* physics in this way, at least not for the purpose of characterizing physicalism. Physics may indeed do that job if physicalism is true, but physicalism is neither an analytic truth, nor is it *a priori* knowable that it is true.

In the face of Hempel's dilemma, along with some other worries, some have argued that we should give up to make any attempt to properly define the physical. According to such pessimists, any definition of the physical, and thus also of physicalism, is doomed to fail (e.g. Crane and Mellor 1990; Daly 1998; Stoljar

---

44 That said, while further revision in such a case seems unintelligible, it may in fact happen because we might come up with the true theory without knowing that the theory is the one that is true. In such a case, while the true theory might be further revised, there would not be any actual progress.

45 It is important to note that this is a different worry regarding the indeterminacy of content of the theory than Dowell's worry discussed above. Here, the worry is that that future physics might count too much as physical, so that physicalism, so construed, comes out *true* in cases in which it should not. In Dowell's case, future physics might count the wrong entities as physical, so that physicalism might come out *false* in cases where it should come out true instead.

2010). I do not think that we should throw in the towel too quickly. At the end of this chapter, I will provide an account that I think fares rather well with regard to the concerns that have been raised against views of the physical in the literature.

One further comment is in order that applies to both the currentist and the futurist account of physical properties. As pointed out by several authors (Post 1987: 178–180; Poland 1994: 128; Melnyk 2003: 18), not every predicate that only includes terms corresponding to physics and topic-neutral terms is a physical predicate as relevant for our purposes. The relevant predicates need to be either simple *positive* predicates, like '... has mass' or '... is an electron', or more complex predicates formed from such simple positive predicates via *conjunction*, *disjunction* and *negation*. However, not every predicate formed in this way counts as a predicate of a physical theory. Such predicates must not pick out a property that is *necessarily* had by everything whatsoever, like '... is an electron or not an electron'. If such predicates were allowed, even immaterial souls, if they exist, would count as physical because they certainly have the property picked out by the predicate just considered. A similar problem arises if we allow *entirely negative* predicates like '... is not an electron' to count as predicates of a physical theory, so we need to exclude such predicates as well.

3.2.2 How (not) to be a currentist: Andrew Melnyk's account of the physical

Andrew Melnyk (1997; 2003) is virtually the only one who has provided an elaborate defense of currentism (but see also Vicente 2011). In taking this horn of Hempel's dilemma, he has to account for the worry that physicalism so construed is likely false. Other than one might expect, he does not try to convince us that the concern is unwarranted, and that physicalism so construed is (likely) true, contrary to all appearances. Rather, he bites the bullet and accepts that the physicalism he construes is indeed likely false, and tries to convince us that this does not matter. According to his view, the first horn of Hempel's dilemma is blunt, because in order to be a physicalist, it is not required to believe that physicalism is true. Even more, it is not even required to believe that it is likely true (Melnyk 1997: 624). He tries to support this claim by suggesting that somebody who assigns a probability of 0.9 to the truth of each of ten independent propositions, and thus believes that each one of them is likely true, is also likely to believe the conjunction of these ten propositions, although the conjunction's probability is only $0.9^{10} \approx 0.35$, and thus is more likely false than true (1997: 630). If we can believe the conjunction although it is more likely false than true, why shouldn't the same hold for physicalism?

Montero (1999: 189) states that Melnyk's physicalist seems to be committed to something like the thesis that "everything is physical, but I don't believe it", which sounds somewhat paradoxical.[46] Melnyk (2003: 233) answers, rightly I think, that given the way he construes the notion of belief, his physicalist is not committed to such a thesis. As we have seen in the last paragraph, Melnyk indeed claims that the physicalist believes the thesis of physicalism, but takes belief not to require assigning a probability of at least 0.5 to the respective proposition. So what Melnyk's physicalist would say is rather that they believe physicalism, but do not believe that physicalism is (likely) true, which also has a paradoxical moment. I think that Melnyk, confronted with somebody like Montero (and me, for that matter) who has a strong inclination to intuitively associate the term 'belief' with at least a high subjective probability of truth, can still simply give up talking about belief and talk about *acceptance* instead. On this reading of Melnyk's view, then, the physicalist *accepts* physicalism, but need not *believe* physicalism, where believing *p* entails believing that *p* is (likely) true. Still, this is not how Melnyk talks about belief, so I will in the following stick with his conception of belief.

Believing physicalism, according to Melnyk, consists in taking a certain *attitude* towards physicalism. This is the attitude "which those who have broadly scientific realist and antirelativist intuitions take toward what they regard as the best of current scientific hypotheses" (Melnyk 1997: 625; 2003: 227).[47] Melnyk further argues that it is plausible to take physicalism to be a scientific hypothesis, or at least to be something that is like one in the relevant respects, and fur-

---

46 Clearly, this is reminiscent of Moore's paradox (Moore 1942: 543).
47 Bas van Fraassen (2002) also proposes an attitudinal view, and thinks that to be a physicalist (or materialist, which is the term he uses) is to take a realist/antirelativist attitude, or stance. However, and this is a crucial difference to Melnyk, from his point of view physicalism is not a truth-apt thesis. Alyssa Ney also focuses on attitudes, but takes physicalism itself (rather than being a physicalist) to be an attitude with respect to ontological commitments. According to her, physicalism is nothing more than the following oath: "I hereby swear to go in my ontology everywhere and only where physics leads me" (Ney 2008b: 9). Like van Fraassen, she denies that physicalism is a truth-apt thesis. I hardly find such accounts persuading. After all, this renders many of the debates in philosophy of mind completely pointless. Philosophers would be arguing for and against the truth of something that could not possibly be true or false in the first place, and thus make a category mistake. I certainly admit that many physicalists are inclined to have such an attitude, with the caveat that most of them would not go as far as even accepting immaterial souls in their ontology if physicists were to start postulating such things, but I do not agree that this attitude is to be identified with physicalism (or with being a physicalist, for that matter). Duško Prelević (2018) proposes a related account that takes physicalism to be a research program, and suffers from similar problems.

ther argues that the abovementioned attitude is identical to what he calls the 'SR attitude'. Melnyk stipulates that (1997: 625; 2003: 227)

> (SR) [t]o take the SR attitude towards a hypothesis is (1) to regard the hypothesis as true or false in virtue of the way the mind-independent world is, and (2) to assign the hypothesis a higher probability than that of its *relevant rivals*.

Melnyk does not elaborate on clause (1) of his proposal, but it is clear that this is supposed to be an objectivity constraint that rules out that the truth of physicalism depends on what we believe to be true. He does however further elaborate on clause (2) by spelling out what he means by a relevant rival to a hypothesis (1997: 626; 2003: 227):

> (RR) Hypothesis H1 is a relevant rival to H2 iff (a) H1 is sensibly intended to achieve a significant number of H2's theoretical goals; (b) the hypotheses, H1 and H2, fail to supervene on one another; and (c) H1 has actually been formulated.

Clause (a) is supposed to bring in a certain degree of permissiveness regarding the theoretical goals of different hypotheses. It remains an open question however how closely the theoretical goals of rival hypotheses need to resemble each other. It also serves the purpose of rejecting the mere denial (or negation) of a hypothesis as a relevant rival to it, because the denial of a hypothesis does not share its theoretical goals with the original hypothesis. Clause (b) is supposed to rule out as rivals hypotheses like folk psychology and scientific psychology, which arguably share a significant number of theoretical goals but the one presumably supervenes on the other.[48] Regarding clause (c) Melynk is not very specific. He merely considers the example of Creationism, which he would count as formulated, although it has not been formulated in very much detail, and reminds us of the distinction between formulating a theory and referring to it. Certainly, we can refer to a particular hypothesis without providing any information about the content of the hypothesis. For example, the definite description 'the hypothesis Andrew Melnyk devoted a book-length defense to which was published in 2003' refers to the realization physicalism that Melnyk advances, assuming that it can be considered a hypothesis, but it does not tell

---

48 Usually, supervenience is framed as a relation the relata of which are property types, or sets thereof. Sometimes it is also thought of as a relation between facts. So it might seem odd to talk about one theory supervening on another. If we take the basic idea of supervenience of A on B to be the one that there cannot be a difference in A without a difference in B, what Melnyk means is probably that there cannot be a difference with regard to the truth value of theory A without a difference with regard to the truth value of theory B. For more on supervenience, see section 4.2.

us anything about the content of realization physicalism, i.e., what realization physicalism is about. Fortunately, Melnyk's book provides us with the necessary content of the hypothesis he endorses, so that we can evaluate his views.

Montero (1999: 190) objects that taking the SR attitude towards a hypothesis is certainly not enough for being an advocate of that hypothesis. She provides two examples, one regarding philosophical views and one regarding religious views. A realist about free will who does not self-identify as a Humean compatibilist might still believe that Humean compatibilism regarding free will is superior to all its actually formulated rivals, just because it is the view that contains the fewest contradictions. Similarly, somebody who does not self-identify as a Buddhist might think that among all religions, Buddhism most closely captures their faith. Analogously, Montero claims, taking the SR attitude towards physicalism does not yet make one a physicalist. Melnyk (2003: 233 [fn44]) responds that the Buddhist example is not adequate, since his claim is restricted to *scientific* hypotheses.[49] Regarding the philosophical example, he prefers to bite the bullet. While he acknowledges that one cannot be a Humean compatibilist if one believes that the view is outright contradictory (and thus has a likelihood of truth that is zero), he thinks that somebody who regards Humean compatibilism as the best among the available non-contradictory theories regarding free will just *is* a Humean compatibilist, even if they do not want to admit it. My own intuition is that even in case one considers Humean compatibilism as both non-contradictory and better than its rivals, one need not be a Humean compatibilist. At least, it seems, one might remain agnostic and wait for a theory to be formulated (or formulate one oneself) that one deems worthy of endorsement. Thus, as I understand it, taking the SR attitude to physicalism is not enough to be a physicalist.

In any case, since I am not so much concerned with the question what is required for somebody to be a physicalist, but rather with the question what physicalism is, it seems to me that the foregoing discussion, while closely related, is not our main concern anyway. In the following, I want to focus on those parts of Melnyk's account that directly concern physicalism, rather than being a physicalist.

Let me start with a discussion of the question what Melnyk takes to be the relevant rivals to his currentist physicalism, according to his (RR). He takes

---

[49] Interestingly, although Melnyk rejects Montero's Buddhist example, he uses the example of Creationism to illustrate what he means by a theory that counts as formulated.

physicalism to be the conjunction of two theses,[50] where (R) is his realization physicalism (2003: 235; see also 1997: 633):

> (i) there is some science, S, distinct from the totality of all the sciences, such that every token that falls within the scope of (R) is either a token of a type mentioned as such in the laws and theories of S or an S-ly realized token of some or other functional type, and that
> (ii) S is current physics.

One group of rivals to physicalism as construed by Melnyk are theses that take some other single science than physics as basic, e. g. biology or chemistry. Moreover, the conjunction of some of the sciences also counts, and Melnyk considers the case where S is the conjunction of physics and folk psychology. On his view, the latter is what the traditional dualist accepts. I am not quite sure on what basis one should assign a higher probability to physicalism than to dualism, as the SR attitude requires. At least, it cannot be the empirical evidence, because both physicalism and dualism seem to be likewise compatible with what we know about the world. In any case, if this is Melnyk's view of traditional dualism, then, although he does not mention this view, it seems reasonable to think that he would frame idealism along the same lines, where S is folk psychology.

Another group of theories, which Melnyk only mentions in a footnote, is the group of former physical theories, which have by now been replaced. Certainly, on the available evidence, the truth of these theories is less likely than the truth of physicalism construed via current physics. Still, I find it somewhat odd to think that somebody who endorses (i) and, say, the claim that (ii*) S is the pre-relativistic physics of the late 19th century does not count as a physicalist. Melnyk tries to comfort people like me by arguing that although a view like this does not strictly count as a physicalist view, it is still in what he calls "the spirit of physicalism". He further considers (i) a good candidate for this 'spirit' (1997: 633 [fn21]). If this is what he has in mind, however, I do not see much that remains of the spirit of physicalism. After all, traditional dualism and idealism, construed along Melnyk's lines, also share that very same spirit. Thus, what he has in mind does not deserve the description "the spirit of physicalism". At most, it is something like "the spirit of sparsity" with regard to one's fundamental ontology.

---

50 In his 1997 paper, Melnyk uses a slightly different version of clause (i) than the one quoted here, which is from his 2003 book. The differences in the phrasing focus on the way the dependence relation between the (narrowly) physical entities and other properties is spelled out, which need not concern us for now.

The last group of rivals that Melnyk addresses is the views of what he calls the egalitarian and pluralist camp, which he takes to deny clause (i) of his construal of physicalism. These are the views that certainly do not share "the spirit of physicalism", and are also the ones that Melnyk mainly opposes. Other than traditional dualism, which he takes to claim "that physicalism is very nearly true (since true of everything *except* the mental), though not strictly true (since not true of the mental)" (2003: 4), such pluralist views deny that any science is concerned with entities that are ontologically privileged (i.e. have metaphysical priority with respect to those of the other sciences).

It is somewhat puzzling to see that Melnyk takes the dualist to think that physicalism is true of everything except the mental. While I think that there is indeed something to this construal of the dualist, I have a general worry and one directed at Melnyk's account in particular. The general worry is that if dualism is true, there likely are some domains other than the mental domain for which physicalism is not true. This is because there are domains like the social domain, which depend on what goes on in the mental domain in addition to what goes on in the physical domain. The worry directed at Melnyk's account in particular is that I do not see how his construal of the dualist's view squares with his view that the physicalist need not believe that physicalism is (likely) true. If the physicalist does not need to believe that, why should the dualist do so?

For Melnyk, all these rivals to physicalism as he construes it are less likely true than physicalism. However, as Montero (1999: 190) correctly observes, Melnyk, by introducing clause (c) of his (RR), that relevant rival theories have to be formulated, begs the question against futurist accounts. As Crook and Gillett (2001: 339–341) argue, there is even more trouble to Melnyk's view. There are close descendants of physicalism, which, according to his own characterization of a formulated theory, are to be taken as relevant rivals to currentist physicalism, but have to be taken as more likely true. To show this, Crook and Gillett consider a physical theory that postulates all the entities of current physics, as well as one additional entity not yet discovered that is "similar in nature" (2001: 339) to those entities postulated by current physics – maybe a new kind of particle. Let us call these particles 'schmosons'. This is supposed to introduce a new property, *being a schmoson*. Let us also assume that the property of *being a schmoson* does not metaphysically depend on the properties current physics is concerned with, in order to make sure that it is a property that is missing in current physics, but is required as part of the base on which everything else depends. A physicalist view based on this physics is as well-formulated as current physics with respect to all entities except for that single one, and also seems to provide us with enough information about the remaining one so that we need not worry about the entity to be somehow 'spooky'. We might even think of such a view as the physicalism based on the next iteration of physics, where the part of the theory that postulates another entity has already been formulated but has not yet become part of the widely accepted body of physical theory. Crook and Gillett (2001: 340, esp. [fn14]) then argue that physicalism based on this physics is more likely (or at least *as likely* true) than Melnyk's physicalism. Thus, Melnyk's currentist version of physicalism fails to meet condition (2) of his (SR), which asserts that it needs to be *more likely* true than its rivals.

Melnyk (2003: 236 [fn45]) answers to this worry, but I do not find his answer very compelling. Against the claim that Crook and Gillett's candidate view is more likely than currentist physicalism, Melnyk first considers that the higher likelihood with respect to currentist physicalism might be nullified due to economy considerations along the lines of 'Occam's razor'. However, I take it that considerations of economy can only be applied if two theories are equal with respect to their explanatory (or at least predictive) power, and it seems reasonable to think that Crook and Gillett have in mind a theory that introduces a further entity in order to increase that power. Therefore, it is hard to see how considerations of economy apply in this case. After noting considerations of economy, Melnyk seems to first concede to Crook and Gillett that we should indeed prefer their rival to his physicalism, but then goes on to claim that it would be even better to just consider his physicalism to embody their modification (Melnyk 2003: 236 [fn45]):

> So my main point is that probably we *should* prefer the rival that Crook and Gillett present to realization physicalism as I have formulated it. (Or, better, realization physicalism should be understood as embodying the modification they suggest.) Why would that be bad?

This seems to be an unfair and somewhat desperate move, however, which has the bitter taste of the response of somebody who, confronted with a serious counterexample to their view, just claims, "This is what I meant anyway!" Contrary to what he says in the passage quoted above, at another passage (2003: 15), Melnyk dismisses Crook and Gillett's worries by claiming that while the hypothesis they construct is indeed a rival to physicalism, it is a descendant of physicalism that shares physicalism's 'spirit'. But as we have seen earlier, what Melnyk considers this 'spirit' is also shared by dualist and idealist views, and thus does not capture what it is intended to. In sum, it remains somewhat elusive how Melnyk's response to Crook and Gillett is supposed to work.

Wilson (2006: 65) raises a different concern. She argues that due to the inconsistency of general relativity and quantum field theory, current physics is clearly false, and a false theory, that is, a theory the truth of which has a probability of 0, clearly is not more likely than any of its rivals. Wilson's criticism somewhat misses the point, however, because Melnyk is not concerned so much with current physics being more likely true than its rivals, but with physicalism based on current physics being more likely true than its rivals. The inconsistency of current physics does not entail the inconsistency of a physicalism that is based on current physics.

In summary, the most important concerns regarding Melnyk's currentism are that (1) Melnyk's account has the unintuitive consequence that one can be a physicalist without believing that physicalism is true, that (2) taking the SR attitude towards physicalism is arguably not enough to be a physicalist, that (3) it begs the question against the most prominent rival view in the literature, *futurism*, and that (4) physicalism can be refuted by ordinary progress in physics, such as the introduction a new kind of particle (the schmoson, say). Thus, Melnyk's view that we should define 'physical property' in our definition of physicalism by reference to current physics is not appropriate.

With regard to my catalogue of criteria from section 3.1, Melnyk's currentism fails with regard to at least the following criteria. It neither satisfies the *nontrivial falsity constraint*, since physicalism on this view is indeed (most likely) false, nor does it satisfy the related *progress of physics constraint*, since it makes physicalism vulnerable to be rendered false by normal progress in physics, and since such progress will clearly happen, physicalism as construed by Melnyk is quite obviously false. Moreover, it fails to satisfy the *alien physical properties constraint* because it is unable to capture any property not postulated by current physics. After all, the current physics of the actual world is not supposed to be concerned with such properties, and in order to relativize the currentist account to worlds, we would need to make sense of an appeal to the 'current physics' of some other possible world, and I do not even understand what this would mean. The latter failure is however one for which Melnyk is not to be blamed. His project, as I understand it, is more restricted than mine because he tries to provide a particular account of physicalism which he thinks is true of the actual world.

Nevertheless, the set of those actually instantiated properties that are picked out by the expression '... is a physical property' according to Melnyk's view is a subset of those properties the expression should pick out. It is just that Melnyk's definition is too restrictive. Thus, we need to liberalize the notion of a physical property. Relatedly, and importantly, the considerations of this section do *not* show that Melnyk's view is not a variant of physicalism. After all, intuition tells us that a possible world *w* that is such that the entities postulated by current physics exhaust fundamental reality should indeed be considered a world in which physicalism is true. It is just that most likely, *w* is not the actual world, so physicalists in our world are well advised to believe in some other variant of physicalism.

3.2.3 How (not) to be a futurist: Jeffrey Poland's and Janice Dowell's accounts of the physical

Let me now turn to the view that is usually taken to be the main rival to currentist physicalism: futurism. We have already seen in section 3.2.1 that futurists tie the notion of a physical property to the ultimately true physics. The second horn of Hempel's dilemma is the worry that in doing so, we end up with a thesis of physicalism that is either trivially true, or a thesis that lacks content and is thus vacuous. Moreover, such an account does not provide any restrictions to what might count as a physical property, and opens up the possibility that mental predicates might be incorporated into physics, and the corresponding properties may thus count as physical, contrary to our intuitions. After all, who knows what the ultimately true physics will be like?

Jeffrey Poland, in his 1994 book "Physicalism", tries to provide an account along such lines that is supposed to avoid these worries. To do this, he starts with what he thinks is an appropriate "characterization of physics" (1994: 124):

> [P]hysics is the branch of science concerned with identifying a basic class of objects and attributes and a class of principles that are sufficient for an account of space-time and of the composition, dynamics, and interactions of all occupants of space-time.

If this is supposed to be a *definition* of what physics is, Poland's account does not seem to be adequate. It does not seem to provide any restriction to the objects and attributes that form the base other than that they need to account for what goes on within space-time. So if we plug it into the futurist definition of a physical property in section 3.2.1, and plug that definition into our definition of physicalism, only those possible worlds inhabited by contingent or causal individuals that fail to be occupants of space-time and have properties that are neither required as part of the base nor metaphysically depend on the physical properties will be such that physicalism comes out false of them. So physicalism will come out false of worlds with a contingently existing deity that lives outside of space-time and has certain properties not involved in accounting for what goes on within space-time. But, as Dowell points out, it will not come out false if "there are occupants of space-time that possess miraculous powers" (2006b: 58 [fn25]), even though it should come out false in this case.

If we allow entities like contingently existing deities outside of space-time to be metaphysically possible, then physicalism so construed is strictly speaking neither necessarily true, nor is its truth knowable *a priori*, which is in line with the constraints formulated in section 3.1, but for the wrong reasons. What physicalists have in mind is clearly that physicalism should be a contingent *a posteriori* thesis *even if* we restrict our attention to worlds in which such entities do not exist. However, since Poland's construal of physics is so liberal, if we restrict our attention to such worlds, physicalism, on this construal, comes out as a necessarily true thesis whose truth is knowable *a priori*.

It is not clear however that Poland considers what he says to be a definition of physics. After all, Poland explicitly states that the quoted statement above is a *characterization* of physics, which might mean that he tells us something about a contingent connection between physics and what the actual world is like. In other words, one might think that what he has in mind is that the description he provides *fixes the reference* of the name 'physics', rather than defines what physics is, along Kripke's (1980: 32) lines of distinguishing between definitions and reference-fixing descriptions.[51] A physicalism construed in this way is not trivial in the sense that it is almost an *a priori* doctrine that is necessarily true. Rather, its truth depends on what the actual world is like, and the entities forming the base in other possible worlds can be different to the ones in the actual world.

However, a related important concern remains. Since we do not know what the basic class of objects and attributes in Poland's description is in the actual world, it might be the case that his description picks out entities we intuitively do not want it to pick out. If physicalism, intuitively understood, is true, Poland's description likely applies to physics. But since we cannot just presuppose that physicalism is true, we cannot even use his description to merely fix the reference of the name 'physics'. Physicalism construed in this way is unable to

---

[51] In the case of the name 'Aristotle', we might say "Aristotle is the teacher of Alexander and the student of Plato". Taken as a definition, it makes the name 'Aristotle' *synonymous* with the definite description 'the teacher of Alexander and the student of Plato', but this is certainly not what we want, because it would make the sentence "Somebody other than Aristotle could have been the teacher of Alexander and the student of Plato" an outright contradiction which we could know to be false (or even more: impossible) on *a priori* grounds. But taken as merely a reference-fixing description that helps picking out Aristotle in the actual world via some of his contingent attributes, this unwanted result does not follow.

avoid the objection that it might count entities as physical that should intuitively not be counted as such.⁵²

Let me discuss this worry in more detail. The worry is that in the course of progress in physics, all sorts of things might be 'downward incorporated' (Poland's term) into the body of physics. This concern is frequently attributed to Noam Chomsky (2005: 86):

> We can, however, be fairly sure that there will be a physical explanation for the phenomena in question, if they can be explained at all, for an uninteresting terminological reason, namely that the concept of "physical explanation" will no doubt be extended to incorporate whatever is discovered in this domain, exactly as it was extended to accommodate gravitational and electromagnetic force, massless particles, and numerous other entities and processes that would have offended the common sense of earlier generations. But it seems clear that this issue need not delay the study of the topics that are now open to investigation, and it seems futile to speculate about matters so remote from present understanding.

Let me provide an example that vividly illustrates the problem. Suppose that ghosts, immaterial souls and the like do exist and are indeed part of the fundamental base everything else depends upon. In that case, Poland's account seems to count them (and the corresponding properties) as physical. More specifically, the problem is that on Poland's account, the predicates '… is an immaterial soul' and '… is a ghost' might turn out to be counted as predicates of future physical theory. The same worry arises in less outlandish cases as well. Suppose that, faced with the problem of accounting for mental properties like the phenomenal property of *being in pain*, future physicists might just incorporate the predicate '… is in pain' into physical theory, and thus treat *being in pain* as a property of physics.

What does Poland say about this worry? His reply is "to bite the bullet and allow that indeed it is conceivable that physics might be revised to incorporate

---

52 Note that on Poland's characterization, ghosts, immaterial souls, God and the like might count as physical even if we think that such entities are not themselves *occupants* of space-time, which is not obvious in the first place. Unless 'immaterial' entails 'outside of space-time', why should we think that immaterial souls are not in space-time? Even if we take serious the Cartesian conception of souls as non-extended entities, this does not entail that they are not in space-time. Even Descartes could agree that souls are in time, and while they are not *extended* in space, they could still be located at a particular point in space, and thus in space-time. If one denies that something that does not have an extension in space counts as in space, then fundamental particles like photons, according to the standard model of particle physics, are not in space either.

mental, and other phenomena previously identified as non-mental,[53] into the physical basis" (1994: 331). Poland further points out that the incorporation of such entities by a revision of physics must not be *ad hoc*, just to save physicalism from being refuted. I certainly agree with this latter point, but I wonder whether it bears much relevance. After all, unlike physicalists, physicists (at least *qua* being physicists) do not aim at saving physicalism from refutation, and it is the physicists, not the physicalists, who are entitled to revise physics. So, they are not in the business of saving physicalism anyway. Still, if physicists would revise physics to incorporate mental phenomena by incorporating mental predicates, it would not change the fact that intuitively, physicalism should come out false in certain worlds in which it does not on Poland's definition. Poland goes on to put emphasis on the restriction (1994: 330):

> I cannot emphasize strongly enough the significance of the restriction on *ad hoc* revisions of physics for the problem in hand. To say, for example, that mental phenomena might be downwardly incorporated into the physical basis is not to say that, whenever physicalists run into recalcitrant mental phenomena, they need only re-label the phenomena as 'physical' to escape a potentially serious predicament. Downward incorporation means just that: *incorporation* of the phenomenon into the existing physical framework. This requires significant theoretical motivation from the point of view of physical theory construction, as well as preservation, rather than destruction, of the essential theoretical unity of the existing body of theory. Downward incorporation is no mean feat, and should not be viewed as such by critics of physicalism.

In response, I cannot emphasize strongly enough what I just said: it is not the business of the physicalist to revise physical theory and count recalcitrant mental phenomena as physical. As soon as the physicalist has decided to tie the notion of a physical property to physical theory, it is the physicist's turn to tell us whether something is a physical property or not. If the physicist now incorporates entities into their theories that our thesis is intuitively incompatible with, this only shows that we should not have given them the job in the first place.

That being said, Poland is right that the physicalist must not re-label mental phenomena as physical, that is, just take predicates like '... is in pain' to be physical predicates in order to save physicalism, but not for the reason he provides. To see this, we need to be careful with regard to the distinction between physical *predicates* and physical *properties*. I think that much of the debate concerning whether or not mental properties are allowed in the base rests on a confusion between the two. Contrary to the intuition of some philosophers in the debate,

---

[53] I wonder whether Poland means 'non-physical' here. Both expressions seem to make sense, but the 'non-physical' seems to better account for the 'previously'.

including Crook and Gillett (2001) and Wilson (2006), among others, I think that physicalism is compatible with mental *properties* at the base, and thus even with certain variants of panpsychism,[54] given that these mental properties (on *a posteriori* grounds[55]) turn out to be identical to certain physical properties. But I am not inclined to accept that mental properties might quite trivially count as physical properties just because mental *predicates* like '... is in pain' are counted as physical predicates (and likewise with *concepts*). I will get back to the issue of acceptability of mental properties at the base later in this chapter when I discuss Wilson's account in section 3.3.2, and the closely related question of the compatibility of physicalism and panpsychism in section 3.3.3.

Maybe Poland's requirements for downward incorporation make it at least unlikely for mental properties to enter the base. In order to evaluate this, we need to see what exactly Poland has in mind when he takes construction and preservation of theoretical unity as a key ingredient to downward incorporation. It seems instructive to see what he says about the downward incorporation of electromagnetic theory into the framework of fundamental physics (1994: 143):

> [T]he downward incorporation did not consist in a simple appending of electromagnetic theory to mechanics. Rather, there was substantial theoretical integration: mechanics and electromagnetic theory each make essential contributions to descriptions and explanations of many phenomena that neither can adequately account for alone.

If theoretical integration is the relevant criterion, what exactly are the criteria for a successful such integration? Poland does not say, but we may find some hints in a different futurist account put forward by Dowell (2006b).

---

54 David Lewis argues – convincingly, I think – that physicalism (or materialism in his terminology) should not rule out panpsychism. "[P]sychophysical identity is a two-way street: if all mental properties are physical, then some physical properties are mental. But perhaps not just some but *all* physical properties might be mental as well; and indeed every property of anything might be at once physical and mental" (1983: 362–363). It might be that a panpsychistic physicalism is impossible, but then this is due to something that exceeds a minimal physicalist commitment.

55 Note also that the kind of *a posteriority* I have in mind here is different to the one in the label "*a posteriori* accounts of the physical" above. The former concerns the claim that mental properties might *a posteriori* turn out to be physical properties, similar to the "water = H_2O" case, as the *a posteriori* physicalist (or type-B physicalist in Chalmers' terminology; see his 1996: 165–166) claims. The latter concerns the question whether we might find out *a posteriori* (e. g. by asking the physicists or looking into their writings) that physics incorporates mental predicates into their terminological apparatus. I do not want to rule out the former option, but I do want to rule out the latter one to be in line with physicalism (see also sections 3.3.2 and 3.3.3).

Dowell thinks that she can save futurism by putting constraints on what counts as a physical theory.[56] According to her, any scientific theory, and so also the ideal physical theory, has to have "the hallmarks of a scientific theory" (2006b: 38). She provides four such hallmarks, but leaves it open whether this list is exhaustive. A scientific theory must (1) include "a set of explanatory hypotheses from which empirically testable implications can be derived" (2006b: 38), and must be (2) confirmed (or at least be confirmable) "by the obtaining of a number and variety of the test-implications of its explanatory hypotheses" (2006b: 38). Moreover, a scientific theory must (3) provide "a unified explanation of a variety of empirical generalizations" (2006b: 39), and (4) receive "additional empirical support by its fit with what is antecedently known and independently observable" (2006b: 39). One of her examples for such an explanatory hypothesis is that heat is mean molecular motion. This has the empirically testable implication that if there is a certain amount of heat at some spatio-temporal location, there must be the corresponding mean molecular motion at that very location. Moreover, the theory provides a unified explanation of why it is that heat and mean molecular motion co-vary and fits into the body of antecedent knowledge.

She then goes on and makes explicit her definition of ideal physical theory (2006b: 39):

> Finally, we define 'the complete and ideal physical theory' as the complete and ideal scientific theory of the world's relatively fundamental elements. ('Complete' here characterizes the scope of the theory. A physical theory is complete just in case every property, etc. that can be integrated into its scope has been so integrated. 'Ideal' here characterizes the theory's grounds. A theory is ideal when it is fully well-confirmed.)

According to Dowell, this puts the following 'pretty strong' constraint on what can count as a physical property (2006b: 39):

> To count as basic and physical, a property must be well-integrated into the most complete and unified explanation possible for the relatively most basic occupants of space-time. To be so integrated, its behavior must be highly regular. So it is not enough, on the present account, that a property's instantiations are merely compatible with events explained by the ideal and complete physical theory. It must be well-integrated into its overall pattern of explanation.

---

56 Note that Dowell's focus is on saving futurism from the indeterminate content worry, where she has in mind situations like the one in which the people in the physics departments of the future stop doing proper science and start channeling the dead, see section 3.2.1 above.

I agree with Dowell that her account avoids complete triviality and lack of at least some determinate content insofar as it avoids that properties like *being a miracle-performing angel* (her example) cannot be counted as physical, and so there are some ways a world might be such that physicalism turns out false. Insofar as it is not *a priori* that there are no miracle-performing angels and other entities that defy subsumption under laws or law-like generalizations, Dowell's account does not make physicalism an *a priori* truth. Nevertheless, assuming that a non-miracle-performing angel is a conceptual possibility, Dowell thinks that 'mundane' angels which are fully governed by the laws of nature and thus don't have miraculous powers would be perfectly fine candidates to count as physical, and so, I assume, does the property of *being a mundane angel* (cf. 2006b: 40–42).

If we assume that the picture of theoretical integration Dowell sketches is also what Poland has in mind, neither Dowell's nor Poland's view are able to avoid the concern that most pluralists, and clearly most dualists with respect to mental properties, will agree that the properties they deem non-physical figure in laws or law-like generalizations. Neither Dowell nor Poland provides the means to rule out a case in which mental properties might be counted as physical due to the incorporation of mental predicates into physical theory. In her reply to the objection that physicalism is supposed to rule out fundamental mental properties, Dowell explicitly admits that if mental properties are an integral and explanatory part of a unified theory, they might well be among the posits of ideal physics (2006b: 45).

> So the price of holding that the incompatibility of fundamental physicality and mentality is a posteriori is holding that there is a way the world could turn out to be such that they aren't incompatible. For this to be a reasonable alternative to holding that the incompatibility is a priori, one should identify a scenario plausibly described as one in which some mental property is a basic physical one. On the present account, it is a posteriori that no mental property is a basic physical property, so it is required to identify a scenario plausibly describable as one in which it turns out that some mental property is both basic and physical. [A scenario] in which the ideal and complete physics integrates fundamental mental properties into its unified pattern of explanation, is just that scenario.

I agree with Dowell that we should not include an *a priori* constraint into our definition of the physical that rules out that mental properties might be identical to fundamental physical properties. If it turns out that mental properties are type-identical to fundamental physical properties, i.e. that the properties picked out by mental predicates are identical to fundamental physical properties picked out by physical predicates, or are in the extension of the predicate '... is a physical property', I am happy to accept that physicalism can be true even if it turns out that there are fundamental mental properties. But I do not agree that this also shows that we should accept that physicalism is compatible with fundamental mental properties due to the incorporation of mental predicates into physics.

To see this, consider a scenario where the world is such as David Chalmers (in his property dualist mood, which he calls 'naturalistic dualism' in his 1996 book) conceives it to be. Chalmers is certainly *not* an anti-science lunatic who thinks that there is the physical realm, the inner workings of which are unified by lawful relations, and then, on top of that, there is the mental realm, completely unconnected to the physical realm, in which unpredictable magic happens that does not comply with any law or law-like generalization.[57] On his view, in addition to the physical laws, there are indeed psychophysical and maybe also psychological (or mental-to-mental) laws among the laws of nature, or at least there are psychophysical or psychological regularities. It is only that these laws or regularities are not physical laws or regularities, because mental entities are distinct from physical entities. So, it seems that on Chalmers' view, the goings-on in the mental and the physical realm, taken together, can provide us with an account more adequate to explain certain phenomena (e. g. sociological phenomena) that physics, on his view, is unable to adequately account for alone. Now suppose that future physicists incorporate mental predicates into their theories, such that '… is in pain' counts as a physical predicate. On Dowell's and Poland's construal, such a scenario would be one in which physicalism is true.

Or consider a scenario in which the actual world is such as René Descartes conceived it to be, but future physicists incorporate predicates like '… is an immaterial soul' into their theory. Even such a world may come out as a physicalist world on Poland's and Dowell's construal. After all, the substance dualist can agree to lawful relations between the mental and the physical. Even on Malebranche's Occasionalism (Malebranche 2014 [1674–75]: 448 [6.2.3]) or Leibniz's view of the pre-established harmony (Leibniz 2014 [1714]: 30 [§ 78–§ 81]), there are regularities, or covariations, between mental and physical events, even if there are, strictly speaking, no causal or other more metaphysical dependence relations between the events and the corresponding property types. One might think that such views do not provide us with a sufficiently unified picture, but still, substance dualism remains compatible with lawful relations between the mental and the physical realm.

---

57 Maybe this confusion somehow arises due to our everyday conception of ghosts and angels, which are taken to be somewhat spooky entities, and the association of spookiness with something like randomness, or unlawfulness, as well as the idea that postulating immaterial souls goes against a scientific understanding of reality.

According to Poland's and Dowell's accounts, the incorporation of mental predicates into physical theory would not disconfirm physicalism. But do we really want to say that physicalism might be true even if the world is such as David Chalmers or even René Descartes think it is, just because future physicists incorporate mental predicates into their theories? I do not think so. The considerations rather show that Poland's and Dowell's criteria for downward incorporation are too weak, and cannot avoid the worry that future physicists (not physicalists!) might incorporate predicates into their theory that would make intuitively non-physical entities count as physical too easily. In order to show that *being in pain* is a physical property after all, it is not suitable to just incorporate the corresponding mental predicate into physical theory. Rather, it has to be a matter of *a posteriori* scientific enquiry, probably combined with an abductive inference, analogous to the scientific result that water is H_2O or that heat is mean molecular motion, to find out that the property picked out by some mental predicate is identical to a property in the extension of the predicate '… is a physical property' (which, in the end, I will sharply distinguish from '… is a property of physics', see section 3.4.2).

Crook and Gillett (2001: 343–346) make a related point against Poland's view. They charge Poland of failing to make his futurist physicalism a theory "in good standing – namely, that a theory can potentially be disconfirmed by empirical enquiry" (2001: 345), because Poland accepts that any intuitively non-physical entities might be downwardly incorporated into physics as long as the criteria for downward incorporation are fulfilled, and thus makes it vulnerable to the objection that it is a trivial theory. However, contrary to what Crook and Gillett claim, Poland's view might in principle be disconfirmed by empirical enquiry if it turns out that certain phenomena exist which defy subsumption under any laws. Nevertheless, the above considerations show that Poland's view cannot properly account for the distinction between physicalist and dualist views, and thus is to be rejected nonetheless.

Regarding the catalogue of constraints I formulated in section 3.1, Poland's and Dowell's futurist accounts fail, or at least almost fail, to account for the *nontrivial truth constraint* as well as the *traditional rivals constraint*, because on these accounts, physicalism comes out true of far too many worlds, including worlds in which we would intuitively say that dualism is true. They fare better than currentism with regard to the *nontrivial falsity constraint* and the *progress of physics constraint*, because they make sure that physicalism is not obviously false, and it cannot be rendered false by further progress in physics. At least as long as we construe futurist accounts as tied to the true physics of the actual world, they however fail to account for the *alien physical properties constraint*. Regarding the *nontrivial inclusion of special science properties constraint*, Poland explicitly claims that we should "not characterize physics in a way that is so abstract as not to distinguish it from other disciplines" (1994: 123). Still, at least some special science predicates might count as physical predicates if they get downward incorporated. The degree to which this constraint will be satisfied depends on the degree to which such downward incorporation takes place. So, we must wait and see. Finally, we cannot say much regarding the question whether a possible world that is as Poland's and Dowell's accounts tell us is to be intuitively taken a physicalist world, because it depends on what is going to be downward incorporated into future physics.

3.3 *A priori* accounts of the physical

Other than the *a posteriori* accounts discussed above, *a priori* accounts of the physical do not leave it to the physicists to decide what counts as a physical property. A prototypical example for such an account, albeit for substances rather than properties, is the notion of the material used by early modern materialists and their rivals. As we have seen in section 2.1.1, the properties that were considered essential to material substances were the properties *being extended* and *being solid*. However, in the meantime science has arguably taught us that physical objects don't need to have these characteristics. Moreover, the philosophical debate has moved its focus from physical objects to physical properties. So the question the advocators of *a priori* accounts of the physical try to answer is what it is that all and only physical properties have in common. As we will see in this section, it turns out very difficult to come up with an explicit set of such features.

3.3.1 It is none of that stuff: the *'via negativa'*

One account of the physical that has gained some prominence in the last two decades is what is frequently called the '*via negativa*'.[58] Like the traditional materi-

---

[58] Not all philosophers who argue along the lines of a *via negativa* view aim at providing an account of the physical to be applied to a formulation of physicalism. Rather, given the problems with finding an appropriate notion of the physical, some (e.g. Montero 1999; 2001) try to frame the mind-body problem in terms of the mental-nonmental distinction rather than the mental-physical distinction and to avoid talking about the physical and physicalism at all. Others (e.g. Spurrett and Papineau 1999; Papineau 2002: 40–44) apply the *via negativa* not to a formulation of physicalism, but to what is frequently called the 'causal argument' for physicalism, and

alist account of a material entity, the *via negativa* is an *a priori* account of the physical, but there is one important respect in which these accounts differ: while the traditional materialist accounts define the material by reference to positive characteristics like extendedness and solidity, the *via negativa* defines the physical in wholly negative terms. On a first pass, *via negativa* accounts of the physical take the physical to be whatever is not mental:

P is a physical property *iff P* is a not a mental property.

Of course, such an account requires that we have a good enough grasp of what a mental property is, but advocates of such a view typically claim that the answer is simple: mental properties are either phenomenal or intentional properties (or both).[59] This formulation directly leads to a major problem, however.[60] If physical properties are non-mental by definition, the type identity of mental and physical properties is ruled out as inconsistent on *a priori* grounds. While some opponents of the identity of mental and physical properties argue against identity theory using *a priori* arguments, those arguments always rely on some additional principles to derive the conclusion that mental and physical properties are distinct. For example, some early such arguments rely on the principle that identity of property types requires a semantic link between the expressions used to refer to the properties in question (see Place 1956, who discusses and re-

---

more specifically to the premise that states a completeness or closure principle in that argument (see also Gillett and Witmer 2001; Montero and Papineau 2005). It is not obvious that the notion of the physical involved there is exactly the same as the notion of the physical that is involved in the formulation of physicalism.

59 Some advocates of the *via negativa* have in mind only phenomenal properties (e.g. Smith 1993). Nevertheless, it seems odd to think of intentional properties as non-mental (albeit this is only a terminological issue that can be easily avoided by replacing 'non-mental' in the definition by 'non-phenomenal'), and more importantly, it seems odd to think that intentional properties count as physical by definition (unless, of course, they are also phenomenal).

60 The above formulation is importantly different from "P is physical *iff* P is a non-mental property", which can be interpreted in two ways. It can be interpreted as equivalent to the above formulation, in case we do not allow that a mental property can be identical to a non-mental property. While the claim seems prima facie incoherent, if we mean by 'mental' and 'non-mental' nothing more than that the property can be picked out by mental and non-mental (i.e., biological, chemical, physical, etc.) predicates, a property can very well be mental and non-mental at the same time. Such an understanding is compatible with type identity theory. However, this is not the reading of 'non-mental' advocates of the *via negativa* have in mind, as is clear from the following quote from Montero (1999: 194): "[I]t seems that physicalism is, at least in part, motivated by the belief that the mental is ultimately non-mental, that is, that mental properties are not fundamental properties, while a central tenet of dualism is, precisely, that they are."

jects this principle), others rely on principles like the necessity of identity and a conceivability-possibility principle (Kripke 1980: 144–155; Chalmers 2010: 152). The crude version of the *via negativa*, however, does not require any further principle to rule out the identity of mental and physical properties. The non-identity follows immediately from the definition (see also Montero 2001: 75; Stoljar 2010: 87).

Advocates of the *via negativa* agree that this problem needs to be avoided, and provide more sophisticated versions of the view that are less susceptible to such worries. Early advocators of such accounts of the physical are James W. Cornman (1971: 11–13) and A. D. Smith. Here is Smith's account (1993: 245):

> In fact, the physical can only be defined negatively: as that which in a way contrasts with the mental and conscious realm. But obviously the contrastive definition cannot simply be that the purely physical is that which is wholly non-mental: for this clearly rules out physicalism *ab initio*. Rather, we need to proceed in two stages. First, let us define a *merely physical* individual as any (non-abstract) individual that lacks consciousness, or sentience. A merely physical property is any property that could be possessed by a merely physical individual. A merely physical state of affairs is any that consists in the instantiation of a merely physical property. A *purely physical* state of affairs may now be defined as one which either is merely physical or else is just a complex of merely physical states of affairs. As before, a purely physical property can be defined as any property the instancing of which would be a purely physical state of affairs. A purely physical individual is one which possesses only purely physical properties.

Let me first focus on Smith's notion of a *merely physical* property. A bit more formally, I take it that Smith's notion of a merely physical property can be understood as follows:

> F is a *merely physical* property *iff* there is a possible world w such that there is some (non-abstract) individual x at w such that x has F, but x lacks consciousness.

Notably, Smith does not claim that merely physical properties are those had by a merely physical individual, but those that *could be* had by such an individual, so that it suffices for some property F to be merely physical that there is some non-conscious individual in some metaphysically possible world that instantiates F. Given this definition, it is clear that phenomenal properties, which can only be had by conscious individuals, cannot be merely physical properties. But not only phenomenal properties are ruled out. Suppose that some phenomenal property Q is necessitated by some non-phenomenal property P,[61] where the modality in question is metaphysical modality. Any such non-phenomenal property the instantiation of which necessitates the instantiation of a phenomenal property by the same individual is not a merely physical property either – after all, given that P necessitates Q, there will be no world in which there is an individual x that has P but lacks Q. Hence, the only properties that are merely physical are those that do not necessitate phenomenal properties instantiated by the same individual.

Smith further defines the more encompassing notion of a *purely physical* property in terms of the notion of a merely physical property, but not in a direct way. Rather, Smith takes a detour via the notion of a merely physical and a purely physical state of affairs (cf. 1993: 245):

> F is a *purely physical* property *iff* the instantiation of F is a purely physical state of affairs S.
>
> S is a *purely physical* state of affairs *iff* S is a merely physical state of affairs or is a complex of merely physical states of affairs.
>
> S is a *merely physical* state of affairs *iff* S consists in the instantiation of a merely physical property.

The 'consists in' relation, I assume, is to be understood such that the instantiation of the relevant merely physical property entails that the state of affairs S obtains. It does not suffice that S consists only in part in the instantiation of a mere-

---

[61] It is debatable what the relata of the necessitation relation are. Some frame the notion of necessitation in terms of one proposition p necessitating some other proposition q, such that p necessitates q *iff* necessarily, if p is true, then q is true. Others like to talk of one property type P necessitating some other property type Q (e.g. Stoljar 2010: 111), and I will follow this usage. There are different versions of the claim of property necessitation that we might distinguish. A restrictive one, which some call 'same-subject necessitation' (e.g. Wilson 2002: 56) is that P necessitates Q *iff* for every possible world w, for every individual x in w such that x has P, x has Q. But there are also more liberal versions that do not require the properties to be instantiated by the same subject (see section 4.1 for more on property necessitation). Smith's account of a merely physical property rules out that a property P that same-subject necessitates a phenomenal property Q can be a merely physical property. However, a property P that necessitates a phenomenal property Q according to a more liberal account might still be a merely physical property according to Smith's definition, as long as the individuals that instantiate P and Q are not identical. For example, suppose that P is a property that is instantiated by brains, and Q is a phenomenal property instantiated by the subjects those brains belong to. Even if P necessitates Q according to a more liberal definition that allows for necessitation of properties of different subjects, P may be merely physical because it is not the brain, but the subject, that has the property of being in pain, and brains themselves are non-conscious even in the actual world.

ly physical property. Rather, *S* has to wholly consist in the instantiation of such a property – no other properties are involved.[62] Furthermore, one constraint on a complex purely physical state of affairs *S* is that all of the states of affairs that together form the complex are merely physical state of affairs. Still, it remains somewhat unclear what it means for some state of affairs to be a complex of other states of affairs. Nevertheless, on an intuitive level, it seems clear what Smith has in mind.

Examples of merely physical properties, which can be instantiated by some individual without any phenomenal properties being instantiated, might be the property *having mass*, or the property *having charge*.[63] If *having mass* or *having charge* are indeed merely physical properties, then any state of affairs *S* that consists in their instantiation (by some individual) is a merely physical state of affairs. While neither mental properties nor any non-mental properties that necessitate mental properties in the same individual can be merely physical, such properties can still be purely physical if the states of affairs that consist in their instantiation are complexes of merely physical states of affairs, that is, complexes of states of affairs that consist in the instantiation of properties that, by themselves, do not necessitate phenomenal properties in the same individuals. The idea is that if merely physical states of affairs, which only consist in the instantiation of properties like *having mass* and *having charge*, come together in the right way, they form complex states of affairs that consist in the instantiation of properties that necessitate (or are identical to) phenomenal properties.

So Smith's view does not rule out that mental properties are identical to purely physical properties, i.e. identical to properties the instantiation of which consists

---

[62] This is not to say that the state of affairs cannot have any other entity, such as an object or a point in time, as a constituent.
[63] Even properties like *having mass* or *having charge* might, as some panpsychists claim, necessitate mental properties to be instantiated by the same individual. In such a case, not even a property like having mass or having charge could be merely physical. Smith is aware of a tension between his view and panpsychism: "This definition may seem to beg the question against panpsychism: the view that there are physical things, but no merely physical things. In fact the question is not begged, unless panpsychism is held to be metaphysically necessary-since a merely physical property is here defined as one that *could* be possessed by an insentient individual. I must confess, however, not to be able to give a definition of physicality that would be acceptable to such a radical panpsychist except by a possibly problematic appeal to a *per impossibile* clause" (Smith 1993: 245). If there is no insentient being in any metaphysically possible world that instantiates some of the properties instantiated in our world, then there are no merely physical properties either. The kind of panpsychism that he has in mind is however weaker than the one I just depicted, which ties mental to physical properties via necessitation or even identity relations rather than just claiming that all individuals have both mental and physical properties. I will get back to the problem this raises for *via negativa* accounts below.

in a complex configuration of instantiations of properties that do not by themselves necessitate phenomenal properties. By distinguishing between *merely physical* and *purely physical* individuals and properties, Smith's account is indeed compatible with the traditional identity theory if we take the identity theorist's claim to be that mental properties are identical to purely physical properties.[64] After all, identity theorists claim that mental properties are identical to biological properties like *being in a certain brain state*, and such properties seem to be rather complex configurational properties the instantiation of which requires that multiple simpler properties come together in the right way.

In a similar vein, one can distinguish between fundamental and non-fundamental physical properties, and argue that identity theorists only claim that mental properties are identical to non-fundamental physical properties. This is closer to how things are framed in more recently defended versions of the *via negativa* (see Fiorese 2016: 218; Tiehen 2016: 4). Montero considers an account along such lines (1999: 194):

> [I]t seems that a solution to the body problem, or at least one that helps us to better understand the mind-body problem, is not forthcoming. And I take it this indicates that, at least for the time being, we should focus on questions other than the question "Is the mind physical?" To this end, I would like to suggest a question that, I think, highlights some of the central concerns of both physicalists and dualists. And this is the question of whether the mental is fundamentally non-mental. For it seems that physicalism is, at least in part, motivated by the belief that the mental is ultimately non-mental, that is, that mental properties are not fundamental properties, while a central tenet of dualism is, precisely, that they are.

Importantly, Montero does not aim to provide a definition of the term 'physical' to be used in a definition of physicalism, but rather to provide an alternative way of framing the debate about the place of mentality in the world without making use of expressions like 'physical' or 'physicalism' (Montero 2001: 61; see also Gillett and Witmer 2001: 303 [fn5]):

> [I]t is time to come to terms with the difficulty of understanding what it means to be physical and start thinking about the mind-body problem from a new perspective. Instead of construing it as the problem of finding a place for mentality in a fundamentally physical

---

64 Smith's (1993: 226) original phrasing is a bit odd: "By ['physicalism'] I mean the view according to which everything non-abstract, every individual, property, relation, event, state, or process, is physical and wholly physical. I shall say something later about how we are to understand the notion of what is purely physical." He does not explicitly say that what he means by 'physical and wholly physical' just is 'purely physical'. I take it to be clear from the context however that this is what he has in mind.

world, we should think of it as the problem of finding a place for mentality in a fundamentally nonmental world, a world that is at its most fundamental level entirely nonmental.

Still, let us pretend for the sake of argument that what she aims at is to define the physical as the fundamentally non-mental:

> P is a physical property *iff* P is a fundamentally non-mental property.

In order to understand this definition, we need to understand what it is for a property to be *fundamentally* non-mental.[65] Montero does not specify in detail how to cash out the notion of fundamentality. However, she indicates that her notion of fundamentality is indeed tied to the notion of dependence (2001: 62 [fn1]):

> The term 'fundamental' can, if you like, stand for whatever dependence relation you prefer. That is, when I say that the mind-body problem is the question of whether mentality is fundamentally nonmental you can substitute the question of whether mentality is reducible to (or constituted by, or supervenient on, etc.) the nonmental.

Fiorese (2016: 211), in contrast to Montero, explicitly defends a version of the *via negativa* account of the *physical*. Like Montero, he takes a fundamental property to be one that is not dependent on any other property, where for him, a property is dependent *iff* it is metaphysically necessitated by some other property.[66] He

---

[65] There is a substantial debate about the notion of fundamentality in the recent philosophical literature, and relevant questions include whether or not the notion is primitive, i.e. not reductively analyzable in other terms (as e.g. Wilson 2014; 2016; 2018 proposes), whether, and if so, how, the notion of fundamentality is tied to a notion of metaphysical dependence (as e.g. Schaffer 2009 suggests), and whether or not the notion of fundamentality is unitary, i.e. whether there is a property of fundamentality *simpliciter*, as opposed to fundamentality with respect to a particular kind of hierarchy, such as the mereological or the functional hierarchy.

[66] Note that the necessitation relation is reflexive, so that every property is necessitated by itself. If fundamentality would require that a property is not only not necessitated by any *other* property, but not necessitated by any property at all, no property would ever be fundamental. Note also that what is meant by '*other* property' needs to be more than just a *numerically* distinct property, especially if one accepts conjunctive properties. If *being round* itself necessitates *being round*, it is for example also necessitated by the conjunctive property *being red and round*, which is numerically distinct from *being round*, on the assumption that this is a genuine property.

Furthermore, I assume that Fiorese only considers instantiated properties. For suppose that F is metaphysically necessitated by G, so that in every possible world in which G is instantiated, F is instantiated, but G is not instantiated in the world under consideration. Suppose further that in the world at hand there is no instantiated property other than F itself (and conjunctive prop-

first considers a definition of a physical property slightly different from the one above, according to which a property P is physical *iff* P is not fundamentally mental, and elaborates on what is meant by a fundamentally mental property. He observes that a fundamentally mental property cannot be a property that is both fundamental and mental, because a property that is non-fundamental but exclusively necessitated by mental properties would count as physical on such an account, because it lacks at least one conjunct: fundamentality.

With regard to a simple conjunctive interpretation of the phrasing I derived from Montero's quote above, due to the difference in the position of the negation, these considerations do not apply. If we interpret the definition to assert that the physical is what is fundamental and not mental, rather than what is not both fundamental and mental, this problem does not arise. Non-fundamental properties that are exclusively necessitated by mental properties do not count as physical just because they are non-fundamental, because non-fundamentality is not one of the conjuncts.

There are however other concerns with such an account. Given the way we just interpreted the definition, it is conceptually impossible that any non-fundamental property, that is, any property that depends on other properties, is physical. Even if there are some fundamental physical properties, one might think that we still want to distinguish between fundamental physical properties and non-fundamental physical properties that depend on them. While I certainly agree with the intuition, this does not seem to be a knockdown concern. *First*, we are searching for a notion of the physical for the sake of defining physicalism. For physicalism to come out true, it seems to suffice to have a notion that picks out just those properties on which everything else depends – to include more properties just leads to redundancies. *Second*, even on the assumption that Montero searches for a definition of the physical, it does not seem appropriate to attribute to Montero the simple approach that conjoins fundamentality and non-mentality. Arguing against such an account thus would be arguing against a straw man. I think that the following account is closer to what Montero has in mind:

---

erties of which F is a conjunct) that necessitates F. In such a case, it seems more natural to think of F as fundamental, which requires that one only considers instantiated properties.

3.3 A priori accounts of the physical — 81

P is a physical property *iff* P is a fundamental and non-mental property or there are fundamental and non-mental properties $Q_1, ..., Q_n$ such that P metaphysically depends on $Q_1, ..., Q_n$.[67]

The inclusion of the second clause of the disjunction avoids the problem that non-fundamental physical properties are ruled out. Even mental properties can be physical as long as they are not themselves fundamental and metaphysically depend on fundamental and non-mental properties.

Still, such an account shares a further problem with the simple conjunctive account. It requires that there are fundamental properties on which everything else depends in the first place. Otherwise, there are no physical properties at all, and physicalism is clearly false in any world that does not include any physical properties. So any world in which there are chains of dependence that do not end at some point turns out to be a world in which physicalism is false.

Fiorese (2016: 213) settles for an account of the physical that avoids the problem of presupposing finite chains of dependence:[68]

> A property F is a physical property if and only if either (i) F is fundamental and nonmental, or (ii) for every chain of necessitation whose members ($G_1, G_2, G_3, ...$) belong to N, there is some G_i which is necessitated exclusively by some (one or more) nonmental property.

Here, "N [is] the possibly infinite set which includes all and only the properties that play a part in necessitating property F,[69] where a property plays a part in

---

67 Depending on one's views about conjunctive properties, one can either say that P metaphysically depends on the single conjunctive property $Q_{\wedge(1,...,n)}$ or the individual properties Q_1 to Q_n, taken together. In the former case, it is necessary that if $Q_{\wedge(1,...,n)}$ is instantiated, P is instantiated, whereas in the latter case, it is necessary that if Q_1 to Q_n are jointly instantiated, P is instantiated.
68 Note that Fiorese also switches (albeit without explicitly discussing the switch) from the 'not fundamentally mental' he first discusses to the 'fundamentally nonmental' phrasing in his own formulation. Note that Montero (2006) also provides an account of physicalism based on the *via negativa* that is compatible with infinite chains of dependence. Her account is very similar to the one Fiorese provides, but is stated in a more informal way.
69 Similar to the case of a necessitation-based notion of fundamentality, there are two different readings of what properties the set N is comprised of. On what might be called the 'actualist' reading, which I assume Fiorese has in mind, N only includes properties that are instantiated in the world under consideration. On what we might call the 'possibilist' reading, N can also include properties that are not instantiated in the world under consideration. The possibilist reading provides a more restrictive account. To see this, suppose that F is an instantiated non-fundamental property that is necessitated by some instantiated property G, which is fundamental and non-mental, and no other instantiated property necessitates F. Suppose further that there

the necessitation of F just in case it either necessitates F on its own or jointly (and nonredundantly[70]) necessitates F together with some other property" (2016: 213). Furthermore, he defines a 'chain of necessitation' as follows (2016: 213):

> "C is a chain of necessitation" $=_{df}$ "C is a possibly infinite ordered series of properties (G_1, G_2, G_3, ...) such that G_2 plays a part in G_1 being necessitated, G_3 plays a part in G_2 being necessitated, and so on."

The idea here is that for a property P to be physical, it must either itself be a fundamental non-mental property or the chain of necessitation that leads to P must be such that at a certain point in the dependence hierarchy, no property below that point is mental.

Even if such a formulation can overcome the issue of presupposing fundamental properties, I still have substantial concerns regarding the *via negativa* approach. On the one hand, I think that *via negativa* accounts are too permissive. First, on such an account, physicalism would come out true even in cases where very odd fundamental properties are instantiated that are alien to our world and whose nature does not resemble the nature of any of the properties instantiated in our world. Let me call such properties *ectoplasmic properties*. As long as such properties are not mental, they count as physical. Intuitively, however, I think that we should say that such properties should not count as physical, and physicalism should come out false in such worlds. Rather, if those properties exhaust the fundamental base, *ectoplasmism* is true there. Of course, if the job is only to formulate physicalism with respect to the actual world, ectoplasmic properties are not a problem, at least if we take it as part of the definition of an ectoplasmic property that it is not instantiated in the actual world. But since my aim is to formulate physicalism more generally, the *via negativa* seems to be too permissive with regard to such properties.

Moreover, I have already discussed that I take physicalism to be a view that has some historical roots in the positivist accounts of people like Carnap (1931;

---

is also a non-instantiated mental property H that necessitates F as well, and H is a fundamental property in at least some worlds in which it is instantiated. According to the definition, G clearly is a physical property because it satisfies clause (i). Now, on the actualist reading, F is physical as well, but on the possibilist reading, it is not, because there is a chain of necessitation comprised of F and H, and neither one is necessitated exclusively by some nonmental property.

70 I assume that the inclusion of the nonredundancy clause is supposed to avoid that any property is included in N due to the simple reason that we can conjoin any property G whatsoever with F itself (or any property that necessitates F) to make the conjunction necessitate F, even if G has nothing to do with F.

1932) and Neurath (1931), who first used the term 'physicalism' in their work. Their views focused on the priority of physics relative to the other sciences, including natural sciences like chemistry and biology. To account for this ancestry, I take it that the properties physics is concerned with need to play some substantial role with regard to our notion of the physical that figures in the thesis of physicalism, even if we do want to avoid the problems of currentism and futurism that arise from tying the notion of the physical too closely to physics. The *via negativa* does not account for such a role of physics at all. Special science properties like chemical and biological properties all count as physical, unless they depend on mental properties in the way provided by the definition.

Thus, on the basis of a *via negativa* account of the physical, I do not see how a physicalism *simpliciter* is to be distinguished from a domain-specific physicalism about the mental. To avoid this, one might try to revise the *via negativa* to not only claim that physical properties are not fundamentally mental, but also that they are non-chemical, non-biological, and so forth. But this would require that we are able to define what it is for a property to be a chemical or a biological property, and this will most likely lead to similar troubles as those that currentist and futurist views of the physical struggle with.

On the other hand, and maybe even more importantly, I think that *via negativa* accounts are too restrictive. All *via negativa* accounts of the physical rule out by definition that fundamental[71] properties can be both mental and physical. Advocates of the *via negativa* claim that this is intended, but I am inclined to think that it remains a problem due to the way these identities are ruled out. Not only is the identity of mental and fundamental physical properties ruled out on *a priori* grounds. It is ruled out by definition, so that it becomes conceptually impossible, and thus inconceivable, that such identity relations hold. It seems to me, however, that it should be subject to empirical investigation to find out which properties posited by science are candidates for being identified with mental properties due to their pattern of instantiation. If we found out that some mental property always co-occurs with a fundamental physical property, why should the identification of the mental property with the fundamental physical property – at least without further assumptions – be something that is conceptually impossible?

Moreover, this shows that the solution to the other problem I briefly considered at the end of the last paragraph, i.e. to also include that physical properties are non-chemical, non-biological, and so forth, would make things worse. It

---

[71] In the case of Smith's account, what is ruled out is that mental properties are non-complex physical properties.

might very well be that some or all special science properties turn out to be physical properties. However, this should not follow immediately *a priori* from the definition of a physical property.

Relatedly, Daniel Stoljar considers whether physicalism should be incompatible with panpsychism[72] (2015: section 12.3):

> [I]magine a world in which the fundamental properties are both mental and physical. That is certainly a far-fetched scenario but it doesn't seem to be impossible. Would physicalism be true in such a world? It is hard to see why not; at least it may be true at that world that any physical duplicate of it is a duplicate *simpliciter*. Would panpsychism likewise be true at such a world? Again, it is hard to see why not, since the fundamental properties instantiated at such a world are mental, though of course they are also physical.

It is worth noting that the notion of fundamentality at issue in Stoljar's quote is one that requires that at least part of what it is for a property to be fundamental is to be instantiated by mereologically fundamental entities. The notion of fundamentality that is invoked in Fiorese's and Montero's accounts discussed above, which takes fundamental properties to be those that are not metaphysically dependent on distinct properties, does not by itself entail any conclusion about the mereological level on which fundamental properties in their sense are instantiated, unless one adds the further premise that metaphysically independent properties are those instantiated by mereologically fundamental entities.[73]

David Lewis, one of the most prominent physicalists, less controversially expresses the basic idea Stoljar wants to get across. He also thinks that physicalism (or materialism, as he calls it) is not *per se* incompatible with panpsychism (1983: 362–363):

> It is often noted that psychophysical identity is a two-way street: if all mental properties are physical, then some physical properties are mental. But perhaps not just some but *all* phys-

---

[72] Note that Stoljar's first intuition goes in a different direction: "Imagine the possibility of panpsychism, i.e. the possibility that all the physical objects of our acquaintance are conscious beings just as we are. Would physicalism be true in that situation? It seems intuitively not." I think that we need to be careful here. Other than in the quote in the main text, Stoljar talks about physical and mental objects rather than properties here. I would say that all options are still open in this scenario, and we need to fill in the details about the dependence structure of physical and mental properties to see which view is true.

[73] The fact that some properties are instantiated across all kinds of levels of the mereological hierarchy complicates these considerations if we are take fundamentality to be something attributed to property types rather than their token instances. But I will set aside these worries for the moment.

ical properties might be mental as well; and indeed every property of anything might be at once physical and mental. [...] Maybe Panpsychistic Materialism is indeed impossible – how do you square it with a broadly functional analysis of mind? – but a thesis that says so is more than just Materialism.

Whether or not physicalism is incompatible with panpsychism is an issue that needs to be further addressed. The main problem for the *via negativa* is that even if physicalism is indeed incompatible with panpsychism, a panpsychism understood along the lines of the quotations from Stoljar and Lewis, which we might call a *panpsychist identity theory*, should not come out conceptually incoherent due to the definition of the physical. But given the *via negativa* view of the physical, Stoljar asks us to imagine something that is conceptually impossible, and thus inconceivable. He could have similarly asked us to imagine a world in which there are round squares. Even if one thinks, *contra* Lewis and Stoljar, that physicalism is false in such panpsychist worlds, it seems that one should not take such worlds to be conceptually impossible.

Nimtz and Schütte (2003: 417–418; see also Nimtz 2009: 29–30) nicely illustrate the problem. Both physicalists and panpsychists (or at least panpsychist identity theorists) make use of the notion of a physical property. In order to avoid that physicalists and panpsychist identity theorists talk past each other, the notion of the physical that is used to formulate the thesis of physicalism should be the same as the one used to formulate the panpsychist identity theory. While advocates of the panpsychist identity theory want to allow that mental properties are identical to physical properties even though they are fundamental properties, the advocates of the *via negativa* claim that physicalism should not allow mental properties to be identical to fundamental physical properties. Now, if we want to capture both of these constraints in our definition of a physical property, we end up with an account that is supposed to allow and not allow this identity, which cannot work.

One variant of the panpsychist identity theory which is in tension with the *via negativa* belongs to a family of views called 'Russellian' views. Views along these lines have received increasing attention in recent years, and draw on a consideration in Bertrand Russell's "The Analysis of Matter" (1927), according to which physics only tells us what things that have properties like mass and charge do, i.e. which dispositions entities have due to their instantiating these properties, rather than what the nature of mass and charge is. There is a range of different views within the Russellian family. The one I want to consider is what Chalmers (2017 [2015]: 34) calls the '*Russellian identity theory*'. According to this view, while the reference of terms like 'mass' and 'charge' is fixed via the dispositions bestowed on the bearers of mass and charge, the terms ultimately refer to the categorical properties[74] that underlie the dispositions (see e.g. Chalmers 2017 [2015]: 32–36; Goff, Seager, and Allen-Hermanson 2017: section 2.5). Given such a picture, it seems intuitive to count the categorical properties as physical properties – after all, these are the properties that physics is ultimately concerned with, even though they are characterized by physics only in terms of what they do, or in terms of what dispositional properties they bestow on their bearers. Furthermore, advocates of the Russellian identity theory hold that phenomenal properties are type-identical to the categorical properties that bestow their bearers with the dispositions physics associates with them. Thus, on the Russellian identity theory, there are fundamental physical properties that are type-identical to mental properties. However, given the definition of a physical property provided by advocates of the *via negativa*, this is ruled out as not only implausible or false, but inconceivable. I think that this is too much. A definition of the physical should certainly be neutral with regard to this issue.

What about the catalogue of criteria from the beginning of the chapter? The *via negativa* clearly fails with regard to the *traditional rivals constraint* and the *nontrivial inclusion of special science properties constraint*. While it is able to distinguish physicalism from traditional dualism, it fails to distinguish physicalism from what I call ectoplasmism. Moreover, special science properties are included too easily into the set of physical properties, and the distinction from traditional dualism comes at a high cost: some live accounts in the panpsychist family are rendered conceptually incoherent.

3.3.2 Jessica Wilson's mixed view of the physical

The same problem also arises for a view defended by Jessica Wilson (2006), which she calls the "physics-based NFM account", where 'NFM' stands for 'non-fundamental mentality'. This view combines the *a priori* constraint of the *via negativa* with some aspects of the *a posteriori* accounts of the physical discussed above. Since she combines aspects of both *a priori* and *a posteriori* accounts of the physical, her view can thus be considered a mixed view. Similar to *a posteriori* accounts of the physical, the positive clause of Wilson's definition appeals to properties treated by both current and future physics. In addition, she

---

[74] The terminology is not quite settled. Chalmers (2017 [2015]) talks of '*quiddities*', Montero (2015) uses the term '*inscrutables*' instead.

includes a negative clause that resembles *via negativa* accounts of the physical (2006: 72):

> *The physics-based NFM account:* An entity existing at a world *w* is physical if and only if
> (i') it is treated, approximately accurately, by current or future (in the limit of inquiry, ideal) versions of fundamental physics at *w*, and
> (ii) it is not fundamentally mental (that is, does not individually either possess or bestow mentality)

The first clause (i') is roughly a disjunction of currentism and futurism. Appeal to current physics is supposed to help filling the notion of the physical with content, and to acknowledge that "it is the successes of current physics that motivate characterizing the physical in terms of physics in the first place" (2006: 71). Appeal to future physics, on the other hand, is supposed to save properties that are not yet discovered but are going to be discovered by future physics from being non-physical, and to save physicalism from the fate of being false because of the incompleteness or inconsistency of current physics. Furthermore, Wilson's requirement that the entity has to be treated approximately accurately by some physical theory is supposed to avoid worries like the one Dowell (2006b: 37) depicts, where future physicists go astray and start channeling the dead. The second clause (ii) makes sure that appeal to future physics does not render physicalism compatible with dualism because future physicists might incorporate mental predicates into physical theory. If this would happen, those properties would still not count as physical properties even though they are picked out by predicates of future physics.

Moreover, Wilson tries to accommodate Stoljar's (2010: ch. 4) worry that a general definition of the physical that is not only apt to formulate physicalism for the actual world, but also for other possible worlds in which properties are instantiated that would intuitively count as physical but are not instantiated in our world by relativizing her account of the physical to possible worlds, so that it is always the physics of the world at hand rather than our actual world physics that fixes what counts as physical. While our physics, current or future, clearly cannot adequately treat any property that is not instantiated at our world, the idea is that the physics of the possible world at hand does.

As already indicated above, my main concern with Wilson's account is that just like pure *via negativa* accounts of the physical, her clause (ii) renders certain live views inconsistent. This alone would be enough to reject her account of the physical, but I have further concerns. While I agree with Wilson that we should formulate physicalism in a way that also provides us with the right result when considering different possible worlds, I do not think that her account is successful in doing so. To see why, consider a world that is very much like our world, with the difference that science has never been developed in this world. If physicalism is true of our world, it should certainly be true of that world as well. However, on Wilson's account, 'physics' refers to the physics of the world under consideration, rather than that of the actual world. Since there is no such physics, there are also no physical properties at that world. Thus, physicalism is false at that world whether or not physicalism is true at our world, which is not the adequate result.[75] If 'physics' would instead always refer to actual-world physics, that problem would not arise, but the ability to account for alien physical properties would be lost. Furthermore, I have a hard time understanding what could be meant by 'current physics' with regard to some other possible world, especially if the world at hand develops quite differently to the actual world. So with regard to other possible worlds, what remains is appeal to future or ideal physics. However, this deprives us of the alleged benefit of making reference to current physics to add some content to the notion of the physical.

Wilson's view fares better than the pure *via negativa* with regard to the *non-trivial inclusion of special science properties constraint*. However, the strategy to distinguish physicalism from traditional dualism, as required by the *traditional rivals constraint*, parallels the one of the pure *via negativa*, and is thus similarly costly. Furthermore, her attempt to satisfy the *alien physical properties constraint* leads to some inadequate results.

3.3.3 Should physicalism be incompatible with panpsychism?

I now want to get back to the question whether physicalism should be compatible or incompatible with panpsychism. This is different from the question whether the notion of the physical is to be defined such that fundamental physical properties cannot be identical to mental properties, to which I have already given a negative answer. I am happy to admit that to some extent, the question of compatibility of physicalism with panpsychism is a terminological one. I side with Lewis and Stoljar and thus think that physicalism does not require that mental properties are non-fundamental, either in the sense of being dependent or not being instantiated by mereologically fundamental entities. Others, including the advocates of the *via negativa* view, deny that the term 'physicalism' is to be applied to views that allow mental properties to be fundamental, even if they are identical to fundamental physical properties. Wilson (2006: 70) argues that it

---

[75] One might try to account for this problem by appealing to the closest possible world in which physics has been developed, but that does not make the other issues go away.

is part and parcel of physicalism's being an anti-dualist doctrine that fundamental mental entities are to be ruled out. To substantiate her claim, she provides textual evidence from the literature from both the physicalist and the dualist camp. In principle, this is a fair move, because in case of a terminological dispute with respect to a technical use of a term, the most we can do to argue in favor of one side is to show that a term is typically used in one or the other way in the literature. Still, we need to make sure that the textual evidence is chosen appropriately, and is strong enough to support the claim. So let us have a look at the passages she quotes.

First, Wilson quotes Jaegwon Kim (1996), and says that he "specifies the basic physicalist commitments as including the claim that there are 'no fundamental mental entities'" (Wilson 2006: 70). As Montero (2001: 67 [fn14]) indicates with respect to the same quote, however, Kim thinks that this follows from the supervenience of the mental on the physical. But since identity entails supervenience, I think what Kim actually has in mind in this passage is that physicalists are committed to the claim that there are no fundamental mental *and non-physical* entities.[76]

The next passage Wilson quotes is from Keith Campbell (1997), which is a review of Poland (1994). Campbell suggests that "a dynamics which introduced forces with immanent purpose, and hence teleological causation at the base level, would not sustain a program maintaining the spirit of physicalism" (Campbell 1997: 224). I do not see how the existence of fundamental mental properties immediately entails that there are forces with immanent purpose, nor that there is teleological causation at the base level. Moreover, neither Campbell nor Wilson explains why exactly this goes against the spirit of physicalism.

Wilson further quotes Chalmers (1996), who, when discussing Russellian monism, and more specifically the Russellian identity theory, claims that such a view "admits phenomenal or protophenomenal properties as fundamental, and so remains closer to a version of dualism (or perhaps an idealism or a neutral monism [...]) than to a version of materialism" (Chalmers 1996: 136). In some of his later works, however, Chalmers seems to be more open to the idea of physicalist versions of Russellian monism. Otherwise, he would not consider the Russellian monist option to open up a loophole in the zombie argument, such that the conclusion is not merely that physicalism is false, but that "materialism [i.e., physicalism] is false or Russellian monism is true" (Chalmers 2010: 152). Still, he remains careful and indicates that "because it relies on speculation

---

[76] It is worth noting that I checked in the first, second and third edition of Kim (1996), and was unable to find the quote indicated by Montero and Wilson.

about the special nature of the fundamental properties in microphysics, it is a highly distinctive form of physicalism that has much in common with property dualism and that many physicalists will want to reject" (2010: 152). In another writing, Chalmers wants to remain neutral on the issue how to classify Russellian monism, and claims that the question is largely verbal (2017 [2015]: 33):

> Is Russellian monism a form of physicalism, dualism, or something else? As before, this is a largely verbal question that we need not settle. We could say that it is a form of broad physicalism but not narrow physicalism, and leave it at that. Still, it is interesting to look more closely at the question of whether, on a Russellian monist view, (proto)phenomenal properties (i.e., phenomenal or protophenomenal properties) are physical properties. There are a number of different options available here, depending on what one counts as a physical property, and how one construes the semantics of physical terms such as 'mass.'

Finally, Wilson quotes two passages from Montero. In the first, Montero claims that "most physicalists would take it that panpsychism – the view that mental properties pervade all aspects of the world – is incompatible with physicalism" (1999: 185). The second is that "dualism is the view that mentality is fundamental" (2001: 67). If dualism were indeed the view that mentality is fundamental, I would agree that physicalism is incompatible with panpsychism, given that panpsychism entails that mentality is fundamental.[77] After all, this would mean that physicalism is compatible with dualism, the most prototypical rival of physicalism. But I don't see how a view on which the fundamental mental properties would be type-identical to fundamental physical properties would be a form of dualism. Furthermore, if Montero were right, idealism would be a dualist view. But since idealists think, like physicalists, that there is only a single kind of properties that forms the base, it is better considered to be a monist view. Thus it can only be a necessary, but not a sufficient condition for dualism that mental properties are fundamental.

In summary, it seems that the textual evidence Wilson provides is not compelling. Maybe what actually drives the advocates of the incompatibility claim is the thought that a definition of physicalism is supposed to ascertain that phys-

---

[77] What is at issue here is a panpsychism that focuses on properties rather than individuals. I think that even Montero would agree that a view on which every individual, including each mereologically fundamental particle, has phenomenal properties, but the phenomenal properties are metaphysically dependent on and not identical to their fundamental physical properties, would be a panpsychist form of physicalism, but one on which mental properties are not fundamental even if they are instantiated by mereologically fundamental particulars. The views in question are rather those on which the fundamental phenomenal properties are indeed type-identical to at least some of the fundamental physical properties.

ical properties are strictly metaphysically prior to mental properties. This cannot be satisfied in the identity case, because nothing can be metaphysically prior to itself. But why think so? One reason might be that physicalism is supposed to be incompatible with idealism. If we do not include a strict priority claim in both physicalism and idealism, a world in which every single fundamental property is both mental and physical would be one in which physicalism, idealism and panpsychism would all come out true[78] (see also Stoljar 2010: 43–44). But again, what is so bad about this? Other than with dualism, which is clearly not a form of monism, I do not see why we need to make sure that there is no overlap with regard to the set of worlds in which these views are true, and any world that is structured differently to this one special case will still be one in which idealism and physicalism do not go hand in hand.

Somebody who thinks that physicalism should be incompatible with panpsychism and idealism can still follow a suggestion of Nimtz and Schütte (2003: 421; see also Nimtz 2009: 31) and include something like the NFM constraint into their definition of physicalism, rather than into their definition of the physical. This makes sure that such an account of physicalism is not compatible with dualism, idealism, and panpsychism (or at least the versions of panpsychism I just considered), while remaining neutral with respect to the question whether fundamental physical properties can be mental as well. In case they are, physicalism so defined comes out false. Since I think the main aim of physicalism is to make sure that the world is unified in a way that is in line with our scientific image of the world, and identity relations are perfectly fine candidates for unifying relations, I don't see why we need the additional strict priority commitment for a minimal physicalist account. With regard to mental properties, as with any property that is not itself physical, physicalism only needs to ascertain that physical properties are not metaphysically posterior to them, which is satisfied even in the case where mental properties are identical to fundamental physical ones.

3.3.4 Robert Howell's neo-Cartesian account

In his book "Consciousness and the Limits of Objectivity" (2013), Robert Howell defends a view of the physical that shares with the *via negativa* its *a priori* status. Unlike advocates of the *via negativa*, however, Howell attempts to provide a pos-

---

[78] Maybe such a view also enables us to understand *neutral monism* as the conjunction of idealism and physicalism?

itive definition of the physical. He proposes to call his account of the physical a 'neo-Cartesian' view ('Neocart', for short), because it is reminiscent of the Cartesian idea that the physical is extended (2013: 24):

> Descartes had a crucial insight that tends to get left behind: being physical is closely tied to spatiality. Electrons are not extended, but they are in space. Charge might not require that its bearer be extended, but its instantiation does place requirements on other things that are in space. Put crudely, physical things and properties seem to have, by their very nature, spatial implications. They seem, in fact, to be defined by these implications. What it is for something to have charge (in the basic sense in which an electron is charged) is for it to repel or attract other things, and attraction and repulsion are clearly spatial notions. Consider, on the other hand, what the dualist says about qualia – say the sensation of pain. Something is painful in virtue of how it feels, not by how it causes the bearer of pain to act. How something feels doesn't have any immediate spatial implications – neither does having an intentional state, a state that is about something else.

On the basis of his considerations, Howell proposes to define the notion of a physical property in the following way (2013: 24):

> A property is physical iff it can be fully characterized in terms of the conditions it places on the distribution of things in space over time.

He elaborates on what he means by the conditions a property places on the distribution of things in space over time. If a property is instantiated, certain conditions are placed on the world. These conditions are just those entailed by the laws of nature that feature the property at hand. As I understand it, the idea behind Howell's definition is that the nature of physical properties is purely dispositional. However, not any disposition will do. Only dispositional properties the manifestation of which has an influence on the distribution of things in space over time, and only such an influence, count.

Those who defend a categoricalist view of dispositional properties[79] have criticized that Howell's definition rules out any dispositional property that has a categorical base from being physical. After all, "these categorical bases look to be something over and above the 'conditions' the property places on the dis-

---

[79] The participants in the debate are typically divided into two camps: *categoricalists* and *dispositionalists*. The categoricalists think that each dispositional property requires a further non-dispositional property that makes its bearers have it. For example, a wine glass is fragile all the time, even if it never breaks. But why is it that the wine glass is fragile, or: what is the property that makes the wine glass fragile? The categoricalists would answer that what makes a wine glass fragile is a categorical property that underlies the disposition, typically given the laws of nature, and thus contingently. The dispositionalists deny that non-dispositional properties are required to account for the dispositional properties to be instantiated.

tribution of things in space and time" (2013: 26). Howell takes up the criticism and develops an alternative definition for categoricalists. First, he considers the simple option to restrict the definition to the dispositional aspects of properties, so that a property is physical just in case "the dispositional aspects [of the property] are exhaustively characterized by their spatio-temporal implications" (2013: 26). He quickly dismisses this option due to the following scenario (2013: 26):

> We can imagine, for example, that there is a phenomenal property Q that, given the laws of nature, bestows all and only the powers bestowed by negative charge. On the reading of Neocart that gives categorical bases a free pass, a property like Q will count as physical. Thus, Neocart counts property dualism as a form of physicalism. Again, not good.

As I understand it, on the view that Howell depicts, *having negative charge*, like Q, is supposed to be a categorical property that bestows its bearers with certain powers or dispositions. Both properties bestow their bearers with the same powers, but they are different properties. Moreover, since Howell indicates that Q and negative charge bestow their bearers with the dispositions *given the laws of nature*, in this scenario, Q and *having negative charge* are only contingently connected to the dispositions, at least unless one thinks that the laws of nature tie properties to each other with metaphysical necessity.[80] This is different to

---

[80] The idea that categorical and dispositional properties are only contingently connected to each other is typically driven by considerations regarding the alleged conceivability of situations in which e.g. *having mass* is associated with the disposition that is *de facto* associated with *having charge*, and *vice versa*, roughly analogous to Max Black's case of the switching of two qualitatively identical spheres (Black 1952) that is usually taken to support *haecceitism*. I have to admit that I have trouble conceiving of a situation in which *having mass* and *having charge* switch their associated dispositions. The alleged conceivability of such cases is also taken to support the view that properties like *having charge* are not identical to dispositions. I think that another situation is more easily conceivable that is sufficient to make the point that *having charge* is not identical to the dispositional property it is associated with – one in which some property is instantiated that is not instantiated in our world, but bestows its bearers with exactly the dispositions that we associate with *having charge*. Of course, this requires that the nature of the properties in question (or at least of one of them) is not exhausted by what dispositions they bestow their bearers with. However, other than the switching case, this view is compatible with the claim that *having charge* metaphysically necessitates the dispositional properties we associate it with, in case it is the nature of the categorical properties alone to bestow their bearers with the dispositions rather than contingent laws of nature that establish the connection between the properties. On a view that takes dispositional properties to be functional properties, and categorical properties to be the associated realizer properties (see Heil 2003: 85; Chalmers 2017 [2015]: 34), this corresponds to the well-established idea that functional properties are multiply realizable.

how he characterizes charge earlier, where he seems to take charge to be a dispositional property that is necessarily, and *a priori* (by definition), tied to what its bearer does.

Now, if it is the laws of nature that make the properties connected to each other, rather than the nature of the properties themselves, it remains open what the nature of those properties is. Howell elaborates on this question (2013: 29):

> We need [...] a definition that distinguishes between phenomenal property Q, which bestows the powers of charge, and charge itself. There is, of course, an intuitive difference between the categorical bases of these properties. There is a sense in which the categorical base of Q is "juicy" or thick while the categorical base of charge is empty and thin. Even if the categorical base of charge bestows the powers it does only contingently, within a particular world it appears to contribute nothing more to its bearer than a set of powers. Meanwhile, Q contributes the powers plus a phenomenal feel.

Setting aside the issue that here it sounds again as if Q and charge are not categorical properties but dispositions, because Howell talks of *the categorical bases of Q and charge*, the idea seems to be that there is more to the nature of Q than bestowing its bearers with certain dispositions, whereas the nature of negative charge is supposed to be exhausted by its bestowing these dispositions. In case it is the laws that make Q and charge be connected to the dispositions, it seems that the nature of negative charge is indeed 'empty' – there is nothing to charge other than what is contingently tied to it by the laws. Similarly, it seems, any other physical property would be such an 'empty placeholder' as well on such a view. Howell calls such properties 'thin properties'.

In order to make sure that thin properties can still be properly individuated, Howell introduces the notion of a *trans-world disposition set* (TDS, for short; 2013: 29):

> The TDS of a property is the set of dispositions the property gives rise to in each world. So, for example, charge gives rise to a certain group of dispositions D[1] in world 1, but a different set of dispositions D2 in world 2, etc. The TDS for charge can be characterized as a set of pairs of worlds and dispositions {<w1, D1>, <w2, D2> ... <wn, Dn>}. Even if the powers of a property differ from world to world, its TDS does not – it is a necessary feature of the property.

The individuation condition Howell formulates for thin properties is that P_1 and P_2 are identical if they have the same TDS. Thick properties, on the other hand, are not individuated via their TDS, or at least not only via their TDS.[81]

If we count the contingent connections to dispositions tied to Q and negative charge by the laws as part of their nature by considering them to be part of the TDS of these properties, then Q has the same dispositional aspects as negative charge has, but it also has something more to it than these dispositional aspects. This 'something more' is a phenomenal aspect.

Suppose that the Russellian identity theorist is right that properties like negative charge have a phenomenal aspect to them, although maybe a different one than Q has to it, then the case of negative charge is no different to the case of Q. Howell would think that in this case, physicalism should be false, whereas I would say that it should be true, at least if the same story can be told with regard to all the other physical properties and the rest of the definition of physicalism is satisfied.[82] However, if it turns out that the property of negative charge has something more to it than the TDS, but the 'something more' is not phenomenal, then Q should indeed not count as a physical property. Note that negative charge in this case would not count as physical on Howell's original definition either. In any case, since there is a variant of the story according to which Q counts as physical on the definition even though it should not, Howell correctly dismisses the simple revision of the definition that gives categorical properties a free pass.

---

[81] If one thinks that it is sufficient for a feature like the TDS to be part of the nature of an entity that the entity necessarily has it, claiming that the TDS is part of the nature of a property does not seem problematic. However, if one goes along with the Neo-Aristotelian view that to be part of the essence of an entity requires more than just a necessary connection (Fine 1994), one might worry that including into the nature of each property what dispositions it bestows to its bearer in all the other worlds in which other laws of nature hold bloats the properties' essences in a way that is rather counterintuitive.

[82] This is not to deny that there is still a dualistic flavor to such a case. Suppose it is true that *having negative charge* is a categorical property that bestows its bearer with certain dispositions, but this does not exhaust the nature of *having negative charge*. Rather, part of its nature is phenomenal (or proto-phenomenal), as Russellian monists claim. If these aspects of the nature of the property of *having negative charge* are not tightly intertwined, or in the best case identical, it may well be that there is something dualistic to this view. Still, as long as we are talking about the very same property, the dualism is at most a dualism of aspects of the nature of properties, rather than a dualism of properties of individuals. This might still be considered a problem, but it is not a problem for physicalism construed as a view about properties of individuals. The issue can be accounted for by a metaphysical principle according to which there cannot be a property has two completely independent or wholly distinct aspects of its nature, but it does not seem to be part of one's commitment to physicalism to believe in such a principle.

Those who deny that dispositions need categorical bases, and think that physicalism should come out false in any world in which categorical properties exist, do not have any of these troubles. But I think that a minimal definition of physicalism should not entail that any categoricalist is a non-physicalist. Howell seems to think the same, and tries to accommodate categoricalist views by the following revised definition (2013: 30):

> A property P is physical, iff (a) in the actual world P confers only spatio-temporal powers upon its bearer, and (b) P is a thin property.

So according to Howell's account for the categoricalist, P needs to be a property the nature of which is exhaustively characterized by its TDS, as clause (b) requires, and the element of the TDS $\langle D_@, w_@ \rangle$, where $w_@$ is the actual world, only includes spatio-temporal powers in the disposition set $D_@$, as clause (a) requires.

I do not think that Howell's account is satisfactory with regard to the understanding of physicalism I am concerned with. While it seems to do quite well with regard to many of the constraints I formulated at the beginning of the chapter, it seems that the account does not satisfy the *non-trivial inclusion of special science properties constraint*, at least if special science properties are 'defined' in terms of purely spatio-temporal powers. Any special science property will count as physical in this case. Of course, since Howell is mainly interested in a domain-specific physicalism about the mental, this is not quite his problem. Aside from that, Howell's account seems to exclude certain Russellian monist views from being variants of physicalism that I find acceptable, at least as forms of physicalism about properties. Take the Russellian identity theory again, on which mental properties are identical to the categorical properties that underlie dispositions. Since those categorical properties have a phenomenal aspect and thus their nature is not fully exhausted by conferring spatio-temporal powers, they cannot be physical properties.

There is a further issue that I take to be more worrisome than Howell thinks. In a footnote, he points out but directly dismisses the following concern (2003: 30 – 31 [fn45]):

> There is actually a further problem with Neocart-con that will not affect the debate, since it won't affect the definition of physicalism, but is a problem nonetheless. Suppose dualism is true of this world, and there is a psycho-physical law that C-fibres give rise to the non-physical quale pain. Clause (a) of Neocart-con would seem to imply that C-Fibres are thereby non-physical. This is odd enough, but the non-physicality of C-Fibres will presumably [sic] spread to anything with a disposition to affect C-Fibres, and so on. The result might be that a dualistic world is really, by this definition, a strange sort of idealist world! The

solution to this problem will again depend on particularities of the metaphysics of properties, in particular the trans-world identification conditions of properties. If properties have certain dispositions essentially, then the fix is easy: change (a) to say that P's essential dispositions are spatio-temporal. If properties do not have essential dispositions, the matter is harder, but perhaps the right thing to say is that physicality of properties comes in degrees on this view, and whether or not a property satisfies condition (a) is a contextual matter. These issues threaten to explode beyond what can be covered here, but since the issue of physicalism is not affected I leave the puzzle for a future occasion.

Of course, if the view indeed implies that a dualistic world is a strange sort of idealist world, then dualism, which is a pluralist view, cannot be properly distinguished from idealism, which is supposed to be a monist view. This is more than odd, and given that the notion of the physical that the different rivals in the debate use should be the same in order to avoid that the advocates of the rival views do not talk past each other, this seems to be bad for a physicalist who uses Howell's definition of the physical in their thesis of physicalism as well. Moreover, the easy fix Howell proposes does not in general help, because a minimal physicalism should not presuppose a particular view of properties. Another way to view the issue is that similar to the *via negativa*'s problem of ruling out certain panpsychist views as conceptually incoherent, Howell's view rules out interactionist dualism as conceptually incoherent, if only less directly because it also depends on one's general view about properties. After all, according to the interactionist dualist, mental properties have a phenomenal nature, and interact via laws of nature with physical properties. But on Howell's view, as soon as a property so interacts with a mental property, it cannot be physical. So Howell's view does not quite fail to fulfill the *traditional rivals constraint*, but at least it fails with respect to a closely related constraint: that a view of the physical should not rule out any of the live rival views of physicalism as conceptually incoherent.

I find the first part of his considerations already worrisome enough to move on and to try finding a better definition of the physical than the one Howell proposes. On his view, if dualism is true of the actual world, it might turn out that no property, not even those we would intuitively count as the most prototypical physical properties, such as *having mass* and *having charge*, are physical. As I understand Howell's account, if *having mass* and *having charge* are part of a holistic network of properties connected by laws of nature part of which are also phenomenal properties, a complete story about the dispositions bestowed on the bearers of mass and charge makes reference to such phenomenal properties, which in turn deprives those properties of their status as physical properties. Of course, Howell and I agree that physicalism should come out false in such a world. But the problem is that whether properties like mass and charge, which seem to be prototypical examples of physical properties, count as physical depends on whether dualism is true of our world. This does not seem right. In a different scenario in which it turns out that mass and charge have a phenomenal nature, as the Russellian monist claims, I would understand the reasoning behind the view that in such a case, mass and charge are not physical in the sense required for physicalism, even if I do not agree with the view. But the connection required to make mass and charge non-physical on Howell's view is even weaker: it is sufficient to make mass and charge non-physical that they are part of a network of properties tied to each other by contingent laws part of which are also some phenomenal properties.

Let me consider a different situation that vividly highlights another aspect of the issue. Physicalists typically accept that even if physicalism is true of our world, there can be a dualist world that is a physical duplicate of our world but contains some extra Cartesian souls. Let us say that these Cartesian souls have some phenomenal properties that are not instantiated in our world at all, and there are laws in that world that tie those phenomenal properties to the properties we also have in our world. As far as I can see, this seems to be compatible with the claim that the properties in the actual world are thin properties – the dispositions they bestow on their bearers in other possible worlds need not be merely spatio-temporal, but can also include dispositions to affect Cartesian souls, because clause (b) of Howell's definition does not say anything about the spatio-temporality of the dispositions in a TDS. Thus, the claim that mass and charge are physical properties in our world is not affected by the possibility of such a world. However, what should we say about the other possible world? It seems that we have two options.

Either we take Howell's definition literally and always evaluate clause (a) relative to the actual world. In this case, mass and charge remain physical properties, which is the wanted result. However, this affects the account's ability to satisfy the *alien physical properties constraint*. If a property is not instantiated in the actual world, it does not bestow any dispositions upon its bearers, nor does it bring in any non-dispositional properties. If we understand clause (a) so that such a non-instantiated property already satisfies it, because it does neither confer anything other than spatio-temporal powers nor spatio-temporal powers, then it seems that this might let in too much. Since clause (b) does not say anything about the kinds of dispositions involved, any non-instantiated property that is exhaustively characterized by a TDS will do. If we understand clause (a) so that the property in question has to bestow its bearers with some spatio-temporal powers in the actual world, but not with anything else, then this restricts the set of physical properties too much because alien physical properties become impossible. Alternatively, we can evaluate clause (a) relative to the world in question, so that it is required that *P* needs to bestow only spatio-temporal dispositions upon its bearers in the world under consideration. Then, mass and charge, along with the other properties that count as physical in our world, at the extended duplicate world turn out to be non-physical properties. Is the world under consideration even a physical duplicate of our world, then? I am not quite sure what to say, and it seems to me that we should avoid a view of the physical that has such odd implications.

3.4 A way out: reference-fixing accounts of the physical

3.4.1 Frank Jackson's object-based reference-fixing account

Frank Jackson provides an interesting alternative attempt to avoid the problems that arise for the views discussed above. He dismisses the problems raised in Hempel's dilemma, and points out that we can use some paradigmatic ordinary objects as prototypes to provide an ostensive definition of the physical (1998: 7):

> I think this problem is more apparent than real. For, first, physicalists can give an ostensive definition of what they mean by physical properties and relations by pointing to some exemplars of non-sentient objects – tables, chairs, mountains, and the like – and then say that by physical properties and relations, they mean the kinds of properties and relations needed to give a complete account of things like them. Their clearly non-trivial claim is then that the kinds of properties and relations needed to account for the exemplars of the non-sentient are enough to account for everything, or at least everything contingent.

Here, the idea is that instead of appealing to physics or explicitly providing a list of characteristics that all and only physical properties have in common, we just point at a couple of objects that we intuitively would consider to be physical objects, and ostensively fix the reference to 'physical property' in this way. An overly simplistic version of such an account might be the following:

> *F* is a physical property *iff F* is a property instantiated by some object sufficiently similar to *this* (a table), *this* (a chair), or *this* (a mountain).

One obvious worry with such an account is that it appeals to similarity, and it remains unclear how similar something must be to the examples to be sufficiently similar to them. Furthermore, it remains unclear in which respect they need to be similar, and we cannot say that they need to be similar with respect to their being physical. Moreover, given that the objects fundamental physics is concerned with, like electrons or quarks, are quite dissimilar to the ordinary objects pointed to, the definition may render many of the properties that fundamental physics is concerned with non-physical (cf. Howell 2013: 19).

In order to avoid this concern, one might add electrons and quarks to the list, probably by using a reference-fixing description rather than ostension because it is difficult to actually point at a quark. Another option might be to stick to the original list of paradigmatic objects and to adapt the definition along the following lines (cf. Howell 2013: 19 [fn15]; Stoljar 2015: section 11):

> F is a physical property *iff* F is a property instantiated by some object sufficiently similar to or constitutively involved in the existence of some object sufficiently similar to *this* (a table), *this* (a chair), or *this* (a mountain).

Insofar as quarks and electrons are constitutively involved in the existence of tables, chairs, and mountains, their properties will count as physical.

However, this notion of the physical is still too permissive. *First*, depending on the concrete prototypes, it may count all kinds of special science properties as physical by definition. This might be avoided if we use prototypes that are further down the mereological hierarchy, like electrons and quarks.[83]

In any case, there is a more general problem with any such object-based account. Suppose that some form of panpsychism is true. In such a case, all the mental properties of the objects pointed to and the objects constitutively involved in their existence will count as physical.

Jackson is aware of this issue, but immediately dismisses it (1998: 7):

> There will be a problem for this way of elucidating the notion of physical properties and relations if panpsychism is true (as Ian Ravenscroft reminded me). For then there are no exemplars of the non-sentient. Everything has a mental life. But I think that we can safely set this possibility to one side.

I do not think however that one can so easily get away, given that panpsychism is one of the live options in the debate.

There are certainly some versions of panpsychism that do not pose a problem for physicalism – the prototypical case is the panpsychist version of the identity theory I have discussed in the previous chapter. Another one is a version of panpsychism on which every particular has mental properties, but those mental properties metaphysically depend on physical properties of the particular. If mental properties are however distinct from physical properties in the way the traditional dualist understands distinctness, we have a form of dualist panpsy-

---

[83] How this squares with the *Direction of Priority Constraint* is another question.

chism. We do not know whether or not one of these versions of panpsychism is true. An adequate notion of the physical is supposed to help divide these possibilities into the corresponding camps, but the notion at hand would make physicalism true in all of these cases by counting the mental properties as physical.

Even if I do not think that the object-based account is a viable option, it has something to it that I think is important. It tries to give an account of the physical that is not based upon our theories about the world, but upon the world directly. Physicalism is supposed to be a metaphysical thesis about what the world is like. If we tie the notion of the physical that is plugged into the thesis of physicalism too closely to physics, we bring in an unwanted epistemic component to our metaphysical thesis (cf. Howell 2013: 16).

More generally, we may ask the following question:[84] Is it more plausible to think that (1) physical properties are physical because physics is concerned with them, or rather that (2) physics is concerned with physical properties because they are physical? It seems to me that intuitively, the latter seems much more appropriate. As Howell indicates, if (1) were the case, then "what reason would a physicist have to add something (or eliminate something) from his field of study? The posits of physics would seem to have an air of arbitrariness" (2013: 16). At least, this would be the case if we cannot provide a further non-trivial account of why physics is concerned with the properties it is concerned with. While (2) is much more intuitive, it seems to presuppose that physical properties have something in common: they are physical. But in order to not run in circles, we somehow need to get a handle on what it is that makes them physical.

3.4.2 Appeal to the common nature of physical properties: a property-based reference fixing account

It might seem that we are right back at the starting point and did not make any progress. However, I think that we can derive a solution to the question what it means for a property to be a physical property from what we have learned in the preceding sections. First, we have learned that we should not tie our notion of the physical too closely to physics, but we still need to give physics some role in order to capture the idea that one of the main ancestors of contemporary physicalism is the semantic 'physicalism' of Carnap and Neurath. Moreover,

---

84 Howell calls this a 'Euthyphro' question. This goes back to a dialogue of Plato with the same name, in which Socrates asks Euthyphro whether the pious is loved by the gods because it is pious, or whether it is pious because it is loved by the gods. The question about the physical has the same basic structure.

while it turns out to be difficult to provide an explicit list of positive features that a property must have in order to be physical, even if there are such features, a list of negative features does not seem to work either.

Do we need to provide an explicit list of positive features in the first place? Does it not suffice to somehow fix the reference of the predicate '... is a physical property' in a way that gives us the wanted result without providing an explicit list of positive features? The object-based conception of the physical discussed in the previous section tries to do exactly this, but it fails miserably with respect to the panpsychist option. If we are able to provide an account of the physical along similar lines that is able to avoid the problems of the rival views just discussed, I think that we have at our hands a very promising account of the physical, even if it does not explicitly tell us what it is that makes a property a physical property.

So how might such an account look like? In order to fix the reference appropriately, we need to move from an object-based to a property-based account. Instead of claiming that physical properties are the properties instantiated by prototypical physical objects, we can claim that the physical properties are those properties that stand in a certain relation to the properties of current physics, where the relation is a *sameness-in-kind* relation. As Braddon-Mitchell and Jackson indicate in their defense of an object-based reference-fixing account, "[t]he incompleteness of current physical theory does not imply incompleteness in the *kinds* of ingredients that will be needed to complete the job" (2007: 20).

Along these lines, Esa Díaz-León proposes the following account[85] (2008: 99):

> F is physical$_n$ if and only if F is a property of the same kind as the properties posited by current physics.

Christian Nimtz and Michael Schütte make a similar proposal (2003: 419):

> A property F is physical if and only if F is of the same kind as the properties we singled out as paradigms such as *having a left spin* or *being extended*.

Both of these accounts are fairly close to what I consider to be the most promising account of physical properties that we can come up with. But there are some things that need to be clarified.

---

[85] Díaz-León's notion of a physical$_n$ property resembles what I call a narrowly physical property.

As I understand it, these accounts are based on the idea that, as Galen Strawson[86] puts it, "'[p]hysical' is a natural-kind term – it is the ultimate natural-kind term" (2008 [2003]: 20). What makes a property physical is exactly that (set of) feature(s), or that part of the nature of the prototypical examples, that all the example properties have in common. Understanding the physical in terms of kinds requires that not only particulars can be classified into kinds, but also that property types can be classified into kinds. In other words, what such an account requires is that we can talk of kinds of property types. However, we do not need to put things in terms of kinds. Instead, we can say that the property types that serve as our prototypes need to share part of their nature, and this is what makes them physical properties. As the talk of the nature of properties already indicates, each feature (or kind, or property) in question, in order to belong to the nature of a property type, needs to be one that the property types have necessarily, and that is not necessarily had by any property whatsoever. This avoids that properties like *being a property type considered by current physics* or *being instantiated* may count towards what makes the physical properties physical, since these are only contingent features of those properties. Similarly, it avoids that *being a property*, or *being such that 2+2=4*, may count towards what makes the physical properties physical. These are features that the physical properties share with any property whatsoever.

In a sense, the term 'physical property', according to the property-based reference fixing account, works quite similar to terms like 'water' and 'gold', according to a Putnam-Kripke-style semantics (Putnam 1975a; Kripke 1980). The reference of these terms is fixed by pointing to concrete examples, and, "the rest is done, as it were, by objective relations of sameness and difference embedded in the fabric of the world", as Nimtz and Schütte (2003: 420) put it. Analogously, in order to get the extension of '… is a physical property' right, we use a number of prototypical example properties and extend the range of properties

---

86 As far as I can tell, Strawson's own account is closer to the object-based account, however. He thinks that one can "sufficiently indicate [the reference of 'physical'] by drawing attention to tables and chairs and [...] experiential phenomena" (Strawson 2006: 8), so that "the physical is whatever general kind of thing we are considering when we consider things like tables and chairs and experiential phenomena" (2006: 8). His inclusion of experiential phenomena makes his view inappropriate to capture what is central to the debate about the issue. Strawson is aware of this issue, but he bites the bullet: "It is true that there is a sense in which this makes my use of the term vacuous, for, relative to our universe, 'physical stuff' is now equivalent to 'real and concrete stuff', and cannot be anything to do with the term 'physical' that is used to mark out a position in what is usually taken to be a substantive debate about the ultimate nature of concrete reality (physicalism vs immaterialism vs dualism vs pluralism vs …). But that is fine by me" (2006: 8).

picked out by also allowing for other properties that are of the same kind. We do not need to know what the common nature of the prototypical examples is in order to be able to use the term appropriately. After all, users of the term 'water' who are ignorant of the nature of water that science helped us to reveal, i.e. its *being a molecular compound of oxygen and hydrogen atoms with the chemical structure H_2O*, are also able to use the term appropriately.

Díaz-León thinks that "to decide what properties are of the same sort as those posited by physics [...] the best strategy [...] is to defer to experts in physics: they are the ones who can decide which new properties discovered by physics count as the same kind of properties as those posited by current physics, and which don't" (2008: 100 [fn13]). That seems strange to me. *First*, if one thinks that science is concerned only with dispositional properties, but we also need categorical bases for these dispositions, physicists will be unable to do the job Díaz-León wants them to do. *Second*, since on such a view, objective relations of similarity between properties fix what counts as physical, the job Díaz-León wants the physicists to do is done already by nature.

In order to get an account that is not too restrictive, we need to avoid that the properties that are used as prototypes are too similar to each other. If our only prototype properties were *being an electron* and *being a proton*, we might end up with an account that does not count, say, *being a field* as physical. Thus, in the best case, we include a large variety of rather different properties into our set of prototypes. With regard to this, I think that Díaz-León's approach is more on the safe side. In order to save the account from problems regarding cases in which current physics gets things wrong and considers entities that do not in fact exist, however, we should add the constraint that only instantiated properties count:

> F is a physical property *iff* F is a property of the same kind as the *instantiated* properties posited by current physics.

An alternative way to frame the same idea is the following, where P is basically what makes the physical properties physical:

> F is a physical property *iff* (i) the instantiated properties posited by current physics all have in common a certain non-empty part of their nature P, and (ii) P is part of the nature of F, and (iii) F does not have P as a part of its nature solely due to being a conjunctive property that has as a conjunct a property that satisfies (ii).

Clause (i) fixes what the common nature of physical properties amounts to, (ii) makes sure that the property in question shares that common nature, and (iii) makes sure that conjunctive properties like *being an electron and in pain* do not trivially turn out to be physical properties. Here, current physics is supposed to be the current physics of the actual world, irrespective of the world under consideration. So the physical properties instantiated at different worlds might vary from world to world, and some alien properties that are not instantiated in our world can count as physical as long as they are of the same kind as the physical properties of our world. Thus, the account is able to satisfy the *alien physical properties constraint*. Still, this view avoids that ectoplasmic properties are counted as physical, because they are, by stipulation, different in kind to the properties instantiated in this world. Moreover, it satisfies the *progress of physics constraint*. As long as physics remains postulating further properties that are of the same kind, such properties will count as physical.[87]

Howell (2013: 18) considers a view along such lines, but rejects it because he thinks that it is too vague. It does not provide us with a clue as to what the common nature of physical properties is, nor is it guaranteed that there is such a common nature. I agree with Howell's first point, but I do not think that gives us reason to reject the view, even though I admit that a correct positive account of the physical would be good to have. Regarding his second point, I think that we should not adopt a notion of the physical that makes physicalism compatible with the lack of such a common nature.[88] If it should turn out that the instantiated properties posited by current physics do not have anything in common, so that there is no such sameness-in-kind relation among all the properties of current physics, then I think that there are no physical properties in the sense required for physicalism, and physicalism is false. This is just the right result. *First*, this does not mean that there are no properties of physics – the predicate '… is a property of (current, future, or whatever) physics' will still pick out a collection of properties, even if the predicate '… is a physical property' as defined above does not pick out anything. *Second*, physicalism is supposed to be a form of metaphysical or ontological monism, and this requires that there is something substantial that the properties that form the metaphysical depend-

---

87 Since I think that physics is concerned with certain properties *because* they are of a common kind, I also have the impression that a 'physics' that postulates properties of a different kind than those postulated by current physics does not deserve to be called 'physics' anyway. But nothing hangs on this, since '… is a property of such-and-such (current, future, …) physics' and '… is a physical property' are independent predicates.

88 It is worth noting that Howell's own view is that physical properties do indeed have a common nature – their being such that they have only spatio-temporal implications.

ence base have in common. If there is no such commonality, then we do not have a metaphysical monist picture of what the world is like. In this case, I think that physicalism indeed should come out false.

Some might think that with regard to the *nontrivial inclusion of special science properties constraint*, the account might fail in case it turns out that special science properties are also of the same kind as the prototype properties. My answer to this worry is to concede that it might very well be that some or all of the special science properties are of this kind. However, we did not *trivially* include them because we restricted our prototype properties to the properties of physics, and it is a substantial metaphysical question whether or not those properties are of the same kind as those of physics. If they are, then they count as physical properties, and I think rightly so, because they share the common nature of the properties of physics. If they are not, then the worry remains merely hypothetical anyway.

A similar worry might arise with the *traditional rivals constraint*. Suppose it turns out that Russellian identity theory is true and the nature of physical properties is at least in part phenomenal. Given that I rejected futurism due to its potentially counting mental properties as physical, would that not be a problem for this view of the physical as well? I do not think so. Unlike the futurist scenario, where mental properties might be counted as physical even though they are different in kind from the properties of current physics, mental properties would count as physical properties only because they share their nature with the properties of current physics. Thus, this would not amount to a situation in which a form of substance or property dualism or pluralism is true, unless there are further properties instantiated in our world that do not metaphysically depend on the physical properties. So although the scenario would be one in which the nature of the physical turns out to be very different from what most of us expect, I think that it would be a scenario in which physicalism is true, and rightly so.

More generally, I think the fact that the account is silent about what exactly the nature of the physical is actually is a virtue of the account. After all, this makes the account compatible in principle with a large variety of different views, and that seems to be exactly the way a minimal physicalist account should look like. For example, suppose Howell is correct and the nature of the physical is exhausted by spatio-temporal implications. If this is what the nature of the physical amounts to, i.e. if this is what all properties from the list of prototypes have in common, then the reference-fixing account will just pick out the same properties as Howell's neo-Cartesian account. However, other than the neo-Cartesian account, the property-based reference fixing account is also compatible with views on the other end of the spectrum. If it turns out that the Russellian identity theorist is right in thinking that the ultimate nature of the physical is at least in part phenomenal, then this is fine too. If this is the common nature of the properties posited by current physics, then this is and should be what *being physical* amounts to.

The other constraints I formulated at the beginning of this chapter are also satisfied by the view. Physicalism remains a thesis that is true or false, such that the *truth-aptness constraint* is satisfied, and its truth or falsity is not trivial and depends on what the world is like, as required by the *nontrivial truth* and *nontrivial falsity constraints* and the *contingent a posteriori thesis constraint*. Also, since the notion of the physical does not require a particular direction of priority, it is compatible with different views regarding the order of priority regarding the mereological hierarchy, as required by the *direction of priority constraint*.

3.5 Summary

In this chapter, we have seen that it turns out to be quite difficult to tell what the nature of physical properties amounts to. The views that are most prominently discussed in the literature all turn out to fail with regard to one or the other criterion that a proper account of the physical needs to satisfy. Nevertheless, we do not need to throw in the towel and declare that there is no account of the physical that is satisfactory for the purpose of characterizing physicalism, and that there is thus no meaningful thesis of physicalism either. All we need to understand is that it suffices to just fix the reference properly by using the current physical properties as prototypes, so that we do not need to say what the nature of physical properties is. Some might find it somewhat disappointing that the nature of the physical remains untold, but I think that the property-based reference fixing account provides us with all we need for a minimal physicalist view, and we may even take it to be a feature (rather than a bug) that the view is so liberal.

4 "The bare necessities"

In the previous chapters, we addressed the question what the scope of the thesis of physicalism is, that is, what categories we need to quantify over in order to formulate the thesis, and which categories we also capture implicitly by doing so, as well as the question of how to spell out in detail the notion of a narrowly physical property. We can now move on to the third and final question we need to address in order to properly understand the thesis of physicalism: how should we understand the notion of *metaphysical dependence* that accounts for the idea that some properties are not identical to, but nevertheless *nothing over and above* physical properties? In this chapter, I focus on the modal features that come along with metaphysical dependence, and more generally with physicalism, and investigate whether or not we can spell out metaphysical dependence in purely modal terms.

Let me start by restating the formulation of the thesis of physicalism we have arrived at in chapter 2:

(P) Physicalism is true of world *w iff*
   (a) every positive qualitative property had by any individual at *w* that exists contingently or is causal either
      (i) is a narrowly physical property instantiated at *w* or
      (ii) metaphysically depends on narrowly physical properties and relations instantiated at *w* or
      (iii) is a property that is necessarily had by every individual, and
   (b) every positive qualitative relation had by any plurality at *w* that exists contingently or is causal either
      (i) is a narrowly physical relation instantiated at *w* or
      (ii) metaphysically depends on narrowly physical properties and relations instantiated at *w* or
      (iii) is a relation that is necessarily had by every plurality formed of the same number of individuals.

As clause (ii) of both (a) and (b) indicates, what we are looking for is a notion of metaphysical dependence that picks out a relation (or, as we will see in chapter 5, maybe a family of relations) between the narrowly physical properties and relations of individuals and other properties and relations of individuals that are not necessarily had by every individual whatsoever – those properties and relations that are broadly but not narrowly physical. Moreover, it is important to note that the relata of the relation(s) in question are types of properties and relations, rather than particular instances of properties and relations. As in the previous chapter, I will often omit explicit reference to relations and take it for granted that my use of the term 'property' is to be understood broadly to also capture relations.

As the above phrasing of the thesis of physicalism suggests, the notion of metaphysical dependence associates a single dependent property to a plurality of properties it depends upon. I think this is more appropriate for our purposes than framing metaphysical dependence as a relation between singular properties. In the literature, the relations discussed for this purpose are often taken to take singular relata, but some of those singular relata might be conjunctive properties like *being red and round*, or even much more complex properties like *being a system with such-and-such a microstructure*. However, no harm is done in taking the metaphysical dependence relation to be a one-many relation, given that a one-one-relation is just a special case of a one-many relation. Since we might plausibly want to say that the property of *being red and round* metaphysically depends on the properties *being red* and *being round*, or more generally, that conjunctive properties metaphysically depend on their conjuncts, or that *being a system with such-and-such a microstructure* metaphysically depends on the properties and relations that account for that microstructure, it seems reasonable to think of metaphysical dependence as a one-many relation.

4.1 Necessitation

In order to do justice to the way the debate about physicalism goes, one of the major requirements for our notion of metaphysical dependence is that it must entail that the metaphysically dependent properties are necessitated by the properties they metaphysically depend on, or at least by the whole set of instantiated physical properties taken together. This is sometimes expressed using a creationist metaphor: When God created the world, did they need to fix the distribution of physical properties only to thereby fix all the rest, or did they need to also fix the distribution of further properties, say, phenomenal properties, in addition to the physical properties? The truth of physicalism requires the former, setting aside the creationist part of the story, of course.

4.1.1 Why necessitation is necessary for metaphysical dependence

If we look at the central arguments against physicalism,[89] we find that they typically include such a principle as a part of one of the central premises. Consider the conceivability argument (e.g. Chalmers 1996; 2010: Ch. 6), which in a rather simple form has the following structure:
(1) A world with the same distribution of instances of physical properties as the actual world, but in which no phenomenal properties are instantiated, is conceivable.
(2) If such a world is conceivable, it is metaphysically possible.
(3) If there is a metaphysically possible world with the same distribution of instances of physical properties as the actual world, but in which no phenomenal properties are instantiated, then physicalism is false.
∴ Physicalism is false.

The world that is allegedly conceivable according to premise (1) is typically called a *zombie world*.[90] The argument is obviously valid. But while there is much disagreement with regard to the soundness of this argument between physicalists and pluralists as well as within the physicalist camp, the debate has focused only on premises (1) and (2). So-called *a priori physicalists*[91] deny (1) and argue that such worlds are inconceivable. This typically involves a deflationary account of phenomenal concepts. On such accounts, phenomenal concepts are typically analyzed in causal/functional terms, rather than in terms of *what-it-is-like-ness* (Nagel 1974). Their rivals within the physicalist camp, *a posteriori physicalists*, accept (1) but deny (2), the conceivability-possibility principle, typically on the basis of concerns regarding conceivability-based modal epistemology. They agree with the dualist with regard to the analysis of phenomenal concepts, but still think that each of these concepts picks out the same property as some physical or functional concept.

---

89 Those arguments are mainly advanced against a domain-specific physicalism about the mental. However, since the truth of physicalism *simpliciter* requires the truth of a domain-specific physicalism about the mental, at least provided that mental properties are instantiated at the world under consideration, they can be likewise advanced against physicalism *simpliciter*.
90 Robert Kirk (1974) first introduced the term 'zombie' into the philosophical literature, but David Chalmers (1996; 2010) has contributed most significantly to the debate, so that the current degree of popularity of the term among philosophers of mind is mostly due to him.
91 Importantly, these physicalists are not committed to the claim that physicalism (about the mental) is an *a priori* truth. Rather, they take it to be *a priori* that the physical properties necessitate the mental ones.

Virtually all physicalists and pluralists agree however that (3) is true, and thus that some kind of necessitation principle must hold for physicalism to be true that connects the physical properties with all the rest (for an exception, see Montero 2013; see also the related notion of *ceteris absentibus* physicalism proposed by Leuenberger (2008) discussed in section 4.4.1 below). A structurally similar argument with the same conclusion can be established by considering a world in which the distribution of physical properties is the same as in the actual world, but in which some mental properties are inverted (Shoemaker 1982; Block 1990; Chalmers 1996: 99–101). The above observations regarding which premises are debated also hold for the case of mental property inversion.

In order to move forward, we need to better understand what exactly the necessitation principle amounts to. This requires that we first have a look at the notion of necessitation that applies to propositions, and then move on to a notion of necessitation that applies to properties.

4.1.2 Propositional necessitation and the contingency of physicalism

Strictly speaking, the notion of necessitation primarily applies to propositions rather than to properties. A proposition P necessitates another proposition P^* *iff* necessarily, P entails P^*. In terms of possible worlds, the right-hand side of this biconditional states that in every possible world in which the proposition P is true, the proposition P^* is also true.

Some consider physicalism itself to take the form of one proposition entailing another. Importantly, however, physicalism about world w cannot be the statement 'P entails P^*', where 'P' is a name of the proposition expressing the actual distribution of physical properties at w and 'P^*' is a name of the proposition expressing the actual distribution of all relevant properties[92] at w, because physicalism is supposed to be a contingent thesis (e.g. Horgan 1982; Lewis 1983; Chalmers 1996). Even if physicalism is true, it should not be necessarily true.[93] However, as I will explain below, if physicalism is true of w, it is necessarily true that P entails P^* (and necessarily false otherwise). Thus, that statement cannot be the thesis of physicalism. There is however a contingent statement in the vicinity that is sometimes considered to be equivalent to physicalism: 'the proposition that expresses how instances of physical properties are distributed at w

---

[92] I use the notion of *relevant* properties as shorthand for the positive qualitative properties of contingent or causal individuals, as discussed in chapter 2.
[93] Some have challenged this claim, but the view that physicalism is not a contingent thesis is a minority view (see Levine and Trogdon 2009; Seager 2010; Walter 2011).

entails the proposition that expresses how instances of all relevant properties are distributed at *w*' (where *w* is an indexical that picks out the respective world under consideration). Unlike the statement that *P* entails *P**, this is a contingent statement.

Let me explain why the statement '*P* entails *P**' is necessarily true if true at all. '*P*' and '*P**' are names for particular propositions, those that express how the properties in question are distributed in a particular world, and thus rigid designators of those propositions that express the distribution of properties in that world. Unlike '*P*' and '*P**', the expressions 'the proposition that expresses how instances of physical properties are distributed at *w*' and 'the proposition that expresses how instances of all relevant properties are distributed at *w*' are definite descriptions that refer to different propositions when considering different worlds *w*, depending on which property instances are distributed in which way in the world under consideration, and thus are non-rigid designators.

This is analogous to cases of identity statements discussed by Saul Kripke (1980). The identity relation that holds between, say, *being water* and *being H_2O* holds necessarily, just like the identity relation between *being water* and *being water*, or *being H_2O* and *being H_2O*, for that matter. Still, we can formulate necessary as well as contingent identity *statements* about these properties.[94] The statement '*being water* is identical to *being H_2O*' is a necessary identity statement because it uses rigid designators on both sides of the identity sign, which always refer to the property of *being water* (or *being H_2O*, which comes to the same thing), independent of the world under consideration, as long as the property exists, and never refer to any other property. Thus, if the statement is true, it is necessarily true, and it is necessarily false otherwise. However, the statement '*the property that is essential to all and only the clear drinkable liquid that flows down the rivers and fills the oceans*[95] is identical to *being H_2O*' is a contingent statement, even though the identity relation between the property referred to in our world and itself holds with necessity. This is because the description on the left-hand side of the statement is non-rigid. It refers to different properties in different possible worlds. In our world, it refers to *being H_2O*, and the statement is true. But in a possible world in which the clear drinkable liquid that flows down the rivers and fills the oceans is something different from H_2O, the statement is false. Thus, identity *statements* can be contingent, even though

---

[94] I use the plural form even though strictly speaking, we are talking about a single property here.
[95] Here, I assume that this is a definite description that picks out one particular property, the property of *being H_2O*, in our world. But even if it does not, it should be clear how the line of reasoning works.

the identity relation itself holds necessarily between any entity and itself. Likewise, the entailment from P to $P*$ can hold with necessity, but we can form statements composed of expressions that refer to the same propositions the names 'P' and '$P*$' refer to in the world in question, but to other propositions in other possible worlds. These *statements* will still be contingent (see Stoljar 2010: 130–133 for similar considerations on the link between the contingency of physicalism and Kripke's theory of proper names).

The way physicalism is expressed by my formulation developed in chapter 2 allows it to be a contingent thesis as well. It does not use any proper names in its formulation, but rather uses variables bound to quantifiers to point to the properties in question, so that the properties linked are different from world to world depending on which properties are instantiated in the world in question. Thus, even if physicalism is true of one world, it can turn out to be false in another world in which different properties are instantiated that do not metaphysically depend on physical properties instantiated in that world, and thus can be contingent.

4.1.3 Property necessitation

Even though necessitation strictly speaking primarily applies to propositions, it has become standard in the literature to talk of necessitation not only as a relation between propositions, but also as a relation between properties. According to Daniel Stoljar (2010), who frames things in terms of necessitation as a one-one relation between properties, "one property necessitates another just in case, in all possible worlds, if the first is instantiated the second is instantiated" (Stoljar 2010: 112). Although close, this is not exactly what we want, because this characterization of necessitation still leaves too much wiggle room.[96] Property necessitation properly construed requires that once it is fixed how instances of the necessitating properties are distributed among particulars, there is no wiggle room as to how instances of the necessitated property are distributed. Since Stoljar's formulation does neither put any restriction on which properties are instantiated by which particulars, nor on the way property instances are distributed, it leaves open certain cases we would intuitively like to avoid.

---

[96] I assume that Stoljar is aware of this issue, but uses this formulation because he does not want to decide between the individual and global formulation I discuss below, or takes it for granted that the properties are instantiated by the same individuals.

In order to keep things simple, let us stick to a case of necessitation that relates singular properties. Suppose some property A is instantiated in all the worlds in which another property B is instantiated, so that the right-hand side of Stoljar's definition is fulfilled, but among these worlds there is a pair of worlds in which the pattern of distribution of B is exactly the same, but the pattern of distribution of A is very different, so that the entities that instantiate A in one world do not instantiate A in another. Rather, some other entities do. For example, suppose A is a mental property that is necessitated in such a way by some physical property B. It is compatible with Stoljar's formulation that in one world, people have the mental property in question, whereas in another world, rocks have it, even though the distribution of physical properties is exactly the same. However, the necessitation principle at work in the background of premise (3) of the conceivability argument above clearly requires that such cases are ruled out, and thus Stoljar's formulation, taken literally, is too weak.

One way to avoid this is to appeal to what we might call *individual necessitation* (IN):

(IN) Property B (or: the plurality of properties $B_1, ..., B_n$ jointly) individually necessitate(s) property A *iff* in all possible worlds, whenever B is (or: $B_1, ..., B_n$ are) instantiated by some entity, A is instantiated by that same entity.

One rather uncontroversial stock example in which such a necessitation principle clearly holds is the case of *being red* and *being crimson*. In every possible world, whenever a particular instantiates *being crimson*, that particular also instantiates *being red*.

Another way to avoid the worry with Stoljar's formulation is to frame necessitation in terms of patterns of instantiation, i.e. of distributions of property instances.[97] We can call such an account of necessitation *global necessitation* (GN):[98]

---

97 There is a further question as to whether we mean distribution among particulars, space-time points, or something else, which I leave unaddressed here. For further discussion, see McLaughlin (1995: 32–34).

98 Note that unless further conditions on metaphysical dependence rule out such a case, this opens up the possibility that all relevant properties are narrowly physical or metaphysically depend on the narrowly physical properties, but still, there are some individuals that do not instantiate any narrowly physical properties themselves, even though their relevant properties metaphysically depend on narrowly physical properties and thus are broadly physical. Since an individual is (narrowly) physical only if it has at least one narrowly physical property, this

(GN) Property B (or: a plurality of properties B_1, ..., B_n jointly) globally necessitate(s) property A *iff* all pairs of possible worlds that share the same pattern of instantiation of property B (or: properties B_1, ..., B_n) also share the same pattern of instantiation of property A.

These two ways of spelling out necessitation are also reflected in different attempts to spell out another familiar modal notion that has been influential in the debate about physicalism ever since Donald Davidson first introduced it to the philosophy of mind in his seminal paper "Mental Events" (2001d [1970]): the notion of *supervenience*.

4.2 Supervenience

In the heyday of modal metaphysics, the notion of supervenience has become one of the major candidates for expressing the relation between mental and physical properties that needs to hold in order for a domain-specific physicalism about the mental to be true. In "Mental Events", Davidson argues for a view he calls "Anomalous Monism", according to which mental events are token-identical to physical events. This claim is then supplemented with a supervenience claim. His original formulation of supervenience is as follows (2001d [1970]: 214):

> [M]ental characteristics are in some sense dependent, or supervenient, on physical characteristics. Such supervenience might be taken to mean that there cannot be two events alike in all physical respects but differing in some mental respect, or that an object cannot alter in some mental respect without altering in some physical respect.

Davidson takes the notion of supervenience to express a dependence relation that holds between mental and physical characteristics of events or objects. However, Davidson's terms 'characteristics' and 'respects' are not to be understood as synonymous to 'properties' in a metaphysically deep sense. In his (1993: 4), he explicitly notes that he does "not distinguish concepts from properties or predicates", and rephrases his notion of supervenience in terms of predicates:

---

seems to be an odd case in which property physicalism is true but something like substance physicalism, at least with respect to narrowly physical substances, is false. I do not think that this does any harm to our general physicalist framework, but it is a case that is worth mentioning because it might be interpreted as a somewhat strange situation in which property dualism is false, but substance dualism is true.

> [A] predicate *p* is supervenient on a set of predicates *S* if and only if *p* does not distinguish any entities that cannot be distinguished by *S*.

According to Davidson's account, supervenience is thus a relation between predicates, which are linguistic entities. However, since the metaphysical dependence relation we need for our purposes is a relation between properties understood as worldly entities, rather than a relation between linguistic entities such as predicates, this is not quite what we are looking for.

In a series of papers published in the late 1970s and the 1980s (Kim 1978; Kim 1993d [1984]; 1993e [1987]; 1993f [1988]; 1993g [1990]), Jaegwon Kim develops different versions of supervenience. Other than Davidson, Kim takes the relata of the supervenience relation to be property types, or sets of property types. His account is thus more appropriate for our purposes. In his first paper on the topic of cashing out property supervenience, Kim distinguishes between three notions of supervenience. Two of his notions focus on property instantiations across particular individuals, while the third focuses on distributions of property instances across worlds. Across all variants, the rough idea that underlies the notion of supervenience remains the same: no difference with regard to the *supervenient* properties without a difference with regard to the properties that form the supervenience base, the *subvenient* properties.

4.2.1 Individual supervenience

Kim discusses two versions of individual supervenience, but only one, *strong individual supervenience*,[99] includes a necessitation relation (1993d [1984]: 65):

> A *strongly [individually] supervenes* on B just in case, necessarily, for each x and each property F in A, if x has F, then there is a property G in B such that x has G, and *necessarily* if any y has G, it has F.

A and B are nonempty sets of properties, and F and G are properties that are members of these sets, respectively. The notion above is called *strong* individual supervenience because it has a weaker counterpart, *weak individual supervenience*, which lacks the second 'necessarily' italicized in the above definition (1993d [1984]: 64):

---

[99] Kim calls it just strong supervenience, but I follow McLaughlin and Bennett (2018) in adding the qualifier 'individual' to make the distinction to the global variants more explicit.

A *weakly [individually] supervenes* on B if and only if necessarily for any property F in A, if an object x has F, then there exists a property G in B such that x has G, and if any y has G it has F.

Strong individual supervenience entails weak individual supervenience, but not *vice versa* (1993d [1984]: 67). Weak individual supervenience is considered too weak to express the link between physical properties and other properties required for the truth of physicalism because the relation between *F* and *G* does not have the necessary modal force – it lacks the required necessitation of *F* by *G*. According to weak individual supervenience, the co-instantiation of *F* and *G* is only required across individuals that inhabit the same world, whereas according to strong individual supervenience, it is also required across individuals that inhabit different worlds. Only in the latter case, *G* necessitates *F*. To see why weak individual supervenience is too weak, consider the conceivability argument again. Weak individual supervenience of mental properties on physical properties is compatible with the possibility of zombies, because it only rules out that there are physical duplicates of individuals with different mental properties in the *same* world. Thus, it cannot provide what is required to establish premise (3) of the conceivability argument.

Strong individual supervenience as formulated by Kim involves two necessity operators, and necessity comes in different degrees of strength, the most important of which are *logical necessity, conceptual necessity, metaphysical necessity*, and various forms of *nomological necessity*, depending on which set of laws (e.g. the laws of physics, the physical laws, the laws of nature, etc.) is to be kept fixed. Typically, it is assumed that while the concepts of logical, conceptual and metaphysical necessity differ insofar as not every metaphysically necessary truth is a conceptually necessary truth (e.g. that water is identical to H_2O), and not every conceptually necessary truth is a logically necessary truth (e.g. that every bachelor is an unmarried man), the sets of logically, conceptually, and metaphysically possible *worlds* are the same (cf. McLaughlin 1995: 26–27; Chalmers 1996: 38).[100]

For the purpose of physicalism, the second necessity operator, which is supposed to establish the necessitation of other properties by physical properties, needs to express metaphysical necessity, or at the very least nomological necessity with *just* the physical laws fixed. In the literature, things are usually framed

---

100 This is the reason why the modal operator formulations of supervenience are considered stronger than the possible world formulations of supervenience. While I am aware of this issue, I remain switching between necessity and possible world talk, as is standard in the literature.

in terms of metaphysical necessity, but it is implicitly assumed that we also take into account the physical laws (Chalmers 1996: 33):

> [T]he physical facts about the world encompass all facts about the instantiation of physical properties within the spatiotemporal manifold. It is also useful to stipulate that the world's physical facts include its basic physical laws. On some accounts, these laws are already determined by the totality of particular physical facts, but we cannot take this for granted.

Similarly, Jackson talks about physical duplicate worlds as worlds that are "exactly like our world in every physical respect (instantiated property for instantiated property, *law for law*, relation for relation)" (Jackson 1998: 13; my emphasis; see section 4.3 below for more details on the role of physical duplicate worlds in Jackson's account). I will follow the typical talk of metaphysical necessity in the literature, but we should keep in mind that strictly speaking, what we are talking about is a form of nomological necessity where we keep just the physical laws fixed. This only makes a difference if one thinks that fixing the distribution of physical property instances does not yet fix the physical laws.

It is rather uncontroversial that dualists, or more generally pluralists, can endorse a principle of necessitation with nomological necessity if the laws that are kept fixed include not only the physical laws, but also the laws that connect the physical domain to the other domains in question. Whether dualists can also endorse necessitation of the mental by the physical with metaphysical necessity is far more controversial, and will be addressed in sections 4.4.4 and 4.4.6.

For the first necessity operator, however, metaphysical necessity is clearly too strong. Physicalists want to allow that the properties that are necessitated by physical properties in our world are necessitated by non-physical properties in other worlds. They also want to allow for metaphysically possible worlds in which properties are instantiated that belong to the domain of properties necessitated by the physical properties in our world, but in which there are no instances of physical properties at all. This originally comes from considerations regarding functional properties, which are thought to be multiply realizable by properties from different domains.[101] Even if the tables around here are all physical, it might very well be that there are ectoplasmic tables in some other world, so the functional property of *being a table* is realized by ectoplasmic properties in those worlds. Similarly, consider the case of the mental domain again. Why think that physicalism has to rule out that ectoplasmic creatures in some other world could instantiate mental properties as well, which are necessitated

---

[101] For example, Putnam explicitly states that "the functional-state hypothesis is *not* incompatible with dualism" (1975b [1967]: 436).

by the ectoplasmic properties of the creatures in those worlds, as long as there are no such entities in our world? Maybe they cannot have the very same mental states as we do, as might be the case if psychophysical type identity theory is true with regard to the mental properties instantiated in our world. Nevertheless, we clearly want to allow that ectoplasmic creatures can have at least some mental states alien to our world (cf. Stalnaker 1996: 231). If the first necessity operator expresses metaphysical necessity, however, and A and B are the sets of properties of the mental and the physical domain, respectively, it is required that some physical properties that necessitate the mental properties of those worlds are instantiated in every world in which the mental properties are instantiated.

Individual supervenience claims are arguably too restrictive, however, to serve as a necessary condition for metaphysical dependence. There are cases where properties F and G metaphysically depend on each other but are not instantiated by the very same particulars, as Haugeland (1982) points out. For example, we might want to say that a property of, or relation between, the parts of an entity – e.g. *being organized in such and such a way* – is the supervenience base of a property of the entity composed of the parts. Similarly, if we assume externalism about mental content, it might seem as if we need to take into account certain properties of the environment of an individual that is in a mental state that has content. In order to find an appropriate supervenience base for the mental state in question, we need to take into account properties instantiated by individuals in the environment of the original individual, rather than the original individual itself (e.g. Horgan 1993: 571; Hoffmann and Newen 2007: 309–310).

However, this presupposes that the set of base properties only includes intrinsic properties of the individual in question. If we consider extrinsic properties of the individual as well, we can find an extrinsic property of the same individual in the vicinity that can serve as a supervenience base in order to fit the requirements for individual supervenience. For the mereological example, one might say that whenever there is a whole the parts of which stand in a relation R, the whole has the property of *having parts that stand in relation R*, and this can serve as the supervenience base in question.[102] For the case of mental content, the corresponding property is something like *being such that one's environment has such and such features*.

As soon as we want to say that the extrinsic property of the individual metaphysically depends on the properties of the parts, or on the properties of the individual's environment, however, we still need a less restrictive account of the

---

102 This is what Kim (Kim 1993f [1988]: 124; 1997: 291–292) calls a *micro-based* property.

modal requirements of metaphysical dependence than the one expressed by the notion of strong individual supervenience. As long as the extrinsic properties of the individual on which the other properties supervene are physical properties, it seems good enough for our purposes to require that all properties individually strongly supervene on these extrinsic physical properties of the same individual. However, I have two concerns. *First*, some might want to deny that there is always a extrinsic property instantiated by the individual in question because they are skeptical that *being such that one's environment has such and such features* is a genuine property. That should not be sufficient to rule out that the non-physical properties of the individual have a physical dependence base. *Second*, and more importantly, if metaphysical dependence requires strong individual supervenience, then the relation between the property of *having parts that stand in relation R* and the properties and relations of the parts in virtue of which the whole has the property of *having parts that stand in relation R* cannot be that same relation of metaphysical dependence. Given that metaphysical dependence is a rather general relation between property types, why think that the relation of dependence in play in same-subject cases and different-subject cases is different? So, it seems odd to think that metaphysical dependence of a property on other properties in general requires this kind of supervenience. This seems to indicate that we should avoid a too restrictive notion of supervenience to be entailed by metaphysical dependence.

4.2.2 Multiple domain supervenience

One way to account for supervenience relations between properties of different individuals is to formulate notions of *multiple domain supervenience*. It allows us to link properties of entities of different domains D_1 and D_2 to each other, given that the entities in these domains are related via a particular relation R. For example, we can use it to formulate supervenience theses between properties of parts and wholes, but other relations can be considered as well. As with individual supervenience, there is a weak (MWS) and a strong (MSS) version of multiple domain supervenience (Kim 1993f [1988]: 124):

(MWS) ⟨A, D_1⟩ *weakly supervenes* on ⟨B, D_2⟩ relative to relation R just in case necessarily for any x and y in D_1 if R|x and R|y are B-indiscernible, then x and y are A-indiscernible.

(MSS) ⟨A, D_1⟩ *strongly supervenes* on ⟨B, D_2⟩ relative to relation R just in case for any x and y in D_1 and any worlds w_1 and w_2, if R|x in w_1 is B-indiscernible from R|y in w_2, x in w_1 is A-indiscernible from y in w_2.

$<A, D_1>$ and $<B, D_2>$ are ordered pairs, where the respective first elements, A and B, are again nonempty sets of properties, and the respective second elements, D_1 and D_2, are nonempty domains of individuals. R is a 'coordinating relation' that links the entities in D_1 to the entities in D_2 to which the entities in D_1 are related by R, and R/x is the set of all objects in D_2 to which x is so related. For example, if R is the parthood relation, then R links every entity in D_1 to its parts in D_2. If x is a particular whole in D_1, then R/x is the set of x's parts (given that they are in the domain D_2). If we take R to be the identity relation, and D_1 to be a subset of D_2, the two notions of multiple domain supervenience are equivalent to their individual supervenience counterparts (1993f [1988]: 127). In the case where R is the parthood relation, we get a notion of *mereological supervenience*. Although the notion has some seemingly useful features, multiple domain supervenience did not receive a lot of attention in the literature.[103]

One problem with multiple domain supervenience is that we need to decide on a particular relation R. While the identity relation fits some cases, the part-whole relation fits others. But neither of them seems to fit all cases. Another problem, which multiple domain supervenience shares with individual supervenience, at least as formulated by Kim, is that it seems unable to handle relations. Kim (1993f [1988]: 113 [fn13]) is aware of this issue, and notes that "[f]or simplicity relations are not considered". In order to account for relations, one might define a liberalized notion of supervenience in which the quantifiers the variables x and y are bound to in the definition range not only over particulars, but also over pluralities of particulars, and take the sets A and B to include relations.[104] However, there is another rather simple notion of supervenience that can also handle the other problem regarding the same-individual requirement at the same time: *global supervenience*.

4.2.3 Global supervenience

Just like necessitation, supervenience can be framed globally without making reference to individuals at all. Along with the two notions of individual supervenience discussed above, Kim introduces such a notion of *global supervenience* (1993d [1984]: 68):

---

[103] The same fate is shared by Terence Horgan's (1982; 1993) notion of *regional supervenience*, which is defined analogous to global supervenience but requires that B-indiscernible regions of space-time (instead of whole worlds) are also A-indiscernible for A to regionally supervene on B.
[104] Leuenberger (2013) spells out a non-global relation of strong supervenience analogous to strong individual supervenience that accounts for relations in detail.

> A *globally supervenes* on B just in case worlds that are indiscernible with respect to B ("B-indiscernible," for short) are also A-indiscernible.

Again, in Kim's formulation, A and B are nonempty sets of properties rather than single properties. Since global supervenience of A on B does not require that the properties in the sets A and B are instantiated by the same individuals, this principle is more appropriate than strong individual supervenience to express the modal requirement that goes along with metaphysical dependence. Instead of framing things in terms of whole sets of properties, we can similarly consider single properties as the relata of a global supervenience relation – this is just a special case in which the sets are singletons that only have one property as a member, with the slight caveat that the relata of the supervenience relation are singleton sets that have properties as members in one case, and the properties that are the members of the singletons in the other case.

In order to fully understand the notion of global supervenience, we need to understand what it means for two worlds to be *indiscernible* with respect to (a set of) certain properties. I have already helped myself to another way of framing indiscernibility above by appealing to distributions of property instances, or patterns of instantiation of property types. A pair of worlds (w, w^*) is indiscernible with respect to property F (or: a set of properties B) *iff* w and w^* have the same *distribution of instances* of property F (or: the properties that are members of the set B), or the same *pattern of instantiation* of property F (or: the properties that are members of the set B). These notions can then be spelled out in terms of a *property-preserving isomorphism* between worlds (McLaughlin 1997: 214):

> Let us say that an isomorphism, I, between two worlds w and w^* *preserves B*-properties if and only if, for any x in w, x has a B-property F in w if and only if the image of x under I has F in w^*. We may say, then, that two worlds have the same world-wide pattern of distribution of B-properties just in case there is some isomorphism between them that preserves B-properties.

An isomorphism I is a bijective (i.e., one-to-one) mapping of the particulars in w onto particulars in w^*. A property-preserving isomorphism for a set of properties B (short: B-preserving isomorphism) between two worlds is then a one-to-one mapping of the particulars such that whenever a particular in w has a property F which is a member of the set B, the particular in w^* mapped onto it by the isomorphism also has F, and *vice versa*. This has the consequence that worlds that do not contain exactly the same number of individuals (i.e., worlds that do not have the same *cardinality*) cannot have the same world-wide pattern of distribution of B-properties, because there cannot be an isomorphism between the particulars in w and w^* – some particulars in the world with the higher cardinality would have to be left out.

In section 2.1.2, I said that if one wants to also quantify over properties of events in one's formulation of physicalism, there will be a further problem that will only become apparent later. Now, the problem arises from cardinality difference between our world and a zombie world if we require the worlds to have the same cardinality with regard to events. Suppose physicalism would not only be a thesis about the properties of individuals, but also about properties of other particulars like events. In a zombie world, certain mental events that occur in our world do not occur, so a property-preserving isomorphism that maps events in our world and the zombie world onto each other would not be possible to establish. If physicalism is a thesis about properties of individuals only, this problem does not occur, since the conscious beings can be mapped on the zombies in the other worlds.

On the basis of the notion of a property-preserving isomorphism, we can then distinguish between different notions of global supervenience. McLaughlin (1997: 214; see also Stalnaker 1996; Sider 1999) considers two versions of global supervenience:

> *Strong Global Property Supervenience.* A-properties [strongly] globally supervene on B-properties $=_{df}$ for any worlds w and w^*, every B-preserving isomorphism between them is an A-preserving isomorphism.
> *Weak Global Property Supervenience.* A-properties [weakly] globally supervene on B-properties $=_{df}$ for any worlds w and w^*, if there is a B-preserving isomorphism between them, then there is an A-preserving isomorphism between them.

Aside from these two notions, some have proposed intermediate versions of global supervenience (Shagrir 2002: 182; Bennett 2004: 503) that require that at least one of the B-preserving isomorphisms between w and w^* (given that there are any) is also A-preserving:

> *Intermediate Global Property Supervenience.* A-properties intermediately globally supervene on B-properties $=_{df}$ for any worlds w and w^*, if there is a B-preserving isomorphism between them, at least one B-preserving isomorphism between them is an A-preserving isomorphism.

However, only strong global property supervenience is strong enough to rule out a world B-indiscernible from our world in which the A-properties of some individuals are inverted. Furthermore, only strong global supervenience is incompatible with intra-world variation: B-indiscernible but A-discernible individuals in the same world. An intra-world variation case that physicalism is intuitively incompatible with is the case of two physically indiscernible individuals in physically indiscernible environments, one of which has a particular mental property and the other does not (Shagrir 2002; Bennett 2004).[105] Since these are requirements that the metaphysical dependence relation required for physicalism needs to satisfy, only strong global supervenience seems to remain as a candidate relation to do the required work.

If we look at the statement of global necessitation above, and compare it to a statement of global supervenience where indiscernibility is spelled out in terms of patterns of instantiation, it turns out that necessitation as framed above is a special case of global supervenience where the set of A-properties consists only of a single member. We can thus say that necessitation and supervenience, at least when considered globally, are related in the following way:

> *GN-GS link:* A is globally necessitated by $B_1, ..., B_n$ *if and only if* $\{A\}$ globally supervenes on $\{B_1, ..., B_n\}$.

As with global supervenience, we can in principle distinguish stronger and weaker versions of necessitation. Needless to say, since we have already seen that the only variant of global supervenience that satisfies the requirements needed to capture the requirements of physicalism is a strong global notion of supervenience, the only notion of global necessitation that satisfies the requirements is likewise a strong global notion of necessitation.

Now, can we say that if a property metaphysically depends on some other property, the former also strongly globally supervenes on the latter? Unfortunately, the answer is no. Depending on what we take the set of B-properties to be, there is a problem with both strong global supervenience and strong global necessitation. Take our stock example of *being red* and *being crimson* again. We clearly want to say that *being red* metaphysically depends on *being crimson*. After all, *being red* is intuitively nothing over and above, but not identical to, *being crimson*, and crimson things are red because they are crimson. However, not all things are red because they are crimson. Some are red because they are burgundy, others are red because they are scarlet. But if we take metaphysical dependence of A on B to entail that B strongly globally necessitates A, or that A strongly globally supervenes on B, we have a problem. The property of *being red* does not strongly globally supervene on *being crimson*.

---

105 According to Bennett (2004: 521–522), this also indicates that intermediate global property supervenience captures best the worries that earlier authors had with Kim's less exact notion of global supervenience stated at the beginning of this section.

To see this, consider the following pair of worlds which contain two colored individuals each:[106]

w_1: Ca_1 (and thus: Ra_1) Sb_1 (and thus: Rb_1)
w_2: Ca_2 (and thus: Ra_2) Gb_2 (and thus: $\sim Rb_2$)

We may assume that otherwise, the worlds are exactly alike, or for the sake of simplicity suppose these are the only individuals in these two worlds. Individuals a_1 and a_2 are crimson (C), individual b_1 is scarlet (S) and b_2 is some determinate shade of green, say mint green (G). Now, the only isomorphism that is C-preserving is the one that maps a_1 to a_2 and b_1 to b_2. However, although that isomorphism is C-preserving, it is not R-preserving, because there is an individual in w_1 that is red but the individual mapped to it in w_2 is not red. Thus, *being red* does not strongly globally supervene on *being crimson*. Even more, *being red* does not even weakly globally supervene on *being crimson*. If we extend the supervenience base of *being red* to the set of all determinate shades of red, the problem disappears – after all, w_1 and w_2 are not S-preserving, and since scarlet is a particular shade of red, the considered pair of worlds would not include any isomorphism that preserves all the base properties and thus would not represent a counterexample to strong individual supervenience.

We can also use the slogan form of supervenience to make the point more intuitively. Supervenience requires that there cannot be a difference with respect to the supervenient property without a difference with respect to the supervenience base. But w_1 and w_2 differ with respect to *being red* without differing with respect to *being crimson*, and thus supervenience of *being red* on *being crimson* fails. Thus, when considering worlds in which multiple determinate shades of red are instantiated, it is clearly not enough to keep fixed the pattern of instantiation of one determinate shade of red like *being crimson* to keep fixed the pattern of instantiation of *being red*. We must keep fixed the pattern of instantiation of all shades of red instead.

The problem does not only arise for global supervenience. The property of *being red* does not strongly *individually* supervene on *being crimson* either, but only on the set of all shades of red. According to Kim's definition above, *A strongly individually supervenes on B iff* necessarily, for each x and each property F in A, if x has F, then there is a property G in B such that x has G, and necessarily

---

[106] McLaughlin and Bennett (2018: section 3.2) use an analogous example involving the properties of *being a brother* and *being a sibling* to argue that property entailment is not sufficient for property supervenience. Moreover, Leuenberger (2014b: 231) uses the example of a disjunctive fact and its disjuncts to show that fact Grounding does not entail fact supervenience.

if any *y* has *G*, it has *F*. Now, suppose that *A* is the singleton set that contains *being red*, and *B* is the singleton set that contains *being crimson*. Then, *being red* strongly individually supervenes on *being crimson iff* necessarily, for each *x*, if *x* is red, then *x* is crimson, and necessarily, if any *y* is crimson, it is red. While the necessitation claim in the back is fine, the first part is clearly problematic. We of course do not want to claim that anything that is red is also crimson. So unless we take the first necessity to be a necessity that restricts our view to worlds in which no shades of red other than crimson are instantiated, individual supervenience fails as well. Note also that *being crimson* still individually necessitates *being red*, because individual necessitation only requires that necessarily, everything that is crimson is also red. Individual supervenience and individual necessitation thus come apart in these cases.

What we learn from this is that even though some non-physical property *A* metaphysically depends on certain physical properties $B_1, ..., B_n$, this does not entail that *A* strongly globally supervenes upon $B_1, ..., B_n$, or likewise, that $B_1, ..., B_n$ strongly globally necessitate *A*, if there are alternative dependence bases for A. In other words, the following principle fails:

> MD-GS link: If *A* metaphysically depends on $B_1, ..., B_n$, then *{A}* (strongly) globally supervenes on *{$B_1, ..., B_n$}*.

Note that this is different to the other two cases we need to consider for physicalism. In the case in which a property is identical rather than metaphysically dependent on a physical property, the strong global supervenience of course holds. After all, any isomorphism between a pair of worlds that preserves property *B* preserves property *A* given that *A=B*:

> I-GS link: If *A* is identical to *B*, then *{A}* (strongly) globally supervenes on *{B}*.

Similarly, if a property is necessarily had by any individual whatsoever, it also strongly globally supervenes on any property whatsoever. Any isomorphism between a pair of worlds will preserve a property that all individuals have necessarily, and thus any isomorphism that preserves an arbitrary property will also preserve the necessary property:

> NP-GS link: If A is a property necessarily had by any individual whatsoever, then {A} (strongly) globally supervenes on {B} (for any arbitrary property B).

However, even though the MD-GS link fails, we might be able to make a move analogous to the case of red and crimson. We might just need to keep fixed the pattern of instantiation of all physical properties instead of only those that form the metaphysical dependence base of the dependent property in question.

Thus, even though the direct link between metaphysical dependence and supervenience fails, we can still ask whether physicalism as formulated in chapter 2 entails that every positive qualitative property had by any individual at w that exists contingently or is causal strongly globally supervenes on the set of instantiated physical properties. We will get to understand that this is too strong, but that there are weaker supervenience claims that are more apt to account for the modal requirements of physicalism without unwanted side effects.

4.3 Which supervenience claim is necessary for physicalism?

In this section, I want to further investigate this link between physicalism and strong global supervenience, as well as related notions of global supervenience. The main question is what kind of supervenience claim we should think of being entailed by, and thus necessary for, physicalism.

4.3.1 The contingency of physicalism, epiphenomenal ectoplasm and other extras

As discussed earlier, physicalism is supposed to be a contingent thesis. That is, the truth of physicalism in our world, or some other particular possible world w, is not supposed to require that physicalism is true of any world whatsoever. Rather, the truth of physicalism is supposed to be dependent on the way that particular world is like, i.e., which properties, physical and non-physical, are instantiated at the world in question. Now suppose physicalism is, or at least entails, the following thesis:

> Any two worlds that are indiscernible with respect to physical properties are indiscernible with respect to all other properties.

This corresponds to the thesis that physicalism is equivalent with, or at least entails, the claim that the set of all properties (or likewise each singleton set containing some property) strongly globally supervenes on the set of all physical properties. Then, it seems, independent variation of physical and other properties is not just ruled out for the world w we are interested in, and those worlds similar to this world, but for any world whatsoever. One part of the problem is that *w* is not explicitly mentioned in the claim and thus does not play any special role. It is just one world among many that are compared to each other. Another part of the problem is that the formulation does not make any restrictions regarding which properties are instantiated in the worlds considered, physical or otherwise, and thereby rules out the possibility of certain worlds we do not want to rule out. Specifically, physicalism is not supposed to rule out that traditional property dualism, or more generally property pluralism, is true of some other possible worlds. Unfortunately, if physicalism requires that any two physically indiscernible worlds are also indiscernible in all other respects, independent of which properties are instantiated in them in the first place, such worlds are clearly ruled out (e.g. Witmer 1999: 315–316). Thus, we need something weaker than full-fledged strong global supervenience of all properties on the set of physical properties in order to account for the idea that physicalism is a contingent thesis.

In order to cope with this issue, it has been suggested to take physicalism about world *w* to be, or at least entail, the following thesis:

Any world that is indiscernible from *w* with respect to physical properties is also indiscernible with respect to all other properties.

This corresponds to a thesis of (strong) global supervenience where we keep fixed one element in the pair of worlds, and only universally quantify over the second element. Physicalism so construed entails a modal claim only about worlds similar to the particular world *w* under consideration, rather than about any world whatsoever, and is sometimes also expressed as the claim that any physical duplicate of world *w* is a duplicate *simpliciter* of world *w*, where two worlds are duplicates *simpliciter* if they are qualitatively[107] indiscernible (cf. Jackson 1994: 27–28; 1998: 12). However, as has been argued before, this still rules out too many worlds. Authors in the debate usually agree that the truth of physicalism at a world *w* does not entail that there are no physical duplicates of world *w* that include instances of some extra properties that are neither physical nor necessitated by the physical. For example, the truth of physicalism should not rule out physical duplicates of our world that include some extra im-

---

[107] Once 'two' worlds are not just qualitatively indiscernible, but also indiscernible with respect to non-qualitative (haecceitistic properties), there seems to be no reason to think that they are not numerically identical. Somebody who denies that there can be two (without scare quotes) worlds that do not differ qualitatively may formulate the thesis as follows: Every physical duplicate of *w* is identical to *w*.

material souls with their respective mental properties or extra ectoplasmic properties. This is why some have called the problem at hand the 'problem of extras' (e.g. Witmer 1999; Francescotti 2014). The idea is of course not that physicalism should come out true of those worlds. Rather, it should not be the case that the mere possibility of such worlds rules out the truth of physicalism for our world, or more generally, for any world from which such worlds are accessible.

There are some important remarks to make about these claims which highlight some facts that are easily overlooked. First, if we interpret indiscernibility of worlds in terms of the notion of a property-preserving isomorphism, worlds that contain extra immaterial souls, or more generally, a different number of individuals than the world w under consideration, will not be considered anyway, because we cannot construct an isomorphism between worlds that contain a different number of individuals.[108] However, this does not make the problem of extras go away. The reason is that we also do not want to rule out worlds that include the same number of individuals, which, aside from instantiating the same physical properties as are instantiated by them in w, also instantiate further properties that are neither physical nor necessitated by the physical properties, like certain ectoplasmic properties (cf. Witmer 1999: 319–320).

Even more, we want to allow that such ectoplasmic properties necessitate other properties that are also necessitated by physical properties. If the world w we want to consider is the actual world, an example might be a physically indiscernible world in which, say, rocks have some extra ectoplasmic properties in virtue of which they instantiate mental properties.[109] Such a world would be a world in which the pattern of distribution of mental properties is different to the original world w even though the pattern of distribution of all physical properties is the same in both worlds, and thus even the restricted global supervenience of those mental properties on the physical properties fails. Thus, even if we restrict ourselves to pairs of worlds one of which is the world w under consideration, physicalism fails to be true at w due to the failure of the restricted global supervenience claim unless the physically indiscernible world that contains ectoplasmic rocks with mental properties is impossible. However, intuitive-

---

[108] That is, assuming that the number of individuals in world w is finite. In worlds with an infinite number of individuals, introducing an extra individual does not amount to a change of cardinality.

[109] This is very similar to the problem we had with the failure of global supervenience of *being red* on *being crimson*. We do not want to rule out worlds in which a proper subset of the property instances of a mental property are due to physical properties, but not all of them are. After all, we do not want physicalism to be incompatible with a claim of multiple realizability of mental properties that is not constrained to physical realizers.

ly, as long as the world originally considered does not include any such extra non-physical properties, the mere existence (and accessibility) of such possible worlds should not affect whether physicalism is true of the original world *w* under consideration. As Leuenberger (2008: 146) puts things with regard to a somewhat different case,[110] the "truth [of physicalism] should depend entirely on what God actually did on the first six days, not on what He could have done had He resumed his work later".

A related way to consider the problem is to point out that there are certain properties instantiated in our world merely due to the absence of certain entities or the absence of instances of certain properties, which would not be instantiated in case certain entities would exist or in case certain other properties would be instantiated. Suppose that in the actual world, there are no immaterial souls and no instances of ectoplasmic properties. In this case, I instantiate the extrinsic properties *being such that there are no immaterial souls* and *being such that there are no instantiated ectoplasmic properties* – indeed, every individual does.[111] If physicalism would require that even these properties are necessitated by, or supervene on, the physical properties, then a physical duplicate world that lacks instantiations of these properties due to the existence of further entities or the instantiation of further properties were impossible. Thus, a physical duplicate world in which there are some additional immaterial souls or instantiated ectoplasmic properties would be incompatible with the truth of physicalism, because in such a world, no particular would instantiate the property of *being such that there are no immaterial souls*, or the property of *being such that there are no instantiated ectoplasmic properties*. Of course, these additional entities must not causally or otherwise interfere with the narrowly physical in order to make sure that the world in question is indeed a physical duplicate world – this is why some have called this the 'epiphenomenal ectoplasm problem' (Horgan 1982; Lewis 1983; see also Stoljar 2010: 133–137).

---

110 This is not to say that I agree with Leuenberger with regard to the case he construes, which I will be concerned with in section 4.4.1. In his example, the additional properties make instances of phenomenal properties disappear, which is importantly different to the case at hand, where there are further instances added to the ones already there. For more on such 'blockers', see below. So, in the end, I do not fully agree to the claim Leuenberger intends to make using the metaphor.

111 Importantly, while every individual in the actual world does instantiate such properties, these properties are not had by every individual necessarily. These are only contingent properties of individuals, and thus do not fall into the set of properties that need not be physical or metaphysically dependent on the physical due to being a property that everything has necessarily. In my definition of physicalism, such properties are excluded due to not being positive properties (see sections 2.2.5 and 4.4.1)

In the literature, several attempts to solve the problem are proposed. In the following, I will discuss two accounts. Frank Jackson (1994; 1998) proposes one such attempt, David Lewis (1983) suggests another. David Chalmers (1996) proposes a third supervenience-based account of physicalism that can also handle the problem. Since it differs from the other two accounts with regard to a different problem I will address in the next section, I will address Chalmers' view later.

Instead of requiring that the truth of physicalism entails that any physical duplicate of our world is a duplicate *simpliciter* of our world, which would rule out that there is a possible world that is a physical duplicate of our world but in which some additional properties are instantiated, Jackson restricts his account to *minimal* physical duplicate worlds. According to him, physicalism is the following thesis (Jackson 1998: 12):

> Any *minimal* physical duplicate of our world is a duplicate simpliciter of our world.

On his view, this is both necessary and sufficient for the truth of physicalism. But with regard to the problem we are currently concerned with, it does not matter whether or not it is a sufficient condition. Jackson further explains the notion of a minimal physical duplicate by using a baking recipe as an analogy (1994: 28):

> What is a minimal physical duplicate? Think of a recipe for making scones. It tells you what to do, but not what not to do. It tells you to add butter to the flour but does not tell you not to add dirt to the flour. Why doesn't it? Part of the reason is that no-one would think to add dirt unless explicitly told to. But part of the reason is logical. It is impossible to list all the things not to do. There are indefinitely many of them: don't add bats wings; don't add sea water; don't add .... Of necessity the writers of recipes rely on an intuitive understanding of an implicitly included 'stop' clause in their recipes. A minimal physical duplicate of our world is what you would get if you – or God, as it is sometimes put – used the physical nature of our world (including of course its physical laws) as a recipe in this sense for making a world.

Thus, the minimality condition, just like the baking recipe, includes an implicit "That's all!" clause – what is duplicated is just the physical properties, relations and laws, and nothing else that is not *thereby* also duplicated.

A duplicate *simpliciter* of our world is just a world w^* for which it holds that there is an isomorphism between the actual world and w^* that preserves all properties. However, the notion of a minimal physical duplicate is trickier to spell out in detail. Jackson gestures at the notion, but his considerations above do not provide us with a definition of the notion of a minimal physical duplicate. Gene Witmer (1999: 327) attempts to fill this gap and proposes the following account:

> w_1 is a minimal physical duplicate of w_2 $=_{def}$
> (i) w_1 is a world physically indiscernible from w_2; and
> (ii) any world physically indiscernible from w_1 will have at least the property distribution of w_1.

Clause (i) of Witmer's account can be further interpreted as usual – there is an isomorphism between w_1 and w_2 that preserves physical properties. This is the physical duplication condition. But how exactly are we to interpret clause (ii), which is the minimality condition? What does it mean exactly that a world w^* has *at least* the property distribution of w_1?

Intuitively, the idea is roughly that you leave all the instances of a property that you have in the original world w_1 as they are, and then you may add a few further instances of properties that are non-physical. Let me extend Witmer's account by introducing the new notion of a *($w \rightarrow w^*$)-property-preserving isomorphism*, which helps us capture what Witmer intends in clause (ii) in more rigorous terms.

> An isomorphism, I, between two worlds w and w^* *($w \rightarrow w^*$)-preserves B*-properties *iff* for any x in w, if x has a *B*-property F in w, then the image of x under I has F in w^*.

This is very similar the notion of a property-preserving isomorphism, with the difference that preservation is a one-way street, so that whenever an individual in w instantiates a property F, the corresponding individual in w^* instantiates F as well, but the reverse does not hold, so that it is possible for further individuals in w^* to instantiate F. If an isomorphism I between w and w^* both *($w \rightarrow w^*$)-preserves* and *($w^* \rightarrow w$)-preserves B*-properties, it is a full-fledged *B*-preserving isomorphism as defined earlier.

Using this notion, we can rephrase clause (ii) of Witmer's account as the claim that any world w^* for which there is an isomorphism between w_1 and w^* that preserves physical properties is such that any such physical property-preserving isomorphism also ($w_1 \rightarrow w^*$)-preserves all positive properties in w_1.[112] Similar to the restriction I have introduced in section 2.2.5, I appeal to the notion of a

---

[112] This is analogous to the requirement of strong global supervenience as opposed to the weaker forms of global supervenience. In principle, we could also formulate analogues to the weaker forms.

positive property here, as also appealed to by Chalmers (1996).[113] If we would not add this restriction and appeal to all properties instead, the following problem would arise: Suppose that the superlative property *being the happiest individual* (Witmer's example) is a property of some individual *a* in w_1. Now consider the physically indiscernible world *w**, in which some further ectoplasmic properties are instantiated by some rock that make the rock even happier than *a*'s image in *w**. If *w** is a possible world accessible from w_1, then no isomorphism that preserves the physical properties will (*w*→*w**)-preserve a set of properties that contains *being the happiest individual*, because while *a* has the property in w_1, it loses it to the rock in *w**.[114]

Putting the pieces together, Jackson's supervenience claim can be framed as follows, where *P* is the set of all physical properties instantiated at @, the actual world:

For any world *w* such that
(i) there is a *P*-preserving isomorphism between @ and *w*, and
(ii) any world *w** such that there is a *P*-preserving isomorphism between *w* and *w** is such that any *P*-preserving isomorphism between *w* and *w** (*w*→*w**)-preserves all positive properties in *w*,

it also holds that any P-preserving isomorphism between @ and *w* preserves all properties.

---

113 Witmer (1999: 329) uses the notion of a *resilient* property instance instead that serves the same purpose. He dismisses the notion of a positive property, but the basis for his dismissal is a misinterpretation of Chalmers' notion of a negative property as one on which negative properties are just those that are picked out by "a predicate that is intuitively negative" (1999: 328). If that were Chalmers' notion, then Witmer's worry that the predicate '… is the happiest individual' is not intuitively negative and thus that the property of being the happiest individual would be a positive property would indeed be appropriate. But as we have seen already in section 2.2.5 (see also section 4.4.1 below), this is not Chalmers' notion in the first place.

114 Similar problems arise for friends of properties such as *being non-red*, which most philosophers, including me, find rather dubious anyway. Suppose that both *being red* and *being non-red* are in a set B. In this case, no isomorphism can be (*w*→*w**)-preserving B-properties without also (*w**→*w*)-preserving B-properties, and thus being a B-preserving isomorphism that fixes B-properties both ways. This is simply because whenever an additional individual instantiates *being red* in *w**, that individual does not instantiate *being non-red* in *w** even though it did in *w*, so that the isomorphism does not leave all instances of B-properties untouched that existed in *w*.

In order to avoid cases of intra-world variation, the link between *P*-preserving isomorphisms and isomorphisms that preserve all (positive) properties is again interpreted along the lines of strong global supervenience.

Since we now have a fairly good understanding of the supervenience claim put forward by Jackson, and have seen that it can handle the problem of epiphenomenal ectoplasm and other extras, we have arrived at a notion of supervenience that is a good candidate for being a necessary modal condition for the truth of physicalism.

David Lewis' account of physicalism also allows for physical duplicate worlds with extras, and for the properties had by individuals in worlds that lack these extras. Lewis (1983: 364) takes physicalism to be the following thesis:

> Among worlds where no natural properties alien to our world are instantiated, no two differ without differing physically; any two such worlds that are exactly alike physically are duplicates.

Just like Jackson, Lewis takes this to be both necessary and sufficient for the truth of physicalism. Here, the notion of an alien property is understood as follows (1983: 364):

> Let us say that a property is *alien* to a world iff (1) it is not instantiated by any inhabitant of that world, and (2) it is not analysable as a conjunction of, or as a structural property constructed out of, natural properties all of which are instantiated by inhabitants of that world.

Since worlds with ectoplasmic properties include natural properties alien to our world, such worlds are not quantified over and can thus differ without differing physically. In this way, physicalism so construed allows that there are possible worlds that include entities that instantiate some mental properties without instantiating the corresponding physical properties. Moreover, those physical duplicate worlds that do not contain such alien properties will share the pattern of instantiation of properties such as *being such that there is no ectoplasm*.

The part at the end of Lewis' definition looks familiar. If we interpret duplication in terms of property-preserving isomorphisms, it claims that any pair of worlds for which a certain condition is met is such that every isomorphism between them that preserves physical properties also preserves all other properties. The condition is that the pair of worlds under consideration does not contain any alien natural properties. The notion of an alien property is spelled out rather clearly, apart from the fact that it also appeals to the notion of a natural property, which is the most opaque part of Lewis' definition.

Lewis takes the natural properties to be a sparse set of properties that "carve reality at the joints"[115] (1983: 346), and closely associates them with universals (1983: 347):

> Natural properties would be the ones whose sharing makes for resemblance, and the ones relevant to causal powers. Most simply, we could call a property *perfectly* natural if its members are all and only those things that share some one universal. But also we would have other less-than-perfectly natural properties, made so by families of suitable related universals.

According to Lewis, determinable properties like *being metallic* are less natural than their determinates like *being iron* and *being copper*, for example. Furthermore, he thinks that the perfectly natural properties are the ones that figure in fundamental laws (1983: 368). As Dorr and Hawthorne (2013: 13) point out, Lewis takes "the perfectly natural properties [to] constitute a *minimal* supervenience base for everything". This indicates that Lewis' use of the notion is similar to the way others use the notion of a fundamental property.[116]

I will not attempt to provide any more elaborate explication of Lewis' notion of naturalness here. This is in part because it would lead us too far away from the main topic of this chapter, and in part because he takes the notion of naturalness to be primitive. Although such a notion can be further *characterized* by pointing to examples, considering certain features of the entities to which the notion can be applied, and making clear links between the notion and other more familiar notions, a primitive notion cannot be strictly *defined* in other terms. While such a procedure is commonplace in contemporary philosophy, and is legitimate in principle, I take the fact that Lewis' account appeals to such a somewhat opaque primitive notion to count in favor of the alternative accounts that do without making reference to such notion.

Both Jackson's and Lewis' definition consider only physicalism with regard to our world, the actual world. But we can easily formulate versions of their def-

---

115 Lewis does not take properties to be universals, or tropes, but rather trans-world sets of individuals: "[L]et me reserve the word 'property' for classes – any classes, but I have foremost in mind classes of things. To have a property is to be a member of the class. [...] The property of being a donkey, for instance, is the class of *all* the donkeys. This property belongs to – this class contains – not only the actual donkeys of this world we live in, but also all the unactualised, otherworldly donkeys" (1983: 344). This illuminates why he says that 'members' of a natural property share a universal. Unlike properties, Lewis takes universals to be very sparse: "[T]he world's universals should comprise a minimal basis for characterising the world completely" (Lewis 1983: 346).
116 For further discussion of the link between the notions of naturalness and fundamentality, see Bennett (2017: section 5.7).

initions that generalize the claim to arbitrary possible worlds. In the case of Jackson, the generalized thesis is the following:

Physicalism$_{Jackson}$: Physicalism is true at a world *w* iff any minimal physical duplicate of *w* is a duplicate *simpliciter* of *w*.

Similarly, Lewis' definition can be generalized to arbitrary possible worlds very simply:

Physicalism$_{Lewis}$: Physicalism is true at a world *w* iff among worlds where no natural properties alien to world *w* are instantiated, no two differ without differing physically; any two such worlds that are exactly alike physically are duplicates.

The two definitions are not strictly equivalent, even though they are closely related. Physicalism$_{Jackson}$ has consequences only for worlds that are physically indiscernible from world *w*. Physicalism$_{Lewis}$ however also has consequences for worlds that are discernible from world *w* with regard to the pattern of distribution of properties, as long as the natural properties instantiated in those worlds are a subset of the properties instantiated at *w*.

Some think that the truth of physicalism at a world *w* should put restrictions not only on worlds that are exactly like *w*, but also on worlds that are similar to *w*. For example, Kim worries about the following case with regard to his original definition of global supervenience (1993e [1987]: 85–86):

> But before we accept global psychophysical supervenience as a significant form of materialism we should consider this: it is consistent with this version of materialism for there to be a world which differs physically from this world in some most trifling respect (say, Saturn's rings in that world contain one more ammonia molecule) but which is entirely devoid of consciousness, or has a radically different, perhaps totally irregular, distribution of mental characteristics over its inhabitants (say, creatures with brains have no mentality while rocks are conscious). As long as that world differs from this one in some physical respect, however minuscule or seemingly irrelevant, it could be as different as you please in any psychological respect you choose. Moreover, as we saw, global psychophysical supervenience is consistent with there being within a given world, perhaps this one, two physically indistinguishable organisms with radically different psychological attributes. It is doubtful that many materialists would regard these consequences as compatible with their materialist tenets; it seems clear that they are not compatible with the claim that the mental is determined wholly by the physical.

As we have seen above, the second problem Kim mentions, which is the problem of intra-world variation, can be handled if we take indiscernibility or duplication to require that every isomorphism that preserves the physical properties also preserves the non-physical properties in the worlds under consideration. The first problem Kim mentions, however, which is sometimes called the 'lone ammonium molecule problem' (e.g. Stoljar 2015: section 4.1), is concerned with the question to which extent physicalism about *w* should restrict property distributions at worlds that are not duplicates of *w*, but still so similar to *w* in physical respects that we would intuitively find it strange if they would differ a lot from *w* in other respects.

Insofar these concerns are appropriate, Physicalism$_{Lewis}$ does a better job than Physicalism$_{Jackson}$, even though it does not fully resolve the problem. While Jackson's account does not put any restrictions on worlds that fail to be duplicates of the world *w* under consideration (in Kim's example, the actual world), Lewis account at least requires that worlds like the lone ammonium molecule world are such that all of *their* physical duplicates are duplicates *simpliciter*. Nevertheless, this still allows that such worlds differ significantly in non-physical respects from the original world under consideration. However, it is debatable whether Kim's concern is appropriate in the first place. Robert Stalnaker says the following with regard to Kim's worry (1996: 229; see also Paull and Sider 1992: 841–847):

> Now I agree that no sensible materialist would accept the possibility of a world that differed physically from ours only in this way, while being radically different from it in the distribution of mental properties. But sensible materialists are not only materialists, they are also sensible; one should not define materialism so that there cannot be silly versions of it.

What Stalnaker means is that it is reasonable to think that the world Kim considers is impossible, especially if one commits to a physicalist view, but this is not necessarily due to one's commitment to physicalism. As Stoljar puts it vividly (2015: section 4.1):

> [I]magine that we discover that who has mental properties on Earth *is* in part a function of the behavior of molecules on Saturn. That would of course tell us that we are deeply wrong in our assumptions about how the world works. But it would not tell us that we are deeply wrong about physicalism.

Setting this issue aside, both Physicalism$_{Jackson}$ and Physicalism$_{Lewis}$ do a fairly good job in providing modal restrictions that are necessary for physicalism to be true of a particular world *w*.

That some supervenience claim that enables us to account for the incompatibility of physicalism with zombie worlds is necessary for the truth of physicalism is something that cannot easily be dismissed. Based on this assumption, we have so far focused on the question which supervenience claim can be considered necessary for the truth of physicalism at a world w. I agree with most authors that a modal claim along the lines of the right-hand side of Physicalism$_{Jackson}$ (or Physicalism$_{Lewis}$) is necessary for the truth of physicalism at a world w.

4.4 Can physicalism be fully characterized in purely modal terms?

After having clarified which modal claims we can take physicalism to entail, the next few sections will focus on the question whether such claims are also sufficient for the truth of physicalism at a world w. There is a variety of different reasons to think that a purely modal account of physicalism fails.

4.4.1 The problem of blockers

John Hawthorne (2002) challenges Jackson's and Lewis' definitions of physicalism. Other than the problem of extras, which challenges the claim that physicalism requires a particular supervenience claim, and has led us to Jackson's and Lewis' global supervenience theses, the question raised by Hawthorne's challenge is whether these supervenience theses are sufficient for physicalism. According to Hawthorne, by restricting the physicalist thesis to *minimal* physical duplicate worlds, or to worlds in which *no alien natural properties* are instantiated, Jackson and Lewis fail to rule out certain possibilities that physicalism needs to rule out.

Hawthorne considers a world that is a physical duplicate of our world, but includes instances of some extra property he calls a blocker – a property that, if instantiated, blocks the instantiation of mental properties. Those blockers are stipulated to be nonphysical properties. If they were physical properties, the world in question would not be a physical duplicate of our world. They are not necessitated by the physical properties either, because they would otherwise exist in our world as well. A minimal physical duplicate of the blocker world would be a world in which the blocker properties are not instantiated. Similarly, the blocker world is not to be considered a world in which physicalism is true, according to Jackson's and Lewis' definitions, which is intuitively the right result.

The problem with blocker properties is rather that the blocker world is also a zombie world, a physical duplicate world in which at least some individuals that have mental properties in our world fail to have mental properties. But as we have seen, physicalists think "that the connection between, say, brain states and pain is so strong that nothing could drive a wedge in between the former and the latter" (Hawthorne 2002: 105). This is also in line with premise (3) of the conceivability argument stated above. Thus, a proper definition of physicalism is supposed to rule out the possibility of blockers, but Jackson's definition fails to do so. The same issue arises with Lewis' definition of physicalism. Assuming that the blocker property is an alien natural property, the existence of the blocker world is not ruled out by his account, and since the blocker world is a zombie world, some zombie worlds are not ruled out either. What this shows is that if an appropriate definition of physicalism is supposed to rule out that such a world is possible, as is typically assumed, Jackson's and Lewis' definitions are not enough to capture a sufficient condition for the truth of physicalism. This is however compatible with the claim that they capture a necessary condition for the truth of physicalism.

A third supervenience-based definition of physicalism, offered by David Chalmers (1996: 41), fares better with regard to the blockers problem:

> Materialism is true if[f] all the positive facts about the world are globally logically supervenient on the physical facts.[117]

Chalmers takes global logical supervenience of B on A[118] to hold *iff* "for any logically possible world *W* that is A-indiscernible from our world, [...] the B-facts true of our world are true of *W*" (1996: 40 – 41).[119] This is similar to Jackson's account, although Chalmers uses a notion of logical rather than metaphysical supervenience, which, on his view, in the end amounts to the same except for "an *a posteriori* semantic twist" (1996: 38).

Chalmers explicitly restricts his supervenience thesis to positive facts. We have already seen the notion of a positive property earlier, where I have introduced it to avoid that physicalism needs to account for cases of absence-based

---

117 Note that I changed the *if* into an *iff*. As Hawthorne (2002: 112 [fn11]) also points out, this is clearly intended also by Chalmers since he thinks that the right-hand side is a necessary condition, and not just a sufficient condition, for physicalism. Otherwise, his conceivability argument would not get off the ground, because it would not suffice to show the supervenience thesis does not hold in order to show that physicalism is false.
118 Note that Chalmers uses letters *A* and *B* inversely to my typical usage – in his case, *A*-facts are the subvenient ones, whereas *B*-facts are the supervenient ones.
119 While I find it somewhat strange to attribute truth to facts rather than propositions. However, nothing much hangs on this, and we can simply exchange 'true' with 'exists' to make it more appropriate. I will apply this change in my generalized version of Chalmers' account below.

properties and superlative properties. Let us revisit what Chalmers means by positive facts and properties (1996: 40):

> We can define a positive fact in *W* as one that holds in every world that contains *W* as a proper part; a positive property is one that if instantiated in a world *W*, is also instantiated by the corresponding individual in all worlds that contain *W* as a proper part.

Assuming that each of the positive facts in question is a fact about the attribution of a positive property to an individual, or the attribution of a positive relation to a plurality of individuals, Chalmers could have equally well replaced 'facts' with 'properties' in his definition.

This serves a similar purpose as Jackson's minimality clause. On Chalmers' account, it is not required for the truth of physicalism that properties like *being such that there is no ectoplasm*, which are negative properties since they are not instantiated in every world that includes the actual world as a proper part, supervene on the physical properties (1996: 41):

> The restriction to positive facts is needed to ensure that worlds with extra ectoplasmic facts do not count against materialism in our world. Negative existential facts such as "There are no angels" are not strictly logically supervenient on the physical, but their nonsupervenience is quite compatible with materialism. In a sense, to fix the negative facts, God had to do more than fix the physical facts; he also had to declare, "That's all."

In this way, Chalmers gets around the problem that the truth of physicalism is not supposed to rule out duplicate worlds that contain some extra stuff. The advantage of Chalmers' account over Jackson's and Lewis' account is that it also gets around the problem of blockers. On Chalmers' account, the blocker world just considered comes out as impossible. After all, a blocker world is a world in which certain positive properties instantiated in our world, specifically the mental properties allegedly blocked by the blocker properties in that world, are not instantiated there, which, according to Chalmers' account, is impossible, which is the intuitively correct result.

Let me generalize Chalmers' account of physicalism in the same way I extended Jackson's and Lewis' accounts:

> *Physicalism$_{Chalmers}$*: Physicalism is true at a world *w iff* any logically possible world *w** that is indiscernible with regard to the physical facts, the positive facts that exist at *w* also exist at *w**.

A physical fact is a fact that is wholly about physical properties, so no such fact is partly (or wholly) about non-physical properties. Typically, the facts in question are facts about individuals instantiating a property (or pluralities instantiating a relation), but also more general facts about law-like relations between physical properties might be included.

Stefan Leuenberger (2008) takes the considerations about blockers to have a different upshot. Like Hawthorne, he considers a physical duplicate world that contains a single instance of a blocker property that blocks a particular mental property from being instantiated by a particular. Drawing on the creation metaphor, he claims that "what God could have done after day six ought not to bear on the question whether our world is physicalistic" (Leuenberger 2008: 147), and claims that there is no substantial difference with regard to this consideration between a scenario in which some epiphenomenal ectoplasm is added and a scenario in which blockers are added. On this basis, he proposes to consider physicalism to be the thesis that "The actual physical facts are *ceteris absentibus* sufficient for all actual facts" (2008: 148), where the *ceteris absentibus* clause is supposed to express "sufficiency other things being absent" (2008: 147). This makes physicalism compatible with the possibility of zombie worlds, which seems somewhat strange given that most authors in the debate agree that such worlds need to be ruled out. However, Leuenberger argues that the only zombie worlds that turn out to be compatible with physicalism are the blocker worlds, and considers this acceptable since the typical dualist intuition is rather that mental properties can also be absent in non-blocker physical duplicate worlds.

One way to interpret Leuenberger's considerations, proposed by Stoljar (2010: 138), is to raise a problem for Chalmers' account. Chalmers seems to presuppose that mental properties like *being in pain* are positive properties. But in case blockers are indeed possible, *being in pain* turns out not to be a positive property after all. So, the question is how to respond to the following conceivability argument:

(1) A blocker world is conceivable.
(2) If a blocker world is conceivable, it is metaphysically possible.
(3) If a blocker world is metaphysically possible, then it is false that mental properties like *being in pain* are positive properties.
∴ It is false that mental properties like *being in pain* are positive properties.

The argument is clearly valid. If it were sound as well, it would have the unwanted consequence that Chalmers' definition of physicalism would not require that mental properties are necessitated by physical properties after all. So something has to be wrong, either with Chalmers' definition or with one of the premises of the argument.

Premise (3) follows from Chalmers' definitions. If *being in pain* is a positive property, and is instantiated in some world *w*, then it is instantiated by the corresponding individual in every possible world that has *w* as a proper part. So, by contraposition, if it is false that *being in pain* is instantiated by the corresponding individual in every possible world that has *w* as a proper part, it is also false that *being in pain* is a positive property instantiated at *w*. Now, if a blocker world is metaphysically possible, then there is a possible world in which there is an individual that does not instantiate *being in pain* even though it has *w* as a proper part – this is just what the blocker property is supposed to accomplish. This establishes (3): If a blocker world is metaphysically possible, then *being in pain* is not a positive property.

I find it hard to conceive that a world in which mental properties are instantiated can be a proper part of a different world that lacks mental properties, so there has to be something wrong with one of the first two premises. With regard to the corollary from premise (1) and (2) that blocker worlds are metaphysically possible, Hawthorne claims that "when defining materialism, one should not take a stand on controversial modal issues about which, intuitively, the materialist qua materialist has no commitments" (2002: 110). I agree with his claim, but I am somewhat skeptical as to whether the possibility of blocker worlds is one of those modal issues the materialist *qua* materialist has no commitments about.

To see this, it is important to note that supervenience claims are typically not considered brute, that is, there is typically a further explanation, at least in principle, as to why the supervenience relation holds. In the case of physicalist supervenience claims, it is generally accepted that it makes sense to ask why we should think that the properties of other domains, and in particular the mental domain, supervene on the physical properties. As some have put it, what we are looking for is not supervenience, but "*superdupervenience* – ontological supervenience that is robustly explainable in a materialistically acceptable way" (Horgan 1993: 577; my emphasis).

This can be established by accounting for the supervenience relation by appealing to a further relation between the properties in question. The strongest such relation considered in the literature is a type identity relation. In the case in which such a relation is postulated, it is hard to see how a blocker might work. Given that a property *A* is type-identical to a property *B*, it is clearly impossible to block the instantiation of *A* while leaving the instantiation of *B* untouched. Similarly with other relations that have been considered to underlie supervenience claims. Suppose the relation between mental and physical properties is one of determinable to determinate, as Yablo (1992) proposes. Again, it is hard to see how one could block the mental while leaving the physical untouched. This would be analogous to the claim that a blocker property might block *being red* from being instantiated by certain particulars, but these particulars still instantiate *being crimson*. Again, this is clearly impossible. Or take a functionalist account, according to which mental properties are identical to higher-order properties of the form *having a property that plays causal/functional role C*, and the physical properties are the properties that play these roles. The blocker world would then require that one instantiates the physical property that plays causal/functional role C, but the property of *having a property that plays causal/functional role C* is blocked. Finally, consider a Wilson-Shoemaker-style causal-powers-based account, according to which properties are individuated by the causal powers they bestow on their bearers, and assume that the causal powers of (or bestowed by) mental properties are a subset of the causal powers of (or bestowed by) the corresponding physical properties (Wilson 1999, Shoemaker 2007). In the blocker scenario, the particular that instantiates these properties would need to have the set of causal powers of the physical properties, but not a subset of these powers. In all of these cases, it seems that the blocker scenario is impossible.

Of course, all these views assume more than a mere supervenience relation between physical properties and other properties. Nevertheless, given these considerations, it is more plausible to think that physicalists are committed to the impossibility of blocker scenarios than Hawthorne seems to expect. Nevertheless, if the purely supervenience-based definitions have trouble ruling out such scenarios, but accounts that postulate these stronger relations do, this provides us with a reason to think that metaphysical dependence requires more than mere supervenience.

4.4.2 Can supervenience be a metaphysical dependence relation? Considerations on formal characteristics

Let me take a step back and have a look at some of the more general considerations with regard to the link of supervenience, necessitation, and (metaphysical) dependence. Supervenience, and likewise necessitation, are relations that are *reflexive, transitive* and neither *symmetric* nor *asymmetric* (Kim 1993d [1984]: 67). However, our pre-theoretic intuitions about notions of dependence arguably tell us that a proper dependence relation needs to be *irreflexive* and *asymmetric:*

Irreflexivity: If A (metaphysically) depends on B, then $A \neq B$.
Asymmetry: If A (metaphysically) depends on B, then B does not (metaphysically) depend on A.

Strictly speaking, we do not need to pose irreflexivity in addition to asymmetry, since the former follows from the latter. But it is still worth discussing explicitly since it expresses the very intuitive claim that nothing depends on itself, and thus that the metaphysical dependence relation, like any proper dependence relation, requires its relata to be numerically distinct. Similarly, the asymmetry requirement seems rather intuitive. Bennett (2017: 40–41) argues that to think of what she calls building relations[120] as asymmetric allows us to characterize relative fundamentality in terms of it, which she takes to be a central theoretical virtue of the asymmetry claim. Suppose that if A metaphysically depends on B, then B is in a metaphysical sense more fundamental than A. In this case, asymmetry is an obvious requirement. After all, we certainly do not want to say that there are symmetric cases of relative fundamentality.

While both irreflexivity and asymmetry seem to be very intuitive to many, some have challenged the view that dependence relations need to have these features. Jessica Wilson (2014) argues that the identity relation, which is reflexive and symmetric, is a dependence relation, and more specifically, a dependence relation that might account for the metaphysical dependence of the mental on the physical. Her intuition derives at least in part from the fact that the identity relation is one among the relations that have been suggested to capture the "nothing over and above" locution in sentences like "The mental is nothing over and above the physical" (Wilson 2014: 570–571):

> I think even the supposition of irreflexivity as common to all grounding relations can and should be denied; this result moreover provides additional support to the claim that grounding relations may be symmetric. [...] For, in investigating grounding, we aim to make sense of the usual idioms of metaphysical dependence, and identity claims are paradigmatic of claims taken to establish that certain goings-on are nothing over and above certain other goings-on.

While I agree with Wilson that the 'nothing over and above' locution is sometimes used to express identity, I do not think that this shows that identity is a (metaphysical) dependence relation (or a *grounding* relation, as Wilson puts it). The reason is that the 'nothing over and above' locution does not always express dependence. In cases in which we would say that something is nothing over and above, *but not identical to* something else, it indeed typically expresses

---

[120] Bennett's notion of building is more inclusive than my notion of metaphysical dependence. While I constrain my notion of metaphysical dependence to property types, Bennett also allows entities from other categories such as objects and sets as potential relata of building. I do not want to claim that there might also be a more inclusive notion of building, as she proposes, but it is not my aim here to take a stance with regard to her more liberal account.

a notion of dependence. But that does not suffice to make identity a metaphysical dependence relation. Karen Bennett (2017: 35), when arguing for the asymmetry of what she calls 'building' relations, makes the same point:

> [T]he phrase 'nothing over and above' is a slippery beast [...]. Sometimes the phrase is used to mark that one phenomenon depends on another; sometimes it is instead used to state an identity. If 'nothing over and above' counts as an "idiom of metaphysical dependence" at all, it is a slippery, untrustworthy one that does not always mark the presence of building.

Something similar holds for supervenience (and necessitation): In many cases, there is an underlying relation of metaphysical dependence that accounts for the supervenience of one property on other properties. However, this does not hold in all cases. Sometimes, the underlying relation is an identity relation, and in this case, the presence of a supervenience relation does not indicate the presence of a metaphysical dependence relation.

Others challenge the asymmetry requirement for metaphysical dependence. For example, Ricki Bliss (2014: 248) argues the following:

> Consider, for example, the north and south poles of a magnet: the two are symmetrically dependent upon each other. The fact that the magnet's north pole exists depends upon the fact that the south pole exists, and vice versa.

Bliss frames dependence as a relation between facts, but we can again translate to property talk: the property of *having a north pole* and the property of *having a south pole*, as instantiated by magnets, mutually depend on each other, according to a property-based claim very much resembling the one by Bliss. However, it is at least controversial whether this serves as an appropriate counterexample against asymmetry. For example, Bennett (2017: 37) argues that the seeming interdependence can be explained away by pointing to a common dependence base – (facts about) the properties of the magnetic field.

Jaegwon Kim (1993d [1984]: 67) is also skeptical about supervenience being a relation of dependence, in part because he takes dependence to be asymmetric:

> In most cases of interest supervenience seems in fact asymmetric; for example, although many have claimed the supervenience of valuational on nonvaluational properties, it is apparent that the converse does not hold. Similarly, although psychophysical supervenience is an arguable view, it would be manifestly implausible to hold that the physical supervenes on the psychological. This asymmetry of supervenience may well be the core of the idea of asymmetric dependence we associate with the supervenience relation. For when we look at the relationship as specified in the definition between a strongly supervenient property and its base property, all that we have is that the base property entails the supervenient property. This alone does not warrant us to say that the supervening property

is dependent on, or determined by, the base, or that an object has the supervening property in virtue of having the base property. These latter relations strongly hint at an asymmetric relation.

As becomes clear in this passage, Kim thinks that in order for *A* to depend on *B*, more is required than a mere entailment. It is also required that *A* is instantiated *because B* is instantiated, or that *A* is instantiated *in virtue of B* being instantiated. Supervenience and necessitation do not tell us very much about the order of priority, or relative fundamentality, between their relata. In order to account for this, we need an asymmetric relation that helps us fixing the order of priority between the properties in question.

These considerations indicate that although physicalism entails certain supervenience claims, supervenience and necessitation do not have the right formal characteristics to serve as notions of metaphysical dependence. But there are more concerns with regard to understanding metaphysical dependence solely in terms of supervenience and necessitation.

4.4.3 Necessitation without metaphysical dependence? Fine's challenge to supervenience-based accounts of physicalism

A further reason to think that necessitation is not enough for metaphysical dependence can be derived from an argument that has been originally put forward by Kit Fine (1994: 4–5) to support the claim that there is more to being an essential property of an entity than being necessarily instantiated by that entity.

> Consider, then, Socrates and the set whose sole member is Socrates. It is then necessary, according to standard views within modal set theory, that Socrates belongs to singleton Socrates if he exists; for, necessarily, the singleton exists if Socrates exists and, necessarily, Socrates belongs to singleton Socrates if both Socrates and the singleton exist. It therefore follows according to the modal criterion that Socrates essentially belongs to singleton Socrates.
>
> But, intuitively, this is not so. It is no part of the essence of Socrates to belong to the singleton. Strange as the literature on personal identity may be, it has never been suggested that in order to understand the nature of a person one must know to which sets he belongs. There is nothing in the nature of a person, if I may put it this way, which demands that he belongs to this or that set or which demands, given that the person exists, that there even be any sets.

We can formulate a version of Fine's argument in terms of properties to show that necessitation or supervenience is not enough for metaphysical dependence. Given that Socrates exists if and only if the singleton {Socrates} exists, there are two properties that are had by anything whatsoever just in case these entities exist: *being such that Socrates exists*, and *being such that the singleton {Socrates} exists*. The requirements for necessitation or supervenience are clearly fulfilled in both directions. Take strong global supervenience: Since any entity whatsoever in every possible world will either have both properties or none of them, any isomorphism between individuals that preserves the one property preserves the other. Nevertheless, while we might be inclined to say that *being such that the singleton {Socrates} exists* metaphysically depends on *being such that Socrates exists*, given the reasonable assumption that the singleton exists because Socrates exists, the reverse claim is intuitively incorrect. Alternatively, to avoid the case of properties that everything has, take Socrates' property of *being Socrates*, and his property of *being the sole member of the singleton {Socrates}*. Clearly, the requirements for necessitation or supervenience are fulfilled. Since Socrates has both properties necessarily, and no other particular can have any of these properties, any isomorphism between individuals that preserves the one property preserves the other, and thus the requirements for strong global supervenience are fulfilled. But while we are inclined to say that *being the sole member of the singleton {Socrates}* metaphysically depends on *being Socrates*, the reverse claim is intuitively incorrect – after all, Socrates is the sole member of the singleton because he is Socrates, not the other way around.

This example also shows that it does not help to take metaphysical dependence to *require* an asymmetric modal relation. After all, we want to claim that a metaphysical dependence relation obtains between the properties in question in the case above even though they are symmetrically modally related to each other. If we were to require that metaphysical dependence requires an asymmetric modal link, we would be unable to say that *A* metaphysically depends on *B* even though there is a necessitating link going in both directions.

Another related way to see that supervenience and necessitation are not sufficient for dependence is to consider the case of properties like *being such that 2+2=4*, or *being a philosopher or not a philosopher*. Since everything has these properties necessarily, they turn out to supervene on any property whatsoever. Take the property of *being green*, for example. Since no two worlds (or individuals) can differ with respect to properties that everything has necessarily, *being green* necessitates *being such that 2+2=4* and *being a philosopher or not a philosopher*, or likewise, *being such that 2+2=4* and *being a philosopher or not a philosopher* supervene on *being green*. However, we clearly do not want to say that these properties depend on *being green* in any substantial way, or that *being such that 2+2=4* is nothing over and above *being green* (cf. McLaughlin and Bennett 2018: section 3.5).

Finally, take the case of conjunctive properties and their conjuncts. Anything that has the property of *being red and round* must have the property of *being red*, but we typically do not want to say that *being red* depends on *being red and round*. Rather, it seems that *being red and round* depends on *being red* and *being round* (see e.g. Yablo 1992: 253 [fn23]; Baysan 2015: 251).

4.4.4 Necessitation dualism and the supervenience of emergent properties

A final reason to think that supervenience is not enough to establish a metaphysical dependence relation between numerically distinct properties is based on considerations about a view Stoljar (2010: 144–145) calls 'necessitation dualism'. According to the necessitation dualist, although mental and physical properties are as distinct as the standard dualist intuitively envisages, mental properties supervene with metaphysical necessity on the physical properties. With regard to the first claim, the necessitation dualist agrees with the standard dualist: mental and physical properties are distinct, according to the particular understanding of distinctness required for dualism. With regard to the second claim, the necessitation dualist departs from what the standard dualist thinks. The standard dualist typically thinks that mental properties merely nomologically supervene on physical properties, in the sense that the necessitation of mental by physical properties is restricted to worlds that share the same laws of nature. Here is David Chalmers (1996: 124) on the standard dualist picture he defends:

> [C]onsciousness does not supervene *logically* on the physical, but this is not to say that it does not supervene at all. There appears to be a systematic dependence of conscious experience on physical structure in the cases with which we are familiar [...]. It remains as plausible as ever, for example, that if my physical structure were to be replicated by some creature in the actual world, my conscious experience would be replicated, too. So it remains plausible that consciousness supervenes *naturally* on the physical. It is this view – natural supervenience without logical supervenience – that I will develop.

As becomes clear in the last sentence of the quote, the standard dualist claims that mental properties do not metaphysically (or logically) supervene on physical properties. What Chalmers means by natural supervenience is supervenience restricted to worlds that share their laws of nature with the actual world. Importantly, in the standard dualist's view, the laws of physics do not exhaust the laws of nature. If we would construct nomological supervenience as supervenience in worlds that share with our world the same laws of physics, then the relevant laws linking the mental with the physical domain would be missing, and supervenience would fail. But the necessitation dualist thinks otherwise. On their view, the supervenience is not restricted to a subset of the metaphysically possible worlds. Rather, it holds with full-fledged metaphysical necessity.

Melnyk (2003: 58), who argues for an account of physicalism that appeals to the notion of realization instead of supervenience, rejects a purely supervenience-based account of physicalism based on considerations about a scenario in which necessitation dualism is true of the actual world:

> [Suppose that] the way things are physically [...] necessitates the way things are nonphysically: the distribution of physical tokens necessitates that there be the nonphysical tokens that there are, distributed as they are, and also that they be the *only* such tokens that there are (the physical way things are therefore has a certain *exclusionary* power). Moreover, this necessitation is to be understood as necessitation of the strongest possible sort: *all* possible worlds physically indiscernible from this world also have exactly the same distribution of nonphysical tokens [...] as this world does. But, and here is the crucial point, this necessitation is to be understood as some sort of *primitive and irreducible modal fact*, not to be explained in terms of anything more fundamental. Not only is it inexplicable in terms of the identity of non-physical types either with physical types or with functional types that are always, as it happens, physically realized, but it cannot be explained at all.

In Melynk's scenario, the supervenience relation does not indicate the existence of a further relation that accounts for the fact that the supervenience relation holds. Rather, it is a brute modal fact that the pattern of instantiation of all properties necessarily co-varies with the pattern of instantiation of physical properties, and thus that the supervenience relation holds.

Some (e.g. Wilson 2005: 430; Stoljar 2008: 274) consider the view of the British emergentists (Morgan 1923; Broad 1925; see also McLaughlin 1992; Stephan 1999: part I, esp. § 3.4) to be along the lines of a necessitation dualist view. Emergentism is usually taken to be a form of dualism, but it is a form of dualism that claims nevertheless that mental properties supervene on physical properties (Kim 1998: 12):

> [B]oth emergentism and the view that the mental must be physically realized (we can call this "physical realizationism") imply mind-body supervenience. But emergentism is a form of dualism that takes mental properties to be nonphysical intrinsic causal powers, whereas physical realizationism is monistic physicalism.[121]

---

[121] It is interesting to see that Kim nevertheless seems to think that minimal physicalism can be understood in terms of supervenience (1998: 14–15): "[M]ind body supervenience captures a commitment common to all positions on the nature of mentality that are basically physicalistic. For it represents the idea that mentality is at bottom physically based, and that there is no free-floating mentality unanchored in the physical nature of objects and events in which it is manifested. This is an idea that can be shared by many diverse positions on the mind-body problem, from reductive type physicalism at the one extreme to dualistic emergentism on the other. In

Everybody in the debate indeed agrees that both emergentism and physicalism require supervenience. It is however disputed what the modal strength of the necessitation relation is that comes with supervenience in the emergentist case. For example, van Cleve (1990: 222) claims the following:

> If P is a property of w, then P is emergent iff P supervenes with nomological necessity, but not with logical necessity, on the properties of the parts of w.

Here, what van Cleve has in mind is a notion of multiple domain supervenience. The reason why he thinks that supervenience with logical necessity is off the table for the emergentist view is that "an emergent property is one that is not deducible from the properties of the parts of w" (1990: 222). This is in line with the way Broad (1925: 61) frames emergentism:

> Put in abstract terms the emergent theory asserts that there are certain wholes, composed (say) of constituents A, B, and C in a relation R to each other; that all wholes composed of constituents of the same kind as A, B, and C in relations of the same kind as R have certain characteristic properties; that A, B, and C are capable of occurring in other kinds of complex where the relation is not of the same kind as R; and that the characteristic properties of the whole R(A, B, C) cannot, even in theory, be deduced from the most complete knowledge of the properties of A, B, and C in isolation or in other wholes which are not of the form R(A, B, C).

However, if we take van Cleve's notion of logical necessity to mean metaphysical necessity, it is far from clear that it entails deducibility. Supervenience with logical or conceptual necessity clearly allows for deducibility, but this is not what is at issue. As Wilson (2005: 436) indicates, van Cleve's example that "the shape of an object is a logical consequence of the nature and arrangement of its parts" (1990: 218) shows that he most likely has in mind metaphysical necessity rather than conceptual or logical necessity. However, we know that there are metaphysically necessary relations for which deducibility[122] fails at least since Kripke

---

contrast, mind-body supervenience is inconsistent with more extreme forms of dualism, such as, Cartesian dualism, which allow the mental world to float freely, unconstrained by the physical domain. Thus mind body-supervenience can serve as a useful dividing line: it can be viewed as defining minimal physicalism." Here, it seems that Kim counts emergentism as a form of physicalism even though he classifies it as 'dualistic'. Moreover, in Kim (1999: 4), he claims outright that "[i]t is evident that emergentism is a form of what is now standardly called 'nonreductive materialism', a doctrine that aspires to position itself as a compromise between physicalist reductionism and all-out dualisms".

122 Since deducibility strictly speaking applies to statements rather than properties and relations, what is meant by the failure of deducibility is that the statement that the supervenient

(1980) has forcefully argued for the existence of statements that are necessary but *a posteriori*. So van Cleve's argument against the view that emergent properties might be necessitated with metaphysical necessity by physical properties fails, and thus his considerations do not provide a reason to think that necessitation dualism is not a viable option.

As Wilson (2005: 437–438) argues, the issue of bringing out the distinction between physicalism on the one hand, and dualism on the other hand, in terms of the modal strength of the necessitation relation is particularly problematic if one adopts Shoemaker's (1980; 1998) account of property individuation and his related necessitarian account of causal laws. According to this view, at least those properties that figure in causal laws are individuated by the causal powers they bestow on their bearers, and thus have their powers essentially. Shoemaker thinks that two worlds that share the same instantiated properties share the same causal laws, and if a causal law in one world relates two properties, the same law relates them in all metaphysically possible worlds in which they are instantiated (1998: 70):

> Different things can be true of a property at different places, and at different times. E. g., the frequency of its instantiation can be different, and it can be coinstantiated with different properties, insofar as this is compatible with the laws. But it cannot be governed by different laws at different places or at different times. Applying again the principle that constraints on intra-world variation are also constraints on inter-world variation, we get the conclusion that the same property cannot be governed by different laws in different worlds. Since I take it that the causal features of properties are features they have in virtue of the laws that govern their instantiation, this is equivalent to my claim that the causal features of properties are essential to them. And it implies that causal necessity is a special case of metaphysical necessity.

We need to be careful not to confuse two different claims here: there is (1) the claim that the metaphysically possible worlds are the nomologically possible worlds, and (2) the claim that the metaphysically possible worlds that share the same instantiated properties are the nomologically possible worlds that share the same instantiated properties. Shoemaker's view does not entail (1), but it does entail (2). Worlds in which alien properties are instantiated are not ruled out by the view, and remain metaphysically possible, but since different laws govern these alien properties, those worlds are not nomologically possible. The important thing for the issue at hand is that if Shoemaker's view is correct, any metaphysically possible world in which the physical properties are instanti-

---

property is instantiated cannot be deduced from the statement that the subvenient properties are instantiated. This means that it is not *a priori* that the supervenience relation holds.

ated will be such that the emergent properties are instantiated, even though the link between the emergent properties and the physical properties is established by a causal law. A similar story might be told by the necessitation dualist more generally to support their claim.

The moral of the above considerations is that if necessitation dualism is a coherent view, it clearly poses a problem for those who think that necessitation or supervenience is sufficient for metaphysical dependence of the mental on the physical, and thus for physicalism so construed. For if this is all that is required for physicalism, the right-hand side of our definition of physicalism seems to be satisfied if necessitation dualism is true, even though we do not want to say that necessitation dualism is a variant of physicalism. In the next section, I will address an attempt to make a distinction between physicalism and necessitation dualism in epistemic terms. Afterwards, I will address the question whether necessitation dualism is a coherent view in the first place.

4.4.5 Explanation to the rescue of an ontological stalemate?

Stoljar (2008: 274–275; 2010: 155–157) considers one way to remedy this deficiency, which we might call the 'epistemic route'. On this view, we need to add an epistemic component to our definition of physicalism. Emergentists argue that there is no explanation to be had as to why the dependent properties are instantiated whenever the properties they depend upon are instantiated. On the basis of this claim, one might be drawn to the idea that emergentism, or more generally necessitation dualism, makes the same metaphysical claims as physicalism does, but differs from physicalism with respect to the explanatory link between the mental and the physical. This is the core claim of the epistemic route. The physicalist needs to be able to explain why the supervenience relation holds, whereas the dualist cannot provide such explanation.

Prima facie, this seems to be in line with the notion of superdupervenience introduced by Horgan (1993) I already mentioned in section 4.4.1, which asks for a robust and materialistically adequate explanation of the supervenience relation as a requirement for physicalism. But the idea of taking the superdupervenience requirement to the epistemic route is misguided – the difference between physicalism and dualism has to be a metaphysical difference, not an epistemic one. After all, the one is a metaphysical monist view, while the other one is not. A 'pure' or 'metaphysically brute' supervenience claim, just like the one Melnyk considers in the quote discussed earlier, combined with an explanation as to why the supervenience relation holds that does not require any further metaphysical commitments, is not what Horgan asks for, however. Rather, superdu-

4.4 Can physicalism be fully characterized in purely modal terms?

pervenience requires that the physicalist appeals to a further *relation* between the properties in question, and it is this relation that accounts for the link between the dependent properties and the properties on which they depend, and thereby explains why the supervenience relation holds. Kim (1998: 14; see also Kim 1993a: 167–168; Heil 2011: 36) suggests such an understanding of what the 'explanation' of supervenience comes to:

> [M]ind-body supervenience itself is not an explanatory theory; it merely states a pattern of property covariations between the mental and the physical and points to the existence of a dependency relation between the two. Yet supervenience is silent on the nature of the dependence relation that might explain why the mental supervenes on the physical. Another way of putting the point would be this: supervenience is not a type of dependence relation [...]. Any putative account of the mind-body relation that accepts mind-body supervenience must specify a dependence relation between the mental and physical that is capable of grounding and explaining mind-body supervenience.

In order to satisfy the requirements for physicalism, the relation in question can either be a relation of identity, or a metaphysical dependence relation. Thereby, it is explained why the supervenience relation holds, but this kind of explanation is not, or at least not purely, epistemic. The claim that the further relation holds is a metaphysical claim, not an epistemic one, and whether or not this relation holds is independent of whether we understand why the relation in question holds. What is relevant for distinguishing physicalism from dualism is *that* a relation of identity or metaphysical dependence holds between the mental and the physical that accounts for the supervenience link, not that we understand *why* it holds.

This is not to say that making plausible that the postulated further relation holds between these properties by explaining why it holds is a trivial and unimportant explanatory endeavor which physicalists who have particular views regarding the nature of the relation that holds for a particular domain of properties do not need to pursue in order to make plausible their view. However, independent of whether they are successful in doing so, if there is a further identity or metaphysical dependence relation that accounts for the supervenience of the dependent properties on physical properties, this is sufficient to make the difference between physicalism and its rivals rest on purely metaphysical grounds.

Stoljar (2007: 275) puts forward similar considerations with regard to the difference between physicalism and emergentism and the introduction of an epistemic criterion for distinguishing the two:

> [I]t is difficult to shake the feeling that the distinction between the emergentist and the nonreductive physicalist is a matter of metaphysics, and not a matter of explanation or epistemology. After all, many contemporary philosophers hold that you cannot deduce psycho-

logical facts from physical facts, even if those facts are strictly identical. In view of the commitment to the identity of psychological and physical facts such philosophers are physicalists by anyone's lights; in fact, they are *reductive* physicalists. But in view of their commitment to a failure of deducibility they would be counted – mistakenly counted – as emergentists by the criterion Broad introduced.

As Stoljar indicates, even if mental properties are identical to physical properties, it might be the case that there is no explanation available as to why the identity relation holds between those properties, at least if we require deducibility as opposed to an inference to the best explanation or something similar. But we certainly do not want to say that physicalism is false even though we have strict type identities just because of the lack of deducibility. Moreover, if even the identity theorist may lack this kind of explanatory link, why should we think that a non-reductive physicalist who argues for a weaker link than identity has to offer such an explanatory link? This is not to say that the identity theorist should not try to provide an explanation as to why we should think that the identity theory is true, and similarly with relations of metaphysical dependence. But if such a view is true, even if we do not have an explanation as to why we should believe that it is true, there is nothing that tells against physicalism. We certainly do not think that a form of dualism might be true even though identity theory is true, just because we have no explanation as to why the relevant identity relations hold.

Furthermore, contrary to the epistemic route, dualists might offer explanations as to why a supervenience relation holds between mental and physical properties. For example, they might explain the link by making reference to certain causal laws that link the properties in question. Such explanations would not be *a priori*, nor would they be materialistically adequate, as Horgan's superdupervenience principle requires for physicalism, but it is hard to see how to spell out which explanations are materialistically adequate and which are not without having a prior understanding of what the difference between physicalism and necessitation dualism amounts to (see also Stoljar 2010: 155). Still, there would be some explanation, and if one holds a view like Shoemaker's necessitarianism about laws, the necessitation dualist's claim that the necessitating link between mental and physical properties holds with metaphysical necessity is no more *ad hoc* than the corresponding claim for any other causal link between properties.

The upshot of these considerations is that if necessitation dualism is a coherent view, then we have a further reason to believe that supervenience is necessary, but not sufficient for metaphysical dependence. In order to see whether necessitation dualism is coherent, we need to further investigate what the necessitation dualist means by claiming that mental and physical properties are distinct, and whether it is coherent to claim that even though mental and physical properties are distinct, they are necessarily connected.

4.4.6 Necessitation dualism and Hume's dictum

Concerns about the coherency of the distinctness of properties with a necessary connection between them are closely related to a metaphysical principle that is frequently called 'Hume's dictum' (e. g. Wilson 2010a; Stoljar 2008; 2010: 148–150). Wilson (2005: 441) claims that it is one of the major principles put forward against necessitarianism about laws, and Stoljar takes belief in this principle to be "the main reason" (2010: 149) to think that necessitation dualism is incoherent, or at least impossible.

Stoljar frames Hume's dictum as the thesis that "there are no necessary connections between distinct existences" (2008: 263), and argues that the principle can also be applied to property types, since 'existences' is broad enough to include such entities. Thus, for property types, Hume's dictum is the claim that there are no necessary connections between distinct property types. Since necessitation dualism claims that mental and physical property types are distinct but necessarily connected in the sense that the mental properties supervene with metaphysical necessity on the physical properties, we can assess the view's coherence on the basis of distinguishing between different kinds of distinctness. Assuming that the notion of distinctness involved in the formulation of necessitation dualism is the same as the notion of distinctness involved in Hume's dictum, we can ask what notion of distinctness makes Hume's dictum plausible and necessitation dualism incoherent. Furthermore, we can ask which notion of distinctness both physicalists and dualists might agree to that helps distinguishing between physicalism and necessitarian versions of dualism.

Both Stoljar (2008; 2010: 150–153) and Wilson (2010a) assess the plausibility of Hume's dictum relative to how the notion of distinctness is further spelled out. The first notion they consider is *numerical distinctness*. After all, this is what is most frequently meant by 'distinctness' in ordinary language. For example, if we say that crimson and scarlet are two distinct shades of red, we mean that they are numerically distinct. However, if we take distinctness to mean *numerical distinctness*, then Hume's dictum is quite obviously false. The example of determinate and determinable colors is a clear case for which this interpretation of Hume's dictum fails. The properties *being red* and *being crimson* are clearly distinct properties – it is possible that *being red* is instantiated but *being crimson* is not. But there is a necessary connection between *being red* and *being crimson* if we take the other direction: it is impossible that *being crimson* is instantiated but *being red* is not. So if what was meant by distinctness as required by the necessitation dualist were numerical distinctness, we would have good reason to give up Hume's dictum.

If necessitation dualism were the thesis that mental and physical properties are numerically distinct but necessarily connected, then it would be a perfectly coherent claim. But non-reductive physicalists[123] agree that there are instantiated properties that are numerically distinct from physical properties. After all, there would otherwise not be any reason to include the clause on metaphysical dependence in our definition of physicalism. In this case, the correct judgment would be that necessitation dualism is a form of physicalism after all, and the name 'necessitation dualism' is just a misnomer. Even more, since the distinctness claim is what necessitation dualism has in common with traditional dualism, this judgment would extend to traditional dualism as well. However, this does neither seem to be the view the necessitation dualist actually defends, nor do we want to say that the advocator of Hume's dictum defends an obviously false thesis.

Stoljar (2008) further considers two modal notions of distinctness – weak (2008: 265) and strong (2008: 266) modal distinctness:

> F is weakly modally distinct from G if and only if it is possible that F is instantiated and G is not *or* it is possible that G is instantiated and F is not.
>
> F is strongly modally distinct from G if and only if it is possible that F is instantiated and G is not *and* it is possible that G is instantiated and F is not.

The difference between weak and strong modal distinctness is the way the two parts of the thesis are connected. While weak modal distinctness takes the form of a disjunction, strong modal distinctness takes the form of a conjunction. The example of color properties exemplifies the difference between the two kinds of distinctness: *being red* and *being crimson* are weakly modally distinct, but they are not strongly modally distinct. Since there is a necessary connection between these properties, the example again provides a counterexample for Hume's dictum understood in terms of weak modal distinctness. Thus, if Hume's dictum is the claim that there are no necessary connections between weakly modally distinct entities, we have good reason to deny its truth.

---

123 The term 'reduction' is used in different ways in the literature. Here, I take non-reductive physicalism to be any physicalist view that does not take the relation between physical and mental properties to be the relation of type identity.

If necessitation dualism were the claim that mental and physical properties are weakly modally distinct but necessarily connected, then it would again be perfectly coherent. However, necessitation dualism would come out as a non-reductive form of physicalism. Those physicalists who deny identity of mental and physical properties also typically agree that mental properties are weakly modally distinct from physical properties: While the mental supervenes on the physical, most physicalists think that the reverse does not hold. Again, necessitation dualists seem to require more than the weak modal distinctness of mental and physical properties, because we do not want to count them towards the camp of non-reductive physicalists.

For strong modal distinctness, things are different. If we take Hume's dictum to be the thesis that there are no necessary connections between strongly modally distinct entities, it is clearly a necessary and *a priori* truth. This reading thus makes sense of the claim that Hume's dictum is an analytic truth. If we take this reading of distinctness seriously, this is bad news for the necessitation dualist, however. If the kind of distinctness required by the necessitation dualism is strong modal distinctness, then necessitation dualism is indeed incoherent. After all, in this case, necessitation dualism is basically the claim that although there are no necessary connections between mental and physical properties, those properties are necessarily connected. However, this is not only false, but analytically so. So while this kind of distinctness makes sense of the idea that Hume's dictum is a very plausible principle, the necessitation dualist is taken to believe in an obvious analytic falsehood.

Aside from notions of mereological distinctness and spatio-temporal distinctness (see Wilson 2010a: 605), which I will set aside because they are difficult to apply to property types, there is another kind of distinctness considered by Stoljar (2008: 267; 2010: 151): distinctness in *essence*. He frames this notion of distinctness as follows:

> F is distinct in essence from G just in case the essence of F is wholly distinct from the essence of G.

Here, the essence of a property is "the totality of all its essential properties" (Stoljar 2010: 151; see also 2008: 267). In order to avoid the term 'distinctness' on the right-hand side of the claim, we can rephrase the statement:

> F is distinct in essence from G *iff* there is no property that is both an essential property of F and an essential property of G.

Hume's dictum, on this reading, says that there are no necessary connections between properties that share none of their essential properties. Whether this reading of distinctness is plausible depends on how we understand the notion of an essential property. If the essential properties of an entity are just the necessary properties of the entity in question, then Hume's dictum says that there are no necessary connections between properties that share none of their necessary properties. Stoljar considers this option briefly, and notes that "if that is what is intended, then this interpretation is no advance and necessitation dualism remains incoherent" (2010: 152).

It is not exactly clear to me what Stoljar has in mind here, but one clear difficulty for this view is that it is hard to see how to find any pair of properties that satisfy the requirement. After all, we can come up with any number of examples for necessary properties that any pair of properties share: for example, it seems to be a necessary property of any property *to be such that 2+2=4*, or *to be self-identical*. If this is so, then Hume's dictum turns out to be vacuously true because the antecedent requirement of not sharing any essential property is not fulfilled by any pair of properties whatsoever. Furthermore, necessitation dualism comes out necessarily false, because mental and physical properties cannot be distinct on this reading.

Those who consider an essence-based notion of distinctness as the basis for either Hume's dictum or necessitation dualism are thus well advised to claim that the essential properties of an entity are not just its necessary properties. This view has been championed by Fine (1994). Fine argues that although the essential properties of an entity are among its necessary properties, some of the necessary properties are not essential to the entity in question, based on an argument that I have already discussed above (see section 4.4.3). The properties just considered are typical examples. While it is necessary to any entity *to be such that 2+2=4*, and *to be self-identical*, these are not properties that 'define', in the sense of what Fine calls a 'real definition' as applied to entities rather than words, what the nature of the entity in question is, and thus are not part of the essence of the entity in question.

Whether or not Hume's dictum is true on this account of distinctness is somewhat difficult to evaluate. It says that there are no necessary connections between properties that do not share any essential properties. The necessitation dualist, on this view, claims that although mental and physical properties share no essential properties, they are necessarily connected. Our typical color example does not help here, since *being red* and *being crimson* most likely have some essential properties in common, and are thus not essentially distinct. For example, *being a color property* intuitively seems quite essential to both of them. Maybe, a candidate pair of properties that are essentially distinct but necessarily connected are properties like *being such that 2+2=4* and *being self-identical*. It is at least far from obvious that these properties share any essential properties, even though they are clearly necessarily connected since they are necessarily co-instantiated. If so, a necessitation dualist can plausibly deny Hume's dictum, so construed. But it seems that a physicalist can do so as well. After all, it is not clear whether a physicalist must deny that mental and physical properties do not share any of their essential properties, and thus are distinct in essence. For example, it is not clear that physical properties and higher-order functional properties have any essential properties in common. On the other hand, it is not clear that the dualist must deny that mental and physical properties share at least some of their essential properties, and thus must accept that mental and physical properties are distinct in this way.

Jessica Wilson (2015) argues for a distinction between weak and strong emergence, where the former is acceptable to the physicalist where the latter is not, and can serve as our dualist case in which some essential properties are shared between mental and physical properties. On her view, weakly emergent properties are numerically distinct from the properties they depend upon, but the causal powers they bestow on their bearers are a subset of the causal powers bestowed by certain physical properties. Strongly emergent properties however bestow some further causal powers to their bearers that are not within the set of powers bestowed by physical properties. But even in the strong emergentist case, at least some of the causal powers bestowed by the emergent properties might be within the set of powers bestowed by physical properties, as long as not all of them are. If we combine this with a powers-based view of property individuation, it seems that both the physicalist and the dualist are able to claim that some essential properties can be shared. After all, all the strong emergentist needs, according to Wilson, is that some of the causal powers of mental properties are not also part of the essence of any physical property, so that there is no set-subset relation between the powers of physical and mental properties, respectively. It thus is rather controversial whether distinctness in essence helps drawing the boundary between the views.

Stoljar (2010: 152–153) also briefly considers the idea that the notion of distinctness involved in the necessitation dualist case is primitive. While this is certainly an option, somebody who worries that necessitation dualism is an incoherent view will most likely not be impressed. Thus, as Stoljar rightly points out, it is a dialectically weak position when one's opponent is skeptical about the coherence of necessitation dualism, and will most likely be skeptical about the coherence of the primitive notion as well. Moreover, we should be wary of being too liberal with regard to introducing primitive notions, and adhere to an Occam's razor-like principle of parsimony: "Primitive notions should not be multiplied without necessity!"

This completes the discussion of variants of distinctness discussed in the literature. Only one variant renders Hume's dictum obviously true and necessitation dualism incoherent. However, on this view, the incoherence of necessitation dualism is so obvious that it is hard to see how anybody might hold the view in the first place. All other variants considered so far are either such that Hume's dictum comes out false, and thus provides no reason to think that necessitation dualism is incoherent, but necessitation dualism comes out as a version of physicalism after all, or make it somewhat difficult to judge conclusively whether Hume's dictum is false and whether the physicalist can also agree to the notion of distinctness in question. I now move on to consider two notions of distinctness that have not been addressed in the literature. The first one turns out to be a non-starter, but the second one is promising.

On the basis of the notion of a physical property discussed in the previous chapter, one might think that the kind of distinctness the dualist requires is that mental properties do not share the set of essential properties that all the physical properties share with each other. The dualist clearly does not want to say that mental properties share with the physical properties those properties that make the latter physical. After all, in this case, those properties would themselves be physical properties. However, even though it is true that the necessitation dualist claims that mental properties do not share those properties with the physical properties, and that mental and physical properties are still necessarily connected, this is just a variant of the case of numerical distinctness discussed earlier, and does not help distinguishing the physicalist from the necessitation dualist. For example, if higher-order functional properties are multiply realizable, so that they are also instantiated in worlds that do not include any physical properties, they also do not share those properties. Still, physicalism is perfectly compatible with the instantiation of higher-order functional properties.

Let us get to the final understanding of distinctness I want to consider. When the necessitation dualist claims that mental properties are distinct from physical properties although there are necessary connections between them, this is supposed to entail the denial of physicalism as construed in chapter 2 conjoined with an acceptance of the purely modal commitments that go along with it. Since mental properties are not among the properties that anything whatsoever has necessarily, the claim is basically the following:

A is distinct from B iff for some F in A, there is no G in B such that $F = G$, and there is no plurality $G_1, ..., G_n$ formed from members of B such that F metaphysically depends on $G_1, ..., G_n$.

4.4 Can physicalism be fully characterized in purely modal terms? — 161

Here, *A* is the set of instantiated mental properties, and *B* is the set of instantiated physical properties. We can also formulate a stronger notion of distinctness that conjoins the distinctness of *A* from *B* with the distinctness of *B* from *A*. Dualists need to appeal to this stronger notion to also distinguish themselves from idealists, but as long as we do not take distinctness in the above sense to be sufficient for dualism, this should not lead to any problem.

While such a notion of distinctness does not provide us with an independent reason to accept that necessitation dualism is a coherent view, it at least allows us to make sure that it cannot turn out to be a version of physicalism. However, given that in sections 4.4.1 to 4.4.3, we have already collected further independent reasons to think that metaphysical dependence requires more than can be provided by merely modal claims, but is intuitively compatible with there being necessitating links between properties that do not metaphysically depend on one another, this is something we can live with. Moreover, even if it turns out that our notion of metaphysical dependence is primitive, we at least have not introduced a *further* primitive notion of distinctness in addition to metaphysical dependence.

Stoljar (2010: 159–160) tries to formulate a version of physicalism that accommodates the views of both those who think that necessitation dualism is incoherent because the notion of distinctness employed in Hume's dictum and necessitation dualism is strong modal distinctness, and thus that physicalism can be distinguished from dualism in purely modal terms, and those who think that necessitation dualism is indeed coherent, but that some other notion of distinctness is employed that allows us to draw the distinction between the necessitation dualist and the physicalist properly. To do that, he adds to his necessitation-based formulation a further clause which requires that no property is metaphysically distinct from some physical property (2010: 160):

> Physicalism is true at *w* if and only if for every property *F* instantiated at *w*, there is some physical property *G* instantiated at *w* such that (a) for all possible worlds w^* if *G* is instantiated at w^*, then *F* is instantiated at w^*, and (b) *F* is not metaphysically distinct from *G*.

If one thinks that (a) expresses the modal commitments of physicalism appropriately, and that (a) is sufficient for (b), then one thinks that physicalism can be expressed in purely modal terms, and that necessitation dualism is incoherent. But even though (b) is redundant on such a view, it can still be accepted. If one thinks that (b) adds something to (a), and thinks that (a) expresses the modal commitments of physicalism appropriately, one can similarly well accept the definition.

My own definition of physicalism might be interpreted in a similar way. If one thinks that the notion of metaphysical dependence is such that it can be expressed in purely modal terms, then one might accept that, say, a modal formulation like Physicalism$_{Chalmers}$ is not only entailed by, but also entails physicalism as construed by me. However, I think that this is a case where we in the end need to take sides. One reason why I think that we need to take sides is that although Stoljar's thought seems very ingenuous, it occludes an important difference between views that need to be kept separate to understand where the border between physicalism and dualism is to be drawn. So, although I think that Stoljar's move is well-intended, I also think he should include a further clause (c), which says that (a) does not entail (b), in order to avoid confusion. This of course is against his intention, but what I want to express is that I side with those who think that a purely modal account of physicalism cannot be provided.

4.5 Summary

To sum up, I have so far argued that physicalism has certain modal consequences captured by the accounts of Jackson, Lewis and Chalmers. This is indeed required for any proper physicalist account since the truth of physicalism at a world with creatures that have phenomenal properties needs to rule out physical duplicate worlds that lack such properties. However, such purely modal claims are unable to capture the requirement that non-physical property instantiation does not merely necessarily co-vary with physical property instantiation, but that non-physical properties are instantiated *because* certain physical properties are instantiated. Both identity and metaphysical dependence go beyond what can be captured by a purely modal claim. Thus, physicalism is not entailed by a purely modal thesis of supervenience or necessitation along the lines of the accounts of Jackson, Lewis and Chalmers. In the next chapter, I will investigate alternative options to understand the notion of metaphysical dependence that are more fine-grained than modal notions.

5 "Higher Ground"

Once it is established that purely supervenience-based formulations of physicalism are inadequate to capture the commitment of physicalists that the relevant non-physical properties are instantiated *in virtue of* the instantiation of physical properties, or are, though not identical to them, still *nothing over and above* physical properties, we need a notion of metaphysical dependence that goes beyond what can be expressed in modal terms. In the philosophy of mind literature, many authors appeal to one or the other notion of realization (e. g. Levine 2001: 12; Melnyk 2003: ch. 1; Shoemaker 2007: 1), which supposedly allows for more fine-grained distinctions than supervenience and necessitation. I will address such accounts below, but I want to embed my discussion of these notions in an examination of another candidate notion of metaphysical dependence that has recently gained much attention.

In the recent years, an increasing number of authors have focused on developing a general notion of metaphysical dependence: Grounding.[124] Accordingly, it is no surprise that some have put forward the idea that Grounding is the notion of metaphysical dependence we need to frame physicalism:[125]

- Jonathan Schaffer claims that Grounding "is the notion the physicalist needs to explicate such plausible claims as 'the fundamental properties and facts are physical and everything else obtains *in virtue of* them'" (2009: 364; the encapsulated quotation is from Loewer 2001: 39).
- In a list of potential examples for Grounding claims, Fabrice Correia and Benjamin Schnieder list the claim that "[m]ental facts obtain because of neurophysiological facts" (2012: 1).
- Stephan Leuenberger advances the claim that "physicalism is naturally taken to be the claim that all facts are grounded in some physical facts" (2014a: 151).
- Shamik Dasgupta claims that the rough picture of physicalism is that "at some basic level the world is constituted wholly out of physical stuff, and

---

[124] I use a capital letter 'G' to talk about this notion. This is similar to Wilson's talk of "'Big-G' Grounding" as opposed to "'small-g' grounding", the latter of which Wilson uses as an umbrella term to capture a wide variety of different relations (Wilson 2014; 2018).

[125] Aside from these statements in print, I have noticed that many philosophers of mind and metaphysicians nowadays tend to frequently use the term 'grounds' in the relevant contexts during talks and discussions at conferences. This observation might however be somewhat biased due to the sample of conferences I attended.

everything else – football matches, string quartets, consciousness, values, numbers – somehow 'arises out of' that physical stuff" (2014: 557), and considers whether "we should [...] understand it in terms of *ground* – that is, as the thesis that facts about football matches and string quartets and natural numbers are grounded in purely physical facts" (2014: 558).
- Daniel Stoljar, in his Stanford Encyclopedia article on physicalism, discusses Grounding as an option to define physicalism,[126] and provides the following Grounding-based definition: "[p]hysicalism is true at a possible world *w* iff every property instantiated at *w* is either a physical property or is grounded in a physical property" (2015: section 10.3).
- Philipp Goff argues in his recent book that we should spell out physicalism in terms of Grounding. On his view, we can understand physicalism as "the thesis that all facts that are not narrowly physical facts and that are substantive (i.e., apt to be grounded) are wholly constitutively grounded either in narrowly physical facts alone, or in facts that are autonomous *and* in narrowly physical facts" (2017: 54).
- In response to some of these suggestions, Jessica Wilson (2014; 2018) and Andrew Melnyk (2016) explicitly address and reject Grounding-based accounts of physicalism.

In the following, I will assess whether a notion of Grounding is better suited to capture what we mean by the metaphysical dependence of other properties on the physical properties than the purely modal notions of supervenience and necessitation, as well as other notions of metaphysical dependence, like notions of realization. If so, an appropriate understanding of the notion of Grounding allows us to make the following claim:

$MD_{Grounding}$: A metaphysically depends on $B_1, ..., B_n$ iff $B_1, ..., B_n$ jointly Ground A.

I will first look into the characteristics of Grounding suggested in the literature, and assess whether these characteristics fit the requirements that a notion of metaphysical dependence as required for physicalism must satisfy. I then discuss potential problems of a Grounding-based account that need to be accounted for.

---

[126] Melnyk complains that Stoljar's devoting a subsection of his *Stanford Encyclopedia* entry treats a Grounding-based formulation of physicalism "as if it were a standard approach – which it isn't" (2016: 250 [fn1]).

5.1 The characteristics of Grounding: Taking stock

Other than the notions discussed so far, the notion of Grounding is typically supposed to be primitive. However, this does not mean that we cannot say anything about the notion at all. Virtually all authors agree that Grounding cannot be analyzed in purely modal terms, and few have attempted to provide a definition of Grounding. One notable exception is Fabrice Correia (2013), who considers defining Grounding in terms of essence, although without taking a particular stance with regard to whether such an approach is ultimately successful.

If the notion is primitive, we are supposed to grasp the concept by looking at particular example cases and the formal features of the relation in question. Examples of claims that can allegedly be understood in terms of Grounding are numerous and diverse. Here is a list of examples from Correia and Schnieder (2012: 1; my emphasis):

1. Mental facts obtain *because of* neurophysiological facts.
2. Legal facts *are grounded in* non-legal, e.g. social, facts.
3. Normative facts *are based on* natural facts.
4. Meaning *is due to* non-semantic facts.
5. Dispositional properties are possessed *in virtue of* categorical properties.
6. *What accounts for* the existence of a whole is the existence and arrangement of its parts.
7. A set of things *is less fundamental than* its members.
8. *What makes* something beautiful are certain facts about the reception of its beholders.
9. A substance *is prior to* its tropes or modes.
10. That snow is white is true *because* snow is white.

I have already pointed to the first alleged example, which is the most important one for our purposes, in my list of statements of authors who suggest understanding physicalism in terms of Grounding above. But let us look at some features of the listed examples in more detail. *First*, it is noteworthy that only one of the examples uses the expression 'grounded'. Various other expressions are considered to indicate cases of Grounding as well. The most commonly considered ones are 'in virtue of' and 'because', the latter of which comes with the caveat that it is also often used to express a causal relation,[127] which most authors (including me) want to segregate from Grounding (for an exception, see Bennett

---

[127] These two uses do not even exhaust the options. For example, 'because' is also used in reason explanations or teleological explanations, which some take to be distinct from causal explanations. But segregation of uses that point to a Grounding relation from those uses that point to a causal relation is most relevant for the issue at hand.

2017: ch. 4). *Second*, while in many of the examples the relata of the Grounding relation are facts, other examples include properties, objects, sets, and propositions as relata, and not all examples are such that the relata are all of the same kind.

However, it is far from uncontroversial whether all of these alleged examples are really cases of Grounding. What the proper relata of the Grounding relation are is a matter of debate.[128] While some authors opt for a restrictive facts-only policy, others hold the more liberal view that the Grounding relation can hold between different kinds of relata (Schaffer 2009: 376 [fn33]; 2010: 36). In order to make sense of a Grounding-based notion of metaphysical dependence that can figure in the definition of physicalism I proposed, we need to make sense of Grounding as a relation between property types. This means that one has to adopt a more liberal view of Grounding, or at least accept that even though Grounding strictly speaking is properly construed as a relation between facts, we can make sense of property Grounding talk derivatively, in something like the following way:

Property-Fact link: $B_1, ..., B_n$ jointly Ground A *iff* at least in some cases, the fact that A is instantiated is Grounded in the fact that B_1 is instantiated, ..., the fact that B_n is instantiated.

For example, *being red* and *being round* Ground *being red and round* just in case at least in some cases, the fact that *being red and round* is instantiated is Grounded in the fact that *being red* is instantiated and *being round* is instantiated. The restriction to 'some cases' is necessary to allow for something we might call *mul-*

---

128 The situation is actually even worse. In the Grounding community, two camps have developed proponents of which address Grounding talk in two substantially different ways. One group of authors (e.g. Fine 2001; 2012), who defend what Correia and Schnieder (2012: 10) call the *operational* view, frame things in terms of a non-truth-functional sentential connective, whereas the group of authors who defend the *predicational* view (e.g. Schaffer 2009) frame things in terms of a relational predicate. The canonical form of Grounding claims, according advocates of the operational view, is something like 'p because q' or maybe 'p because $q_1, ..., q_n$', where $p, q, q_1, ..., q_n$ are sentences, and the 'because' is to be understood in terms of metaphysical priority rather than in terms of causation. According to advocators of the predicational view, the canonical form is rather something like 'f is grounded in g', or 'f is grounded in $g_1, ..., g_n$'. Here, I will talk about Grounding along the lines of a predicational view. While the predicational view is metaphysically speaking more committal than the operational view, since it presupposes the existence of relations between whatever the relata of the Grounding relations are, as well as the existence of the relata themselves, this does no harm in our case since physicalism requires commitment to such entities anyway in order to be a properly metaphysical thesis.

tiple *Groundability*, analogous to the idea of multiple realizability. The following example illuminates what I mean. If metaphysical dependence is understood in terms of Grounding, *being crimson* Grounds *being red*, and *being scarlet* Grounds *being red* as well. Now, the fact that the book cover of the book on my table is red is Grounded in the fact that the book cover of the book on my table is crimson, but the fact that the shirt I wear today is red is Grounded in the fact that the shirt I wear today is scarlet. If we would require for property Grounding that the properties $B_1, ..., B_n$ feature in all facts that Ground a fact in which property A features, these two cases would already amount to a counterexample of the claim that $B_1, ..., B_n$ jointly Ground A, because the fact about the book does not feature *being scarlet* and the fact about the shirt does not feature *being crimson*.

Note that in the previous paragraph, I have moved from talking about the *notion* of Grounding to talk about the *relation* of Grounding. When I talk about the notion of Grounding, what I primarily have in mind is a generic *concept* of Grounding, but I sometimes also use the term 'notion' when I want to remain neutral about whether we talk about the relation or the concept. Friends of Grounding typically assume that the notion (or concept) of Grounding picks out a single generic relation of Grounding. In this case, 'Grounding' may be taken as a rigid designator of that single generic relation. Alternatively, one might think that the concept of Grounding is generic only in the weaker sense that although it non-rigidly picks out different relations on different occasions, those relations have certain commonalities that make them fall under the generic concept. When discussing the features of Grounding in the next paragraph, I use the singular form for ease of exposition, but most of what I say can also be applied to the weaker variant according to which different relations are picked out by the generic concept that all share those formal features. Nevertheless, we should keep in mind that this is not what most advocates of Grounding want to claim. They want to establish that there is a generic Grounding relation.

What exactly are the formal features of Grounding? If there is an orthodox view about the formal features of Grounding at all, it is the view that the notion picks out an *asymmetric* and *irreflexive* relation. Furthermore, the Grounding relation is typically thought to be *transitive*, so that if A Grounds B and B Grounds C, then A Grounds C (Schaffer 2009: 376; Fine 2010: 100). Transitivity and irreflexivity together entail that Grounding is a *strict partial ordering* relation. Furthermore, Grounding is often thought of as a *non-monotonous* relation: it is not the case that if A is Grounded in B, then A is Grounded in B conjoined with C as well.[129] The idea behind this is that it conflicts with our pre-theoretic intu-

---

[129] This is not to say that there cannot be any such cases. The typical case put forward by

itions about dependence if we allow that one can add arbitrary irrelevant stuff to the base (Raven 2013). For example, it seems odd to say that if *being red* depends on *being crimson*, it also depends on *being crimson* conjoined with *being square*. A final claim about Grounding is that it is *factive* (e.g. Schaffer 2016: 149; see also Fine 2012: 48–50). In the case of facts, this means that the Grounding relation requires its relata to exist. In the case of properties, the analogue idea is that Grounding requires its relata to be instantiated in the world under consideration.

There is broad agreement among friends of Grounding with regard to the claim that Grounding is not a purely modal notion. After all, the main reason to think that there is a distinctive relation of Grounding is that purely modal relations like supervenience and necessitation are too coarse-grained to distinguish between cases of nothing-over-and-above-ness and something-over-and-above-ness. Still, most authors think that Grounding has certain modal consequences. A number of authors think that Grounding entails necessitation or some form of supervenience of the Grounded entities by or on their Grounds (e.g. Rosen 2010: 118; Fine 2012: 38; see also Correia and Schnieder 2012: 20–22). In order to be a candidate for playing the role of the metaphysical dependence relation that figures in our definition of physicalism, Grounding indeed needs to have certain modal consequences, although as we have seen, it is strictly speaking not required that the metaphysically dependent (Grounded?) entities supervene on their particular dependence base (Grounds?) alone.

A further typical claim of proponents of Grounding is that Grounding is *explanatory*. Fine (2001: 15) puts it in the following way:

> We take *ground* to be an explanatory relation: if the truth that P is grounded in other truths, then they *account* for its truth; P's being the case holds *in virtue of* the other truths' being the case. There are, of course, many other explanatory connections among truths. But the relation of ground is distinguished from them by being the tightest such connection.

Let me translate this notion of explanation to our case, where the dependence relation in question is supposed to hold between property types. The relevant idea here is that the dependence relation between A and B, where A depends on B, is explanatory just in case, at least in some cases of the instantiation of A,[130] A is instantiated *because* B is instantiated, or A is instantiated *in virtue*

---

friends of fact-based Grounding is the case of a disjunctive fact. Given that both disjunct facts exist, even though the disjunctive fact *that p or q* is Grounded in the fact *that p* alone, it is also Grounded in the fact *that q*, and thus Grounded in the pair of facts, taken jointly. This is roughly analogous to cases of overdetermination in the case of causation.

130 Again, this is required to account for 'multiple Groundability'.

of B being instantiated. This indeed is a requirement the metaphysical dependence relation referred to in the thesis of physicalism must satisfy. However, it is a notion of being explanatory that diverges from certain uses of the term 'explanation' we are used to from other contexts. It is a notion that is purely metaphysical. What is explained, and what allegedly does the explaining, is something in the world. Moreover, at least at the face of it, given the way Fine introduces his claim that Grounding is explanatory, this sense of explanation has little to do with epistemic notions we often associate the term 'explanation' with, and which would require that Grounding claims need to be illuminating.

In general, the formal and modal features of the orthodox account of Grounding fit the desired profile for metaphysical dependence required for physicalism. However, for virtually every one of the features the orthodox view ascribes to Grounding there is some author who casts doubt on whether it can be ascribed to the Grounding relation. We have already discussed some of the worries regarding the irreflexivity and asymmetry of Grounding put forth by Jenkins (2011) and Bliss (2014) in section 4.4.2. Schaffer (2012) argues that there are cases of Grounding that tell against transitivity.[131] We will get back to these issues in section 5.3.4 below. Leuenberger (2014a, b) and Skiles (2015) argue against the claim that Grounding entails supervenience or necessitation.[132] Finally, a number of authors challenge the claim that Grounding is explanatory, but mostly in the sense of being illuminating (e.g. Wilson 2014; 2018).

Several authors express skepticism about the prospects of a Grounding-based account of physicalism. On the basis of her general skepticism about the usefulness of the notion of Grounding[133] and the existence of the corresponding relation (Wilson 2014; 2016), Jessica Wilson (2018) expresses her concerns regarding a Grounding-based account of physicalism. Andrew Melnyk (2016) likewise thinks that the prospects for a Grounding-based account of physicalism are

---

131 For replies to Schaffer's examples from defenders of the orthodox view, see Raven (2013) and Litland (2013), which I find quite plausible.

132 Leuenberger does not claim that Grounding and supervenience are completely unrelated. On his view, Grounding entails a form of supervenience, but the relata of the Grounding relation and the supervenience relation are not the same, and the supervenience is restricted to worlds similar to the world under consideration. This is roughly in line with what I said earlier about metaphysical dependence and supervenience (see section 4.2.3).

133 There are other authors skeptical about Grounding, but there is an important difference between authors like Thomas Hofweber (2009), who strictly reject any 'esoteric' (Hofweber's term) metaphysical framework that builds upon primitive metaphysical notions that cannot be spelled out in ordinary language terms, and Jessica Wilson (2014; 2016; 2018), who are sympathetic to primitive metaphysical notions in general but reject the particular notion of Grounding. I here restrict my attention to the latter kind of concerns.

dim, although he understands the notion of Grounding a bit differently to how Wilson does. In the following, I will have a closer look at these concerns.

5.2 Grounding and the zoo of 'small-g' grounding relations

The rhetoric of some of the friends of Grounding suggests that the idea of nothing-over-and-above-ness, or metaphysical dependence, has not been part of the agenda of philosophers until recently, and that no alternatives to a primitive notion of Grounding are available. So it might seem that the view of at least some advocates of Grounding is that Grounding is the only game in town. In the following, I will assess this reading and briefly discuss potential alternative relations of metaphysical dependence.

5.2.1 Is Grounding the only game in town?

Let me start with a number of claims put forward by advocates of Grounding that might be taken to suggest that there are no alternatives to Grounding available. For example, Schaffer says (2009: 347):

> On the now dominant Quinean view, metaphysics is about what there is. Metaphysics so conceived is concerned with such questions as whether properties exist, whether meanings exist, and whether numbers exist. I will argue for the revival of a more traditional Aristotelian view, on which metaphysics is about what grounds what. Metaphysics so revived does not bother asking whether properties, meanings, and numbers exist. Of course they do! The question is whether or not they are *fundamental*.

Similarly, Correia and Schnieder claim that "in fact, it may seem as if the current debate [about Grounding] took up where Bolzano left the issue more than 150 years ago" (2012: 9), and "a serious interest in grounding only arose again at the beginning of the twenty-first century" (2012: 10). Like Schaffer, they associate the alleged disinterest in (non-modal accounts of) metaphysical dependence in the influence of Carnap and Quine, as well as in sustained attempts to spell out metaphysical notions in purely modal terms.

Finally, Fine introduces his "Guide to Ground" with the following claim (2012: 37):

> A number of philosophers have recently become receptive to the idea that, in addition to scientific or causal explanation, there may be a distinctive kind of metaphysical explana-

tion, in which explanans and explanandum are connected, not through some sort of causal mechanism, but through some constitutive form of determination.

Wilson, in her "No Work for a Theory of Grounding", forcefully opposes claims that suggest that until recently, little attention has been paid to the idea of metaphysical dependence (2014: 539):

> Attention to metaphysical dependence is not new: many, perhaps most, contemporary metaphysicians have spent their careers investigating forms of such dependence, typically assumed to go beyond merely modal or causal notions, in service of developing or assessing comprehensive theses such as physicalism (with the status of mentality being a special focus), or of developing or assessing accounts of some phenomena [...] in terms of some others presumed (as a working, speculative, or antagonistic hypothesis) to be more fundamental.

She further argues that there is a plethora of non-primitive metaphysical dependence relations in the metaphysician's toolkit that have been used in different attempts to account for nothing-over-and-above-ness with regard to physicalism (2018: 496; see also 2014: 539):

> Over the past several decades, philosophers working on physicalism have identified and explored numerous non-primitive accounts of metaphysical dependence – call these 'small-g' grounding relations, to distinguish them from the 'big-G' primitive – explicitly assumed to go beyond merely modal, representational, or epistemic notions. These accounts fill in the schematic reference to 'nothing-over-and-aboveness' (or other rough-and-ready idioms of dependence) with specific familiar metaphysical relations, including type and token identity, functional realization, the determinable-determinate relation, the composition relation, the part-whole relation, the proper-subset-of-powers relation, and so on, which serve, against the backdrop of the specified lower-level physical base, to characterize diverse forms of metaphysical dependence in an explanatory and illuminating way.

Nevertheless, she concedes that "the suggestion that there is a distinctive relation or relations [sic] of Grounding is new" (2014: 539), in the sense that advocates of metaphysical dependence who restrict themselves to what Wilson calls 'small-g' grounding relations do not postulate the existence of a generic relation of Grounding that is supposed to capture virtually all cases in which one entity metaphysically depends on another.

So far, even though I do not agree with Wilson with regard to which relations count as metaphysical dependence relations, I do agree to the broad picture she sketches.[134] In the past few decades, and certainly before the notion of Ground-

---

134 As already pointed out earlier (see section 4.4.2), I do not agree to her with regard to the

ing (re)appeared on the philosophical landscape, authors have indeed attempted to provide accounts of physicalism that appeal to a variety of relations that are not purely modal. Since contemporary physicalism requires the metaphysical dependence of properties on other properties, rather than just the metaphysical dependence of particulars on other particulars, in the following, I restrict myself to discussing some of those relations that can be considered to have properties as relata, and leave aside other notions that may belong to a broader family of metaphysical dependence relations, like the part-whole relation understood as a relation between particulars. The relations I discuss are not thought to exhaust the options. Rather, the idea is that there is a variety of different relations that have the relevant features, some of which we may not even know yet.

5.2.2 The higher-order property realization relation

Many authors have claimed that non-physical properties are 'realized', or 'multiply realized', by physical properties. However, there are almost as many different accounts of realization as there are authors addressing the question what realization consists in. Umut Baysan thus suggests that it is hard to believe that realization talk is unitary (2015: 248):

> [T]he term "realization" has become an umbrella term to refer to some dependence relation between higher-level properties or states [...] and lower-level properties or states in the following sense: the instantiation of a higher-level property or a state depends on, and is necessitated by, the instantiation of its lower-level realizer (or realizers). Due to the heterogeneous use of the term "realization", it would be highly ambitious to assume that there can be at most one relation, namely the realization relation, that this term is supposed to denote in each and every case, unless one simply means "dependence" by "realization". Rather, it should be acknowledged that there could be several relations that the term "realization" denotes in different cases.

---

relations that should be considered members of the set of 'small-g' grounding relations. Even though I agree that type and token identity sometimes underlie claims of 'nothing-over-and-above-ness', on my view, they are not metaphysical dependence relations because they fail to be irreflexive and asymmetric. Moreover, since I focus only on metaphysical dependence relations among property types, the part-whole relation and the composition relation, at least if they are taken to be relations between individuals (or pluralities thereof), do not belong to the family of relations I have in mind either. The latter relations, unlike identity relations, might however very well belong to a broader family of metaphysical dependence relations among multiple kinds of relata.

5.2 Grounding and the zoo of 'small-g' grounding relations

To see how different accounts of realization look like, I address two accounts of realization that have received significant attention in the literature. In this section, I focus on the so-called 'higher-order property' account of realization. In the next section, I will discuss an alternative account of realization based on causal powers.

Melnyk (2003; 2006; 2018) has developed the most elaborate account of higher-order property realization to date. Here, I discuss the version he proposes in his book "A Physicalist Manifesto". In a more recent paper (2018), he defends a version of his view that spells out the notion of a functional property in somewhat different terms, but I will set this version aside for the moment and get back to it later (see section 5.4.2 below).[135] In his 2003 book, Melnyk explicates his notion of realization as follows (2003: 21):

> Token *x realizes* token *y* iff (i) *y* is a token of some functional type, F, such that, necessarily, F is tokened iff there is a token of some or other type that meets condition, [sic] C; (ii) *x* is a token of some type that in fact meets C; and (iii) the token of F whose existence is logically guaranteed by the holding of condition (ii) is numerically identical with *y*.

Clause (i) of Melnyk's account links the realized token to a higher-order functional type that is instantiated whenever there is an instance of some other lower-order type that satisfies the condition associated with the functional type, (ii) links the realizer token to a lower-order type that satisfies the associated condition, and (iii) is supposed to make sure that it is *that* very token of the functional type that is instantiated in virtue of the instantiation of *that* very token of the lower-order type.

Importantly, Melnyk understands realization as a token-token relation. He admits that a related notion of "type-type realization [...] could easily be characterized" (Melnyk 2006: 152 [fn1]), but unfortunately does not provide us with a definition. I assume that a Melnyk-style notion of type-type realization would look roughly as follows:

> Type *B* (type-type) realizes type *A iff* (i) *A* is a functional type such that, necessarily, *A* is tokened *iff* there is a token of some or other type that meets condition *C*; (ii) *B* is a type that in fact meets *C*; and (iii) some tokens of *B* realize tokens of *A*.

---

135 To prefigure: Melynk there spells out the notion of a functional property in terms of the notion of a *higher-order essence*, so that "for a token of *M* to exist just is for there to exist a token of some or other (lower-order) state-type such that tokens of that (lower-order) state-type play role R_M, the role distinctive of *M*" (2018: 483–484). I will get back to this account later.

It might seem that we can omit (i) and (ii) because they are already implicitly included in (iii). However, if one token can be a token of multiple numerically distinct types, clauses (i) and (ii) of his definition of token-realization do not ensure that $F = A$ and $G = B$. Furthermore, it is important to note that there is an identity claim in clause (i) that is easily overlooked: A is identical to some functional type, and this identity may be only recognizable *a posteriori* if the concepts we typically use to pick out A are not *a priori* associated with functional concepts that, in case the type identity holds, also pick out A. The claim that a mental property is realized by a physical property, for example, might thus still be knowable only *a posteriori* if we use a phenomenal concept, rather than a functional concept, to pick out the mental property.

Melnyk understands the notion of a functional property type in the following way (2003: 21):

> A *functional property*, P, is a property such that, necessarily, there is an instance of P iff there is a token of some type or other (e.g., an instance of some property or other) that meets condition C.

Being a functional property is *being a higher-order property*, that is, the property of *having one or other (lower-order) property that meets a certain condition* (cf. 2003: 20). This is basically what clause (i) of the definition of realization above says about functional properties. Unless we specify in more detail what kinds of conditions are at issue, this is certainly a very liberal, and arguably too liberal, account of a functional property. Other accounts of functional properties make further assumptions about the kind of condition that needs to be met that are more closely tied to one or the other intuitive understanding of the term 'function'. Typically, the idea is that the condition is to satisfy a particular *causal role* (which again might be understood in several ways), but there are various alternative ways to spell out the notion of a function. Melnyk mentions a few options he takes his account to capture: "meeting a condition could indeed be playing a causal role, but could also be, e. g., standing in a certain spatio-temporal relation to something, or exhibiting a certain internal structure, or having a certain history, or having a certain bio-function" (2018: 484). Likewise, Tom Polger points out that "[t]here is a cornucopia of notions of function in the offing these days. [...] A function may be understood as abstract or mathematical, in any of several causal variations, teleologically, and so forth" (2004: 74). Each of these notions of function can be used to generate a different understanding of higher-order property realization.

Melnyk further defines a notion of *physical* realization that draws on the just defined notion of (token-token) realization (2003: 23):

5.2 Grounding and the zoo of 'small-g' grounding relations — 175

> A token x of a functional type, F, is *physically realized* iff (i) x is realized by a token of some physical type, T, *and* (ii) T meets the associated condition for F solely as a logical consequence of the distribution in the world of physical tokens and the holding of physical laws.

According to Melnyk, it does not suffice for non-physical property tokens to be *realized* by physical property tokens. Rather, non-physical property tokens need to be *physically realized* by physical property tokens. The introduction of clause (ii) is supposed to rule out cases where T meets the condition that is associated with the functional type F in some miraculous way. Melnyk considers the case where T's meeting the conditions associated with F "requires the presence in Australia of five angels" (2003: 23). Note also that Melnyk's talk of 'logical consequence' suggests that the proposition that expresses the distribution in the world of physical tokens and the physical laws that obtain *a priori* entails the proposition that T meets condition C that is associated with the functional property type F.

Since clause (ii) is a further condition on the *types* the realizer and realized tokens are tokens of, we can simply add this clause to our above definition of type-type realization to get a Melnyk-style account of type-type physical realization as well:

> Type B (type-type) physically realizes type A *iff* (i) A is a functional type such that, necessarily, A is tokened *iff* there is a token of some or other type that meets condition C; (ii) B is a type that in fact meets C; (iii) some tokens of B realize tokens of A; and (iv) T meets the associated condition for F solely as a logical consequence of the distribution in the world of physical tokens and the holding of physical laws.

Can such an account of realization be the metaphysical dependence relation we have been looking for? Let me say this much: If we pick a particular understanding of a functional property by focusing on one particular kind of condition to be met, then realization so construed is plausibly sufficient, but not necessary for the physicalist's needs, because not all properties will be plausibly identifiable with functional properties understood in the particular way. Even if all non-physical properties instantiated in our world would be functional properties in this sense, would physicalism be false in a world in which the relevant instantiated properties are identical with functional properties understood in one of the other ways? I think not. Thus, we need something broader to capture the notion of metaphysical dependence required for physicalism.

If the notion of a functional property is framed more broadly, as Melnyk intends, it might be better suited to do the job, but it then more closely resembles an account of metaphysical dependence for which it is not clear whether it still captures what most philosophers associate with the terms 'realization' and 'functional property'. In this case, it might be better to express the account using other terms. This holds especially for the alternative way of framing physical realization Melnyk considers in his more recent work (2018), which is closer to a reasonably general notion of metaphysical dependence (see section 5.4.2 below).

5.2.3 The powers-based realization relation

A second notion of realization has been put forward most prominently by Jessica Wilson (1999) and Sydney Shoemaker (2001; 2007), and is closely associated with, but does not strictly speaking presuppose, Shoemaker's (1980) powers-based account of properties we have already considered earlier (see section 4.4.4). Likewise to the powers-based account of properties, both the realized properties and the realizer properties need to have certain causal features, or bestow their bearers with certain causal powers, but as Shoemaker points out, the account of realization does neither require that these features are part of the essence of those properties (they might have them contingently, given the laws), nor does it require that the causal features exhaust the essence of the properties in question (see Shoemaker 2001: 77–78).

Shoemaker (2001: 78) introduces the realization relation as follows:

> [P]roperty X realizes property Y just in case the conditional powers bestowed by Y are a subset of the conditional powers bestowed by X (and X is not a conjunctive property having Y as a conjunct).

Alternatively, he likes to express things as follows (2001: 79):[136]

---

[136] In his later book "Physical Realization", Shoemaker also includes as an additional requirement that the backward-looking causal features of X are a subset of those of property Y (2007: 12). Here, the order of X and Y in the set-subset relation is reversed. The idea here is that the set of possible causes of the realized properties is larger than the set of possible causes of the realizer, because it needs to capture the possible causes of different realizer properties given that it is multiply realized. Shoemaker includes the further clause to deal with problems that arise from the allegedly possible case of properties that share all their forward-looking causal powers but are distinct with regard to backward-looking causal powers. But by the time the paperback version of his book is published (2009), he already returns to his old account (see the paperback edition of his 2007: 12 [fn5] and his 2011: 17–18 [fn2]) due to objections raised by McLaughlin (2007b).

[P]roperty X realizes property Y just in case the forward-looking causal features of Y are a subset (a proper subset in cases of multiple realization) of those of property X.

The 'forward-looking causal features' of a property are what Shoemaker calls 'conditional causal powers' in his first definition, which he understands as powers an entity would have if it had certain other properties (2001: 77):[137]

> Any property whose instantiation can be a cause or partial cause of something will be such that its instantiation bestows on its subject a set of what I call "conditional powers." A thing's having a power *simpliciter* is a matter of its being such that its being in certain circumstances, for example, its being related in certain ways to other things of certain sorts, causes (or contributes to causing) certain effects. A thing has a *conditional* power if it is such that if it had certain properties it would have a certain power simpliciter, where those properties are not themselves sufficient to bestow that power simpliciter. So, for example, the property of being knife-shaped bestows on its possessor the conditional power of being able to cut wood if it is made of steel, and the conditional power of being able to cut butter if it is made of wood.

One thing to note is that Shoemaker's definition allows for self-realization. Since it is not required that the subset of powers is a proper subset, it might be that $X = Y$. Strictly speaking, Shoemaker's relation of realization is thus not a metaphysical dependence relation since it is not asymmetric and irreflexive. But we could of course add the requirement that X and Y are not identical, which would avoid the self-realization concern.[138]

Just like Melnyk, Shoemaker allows for both token-token and type-type realization. However, for Shoemaker, token-token realization is the derivative notion, which he defines as follows (2007: 12):

> [A]n instantiation of P is realized by an instantiation of property Q just in case P and Q are instantiated in the same thing and Q is a realizer of P.

---

137 I take it that the counterfactual formulation does not rule out that the entity does in fact have the properties in question that form the conditions for having the power.

138 Even if type identity of realized and realizer property are ruled out, it is still allowed that the token instances of realized and realizer property are identical. Another issue with Shoemaker's formulation is that any property that does not have any causal powers will be realized by any property that has such powers. After all, the empty set is a subset of any set whatsoever. So what Shoemaker probably has in mind is that the sets of powers must not be empty. On his powers-based view of properties, there can be no property that does not have any powers, so the problem does not arise if set-subset-realization is combined with the powers-based view of properties (also see McLaughlin 2009: §3).

At least if combined with Shoemaker's powers-based account of properties, it is easy to see that such a view of realization is appropriate to capture that the realized properties are nothing over and above their realizers. If all there is to a property is that its instantiation bestows its bearer with a set of causal powers, and if the causal powers of the realized properties are a subset of the causal powers of their realizers, then it is clear why it is that the realized property is instantiated whenever the realizer property is instantiated. Furthermore, the co-instantiation is no accident: given the set-subset relation, it is clear that the realized property is instantiated *because* the realizer property is instantiated. Such an account also allows for multiple realizability. As long as the causal powers of the different realizers only differ with regard to individual powers that do not belong to the subset that comprises of the powers of the realized property, the instantiation of any of the realizer properties suffices for the instantiation of the realized property.

Without the powers-based account of properties, I have some further concerns regarding the question whether set-subset-realization accounts for nothing-over-and-above-ness. Suppose that properties have powers as part of their essence, but there is more to the essence of these properties than the powers. In addition to the powers, properties might have quiddistic features. Further suppose that there can be distinct properties that share the set of associated powers, but differ in whatever it is that is added to the powers to exhaust their nature. Now, suppose A and B are such properties. It seems that in this case, A and B realize each other, which shows that the realization relation is not asymmetric, and thus no metaphysical dependence relation. Even worse, the part of the nature of A and B that comes in addition to the powers intuitively seems to make A something over and above B, and *vice versa*.

Now suppose that we restrict the realization relation to proper subsets to avoid the mutual realization of A and B. In this case, we can add two further properties C and D that share all the powers of A and B, and have some extra powers in addition. We can even assume that C and D also share all their powers with each other. Now suppose that in the world at hand, whenever C is instantiated, A is instantiated, and whenever D is instantiated, B is instantiated, which has something to do with those parts of the natures of the properties that are added to the powers. Now, C and D each realize both A and B, according to the definition, but it seems that B is something over and above C, and A is something over and above D.

In order to secure that set-subset-realization entails nothing-over-and-aboveness, does it help to deny that two properties can have the same powers? I think not. After all, in a simplified case where we have just two properties, where the one has a subset of the powers of the other, but there is something more to their

5.2 Grounding and the zoo of 'small-g' grounding relations — 179

nature than the powers they bestow on their bearers, it is not even guaranteed that the realized property is instantiated whenever the realizer is instantiated (given the physical laws and perhaps other background conditions), unless their additional features are appropriately related. Thus, since set-subset realization focuses only on powers, it is at least possible that the one is something over and above the other.

Melnyk (2006: 142–143) raises some related concerns. He argues that a version of set-subset realization that tries to save the necessitation of the realized property by its realizers without identifying an individual's having the property with its having a certain cluster of causal powers does not meet the requirements of physicalism. According to him, physicalism requires the guarantee that an individual's having a non-physical property is wholly constituted by its having physical properties, and that the proposition that the individual has the non-physical property is made true by the fact that the individual has certain physical properties.

Wilson (2015: 359) answers that "Melnyk's claims are incorrect: truths about physical constitution or truthmaking, being broadly scientific truths, are neutral as regards whatever non-causal aspects of features there might be; hence the grounds of such truths must also be neutral on whether properties have non-causal aspects". She further elaborates on this claim, and argues that whether or not a property S set-subset-realized by a physical property P has non-causal aspects is irrelevant for conformity of S to physicalism[139] (2015: 360):

> The general pattern, blocking any route to S's physical unacceptability, is as follows: if P is physically acceptable, and every token power of S, on an occasion, is identical with a token power of P, on that occasion, then any causal aspects of S are guaranteed to be physically acceptable; non-causal aspects of S are irrelevant to S's physical acceptability; hence a realization relation satisfying the proper subset condition on powers guarantees S's physical acceptability, in conformity to Physicalism, independent of what account of properties one endorses.

---

[139] Physicalism as construed by Wilson is the claim that "[a]ll broadly scientific goings-on are nothing over and above lower-level physical goings-on" (2016: 1). In her (2010b: 280 [fn1]), she says a little bit more about her notion of a broadly scientific entity: "broadly scientific entities are entities that are among the subject matters of any of the sciences, from fundamental physics up through linguistics, psychology, and beyond. Note that structured or unstructured collections or systems of entities are also entities in this broad sense." I guess she adds the last sentence to include properties like *being a table* as broadly scientific even though not strictly speaking the subject matter of any of the sciences. Still, if non-causal features are irrelevant to physical acceptability given her account of the broadly physical, her understanding of physicalism is too narrow.

Pace Wilson, I think that non-causal features or aspects of properties are relevant for conformity with physicalism. If a non-physical property has non-causal features that go beyond those that physical properties share, it is hard to see how this has no impact on physicalism. The nature of phenomenal properties seems to be the prototypical problem case. Wilson is aware of such a worry, but tries to get around it (2015: 360 [fn15]):

> It is also worth noting that in assuming that only powers are relevant to investigations into the physical acceptability of features, there is no danger of 'leaving out' what is relevant to, e. g., qualitative mental experience; for qualitative and other aspects of mentality do have causal implications (e. g., to produce awareness of qualitative aspects in experiencing subjects), as per the rejection of epiphenomenalism.

Wilson's attempt to account for the problem presupposes the falsity (or even impossibility) of epiphenomenalism. I take it that epiphenomenalism is in principle compatible with both physicalism and dualism, and must not be presupposed to be false (or even impossible) in framing metaphysical dependence. Of course, physicalists hardly ever accept epiphenomenalism, but this is not due to their commitment to physicalism as such.

Given these considerations, it remains safe to say that a set-subset-account of realization, combined with the powers-based view of properties, has the required features to be sufficient for nothing-over-and-above-ness, at least once we add the further clause that realized type and realizer type are not identical in order to ensure irreflexivity. However, since we do not want to say that to be a physicalist, one needs to buy into such a controversial account, it is too much of a commitment for a necessary condition on a minimal account of physicalism.

5.2.4 The determinable-determinate relation

The last metaphysical dependence relation I want to consider is what is typically called the determinable-determinate relation. I have already used a prototypical case of properties that are so related all along: the properties *being red* and *being crimson*. The latter is a determinate of the former, and the former is a determinable of the latter. Other typical pairs of properties so related include the property of *having a shape* and the property of *being spherical*, as well as the property of *having mass* and the property of *having a mass of 10 kg*.

Of course, determinable properties are not determinable *simpliciter*, but only relative to some other property, and a property that is a determinable relative to one property can be a determinate relative to some other property. Both our prototype properties are determinates relative to the property of *being a color*, for

5.2 Grounding and the zoo of 'small-g' grounding relations — 181

example, so that *being red* is a determinable relative to *being crimson* and a determinate relative to *being a color*. However, arguably, not every property that is a determinate relative to some property is a determinable relative to some other property. Some properties seem to be maximally specific. For example, at least *prima facie*, it seems that the property of *having a mass of (exactly) 10 kg* cannot be specified any further.[140]

Stephen Yablo (1992: 250–253) points out that the determinable-determinate relation in a way resembles the identity relation. The identity relation can be understood as follows (1992: 251):

> P is identical to Q iff: for a thing to be P is for it to be Q[.]

Analogously, the determinable-determinate relation, expressed by the two-place predicate '... determines ...', where the first slot is filled with the determinate and the second with the determinable, can be understood as follows (1992: 252):

> P determines Q iff: for a thing to be P is for it to be Q, not *simpliciter*, but in a specific way.

Unlike identity, the determinable-determinate relation is not a symmetric relation. Nevertheless, the properties so related are tightly connected. In both cases, this tight connection brings in certain modal commitments. In the case of identity, the modal link is obviously the following (1992: 251):

> P = Q only if: necessarily, for all x, x has P iff x has Q.

This is basically the individual necessitation principle that we know from the previous chapter taken to hold both ways. Note that the modal requirement is only a necessary, but not a sufficient condition for property identity. If it were sufficient as well, then all properties that are necessarily instantiated by anything whatsoever would be one and the same, for example – a result that we certainly do not want (cf. 1992: 251 [fn17]).

The modal link that comes with the determinable-determinate relation is less strong (1992: 252):

---

[140] I say '*prima facie*' because some might want to argue that there are different ways in which something can have a mass of exactly 10 kg, e.g. by having parts that have different distributions of masses. But I will not pursue this any further.

P determines *Q* [...] only if:
(i) necessarily, for all *x*, if *x* has *P* then *x* has *Q*; and
(ii) possibly, for some *x*, *x* has *Q* but lacks *P*.

The modal connection between determinable and determinate is strictly asymmetric. *P* individually necessitates *Q*, but *Q* does not individually necessitate *P*. Note that this is different from the modal commitments that come with supervenience. Supervenience is neither symmetric nor asymmetric, whereas this relation is strictly asymmetric, and thus incompatible with identity and other symmetric relations. Furthermore, the determinable-determinate relation is transitive. This makes the relation a strict partial ordering relation.

While the asymmetry of the determinable-determinate relation so construed might *prima facie* seem to indicate that it might be a good candidate for being the required notion of metaphysical dependence appropriate for framing physicalism, we need to be careful. While the metaphysical dependence relation in question indeed needs to be asymmetric, this asymmetry arguably should not show in the modal requirements. We do not in general want to rule out cases where necessitation goes both ways, but one property is instantiated in virtue of, or because of, the instantiation of another, as cases in which metaphysical dependence holds (cf. section 4.4.3).

As with identity, the modal criteria only serve as a necessary, but not as a sufficient condition for the determinable-determinate relation to hold. Here is one reason why. Consider the case of conjunctive properties like *being red and square*, and its conjuncts *being red* and *being square*. If the modal requirements stated in clauses (i) and (ii) were sufficient for *P* to determine *Q*, then the conjunctive property would determine its conjunct properties. After all, in accordance with (i), necessarily, if something has the property of *being red and square*, it has the properties of *being red* and *being square*, and in accordance with (ii), there are some things that have the property of *being red* (or alternatively: *being square*) but lack the property of *being red and square*. But this is an unwanted result. After all, most philosophers (including me) would not want to say that something is red because it is red and square, or that it is red in virtue of being red and square. Note that there is a sense in which *being red* is nothing over and above *being red and square*, but this is not the relevant sense, because the notion of nothing-over-and-above-ness relevant for metaphysical dependence must be in line with the corresponding 'in virtue of' and 'because'-claims. What we rather want to say with regard to conjunctive properties is arguably that they are nothing over and above their disjuncts, taken together, although this is also not a case in which a determinable-determinate relation holds between the conjunctive property and its conjuncts. Something has the property of *being red and square* because it has the properties of *being red* and *being square*. Accordingly, it makes sense to say that *being red and square* is nothing over and above *being red* and *being square*, taken jointly. Still, it does not make sense to say that *being red* and *being square* (taken jointly) is *being red and square*, not simpliciter, but in a specific way.[141]

A further potential feature of the determinable-determinate relation is that different determinate properties of a determinable property which do not themselves stand in a determinable-determinate relation cannot be simultaneously instantiated by the same individual. For example, *being crimson* and *being scarlet* are two determinate properties of the determinable property *being red*, but nothing can be both crimson and scarlet at the same time. Some have argued that this does not hold in all cases, however. Armstrong (1997: 48–49) considers the case of tastes. A sauce may be sweet and sour at the same time, even though *being sweet* and *being sour* are determinates of the determinable *being a taste*. Likewise, Wilson (2013: 367–368; see also her 2017: section 2.1) considers the case of an iridescent feather, which shifts in color from red to blue as a function of the perspective of the viewer. This might be interpreted as a case in which the feather is red and blue at the same time, even though both are determinables of the property *being colored* and neither a determinate of the other. Finally, Johansson (2000: 117) argues that if *being a property* is a determinable relative to, say, *being a color* and *being a shape*, then we have another counterexample against the general applicability of the feature at hand. These alleged counterexamples may be disputed, however. In Armstrong's case, for example, one might deny that the sauce is sweet and sour, and claim that there is a third kind of taste, sweet-sour, that is distinct from sweet and sour, which the sauce has. Moreover, with regard to Johansson's case, one might simply deny that we should go as far as taking *being a property* to be a determinable of other properties. Be this as it may, if the feature holds in general, there is additional reason to think that the determinable-determinate relation is too restrictive to do the job of the metaphysical dependence relation required for physicalism. After all, we do not want to rule out cases of metaphysical dependence where two alternative base properties are accidentally jointly instantiated.

Several authors have tried to closely link the relation of determinables and determinates to accounts of realization. Yablo (1992) tries to argue that mental properties are determinables of physical properties that are the former's determi-

---

141 This is already a stretch since the determinable-determinate relation takes single properties as relata. But even if we would allow that a plurality of properties can serve as a determinable of some other property, the example would still not make sense.

nates in order to make a case for the claim that mental properties and the corresponding physical properties are not causal rivals – a feature typically associated with determinables and determinates. The idea is that since having a determinate property is just a specific way of having a determinable property, there is no causal rivalry between such properties (1992: 259; Wilson 1999: 47–48). Since Yablo also associates the link between mental and physical properties with the notion of multiple realizability, on his view, the realization relation turns out to be a species of the determinable-determinate relation (1992: 256). Wilson (1999; 2009), Clapp (2001) and Shoemaker (2001; 2007) associate determination with the set-subset account of realization, and try to account for the nothing-over-and-above-ness[142] of mental properties in terms of such a set-subset realization-based account. Other authors, like Ehring (1996), Funkhouser (2006), and Walter (2006), are skeptical with regard to taking physical properties to be determinates of mental properties. I do not want to engage in this debate. For my purposes, it suffices to say that the failure of mental properties to be determinable properties relative to physical properties does not seem to be sufficient to deny that the former metaphysically depend on, or are nothing over and above (but not identical to), the latter. Thus, the determinable-determinate relation, although sufficient for nothing-over-and-above-ness, is not necessary for it.

5.3 No work for Grounding?

Given all these notions of metaphysical dependence, the motivation for introducing a primitive notion of Grounding cannot be that no other notions of metaphysical dependence have been proposed, so that a primitive notion of Grounding is the only option available. The same holds even more for the claim that this primitive notion picks out a generic Grounding *relation* that exists in addition to the other relations picked out be the more fine-grained notions. Thus, we need a different motivation for introducing Grounding. In the following, I address several moves a friend of Grounding could make to substantiate the claim that appeal to Grounding does enough work to add it to the metaphysician's toolbox, either instead of or alongside the more fine-grained notions.

---

[142] Their main aim is actually to secure the causal relevance of mental properties in the face of the causal exclusion problem (e.g. Kim 1998; Kim 2005). But since they also want to say that set-subset realized properties are nothing over and above their realizers, the two issues go hand in hand.

5.3.1 Grounding as a replacement for 'small-g' grounding relations

Some might think that we can appeal to Grounding *instead* of appealing to the 'small-g' grounding relations, thus taking Grounding as a *replacement* for the 'small-g' relations. Against such considerations, Wilson suggests that Grounding is not sufficiently fine-grained to account for metaphysical dependence on its own (2014: 542):

> Grounding, like supervenience, is too coarse-grained to characterize appropriately metaphysical dependence on its own – indeed, admits of such underdetermination that even basic assessment of claims of metaphysical dependence, or associated views, cannot proceed by reference to Grounding alone. Doing the job requires appeal to the 'small-g' grounding relations that have been traditionally appealed to in investigations into metaphysical dependence – but then [...] we do not need Grounding.

Again, there is something right about Wilson's concern, even though I do not agree to the conclusion she draws from it. The comparison to supervenience is illuminating. As we have seen earlier (section 4.4.5), supervenience relations are typically not brute. When we find that a supervenience relation holds between certain sets of properties, this is due to the fact that there is a further relation sitting in the background that accounts for the modal link that comes with the supervenience relation. In the case of Grounding, we might similarly ask what accounts for the fact that in a particular case in which some property is Grounded in some other properties, the Grounded property is instantiated in virtue of some other properties being instantiated. An illuminating answer to such question involves making reference to one or other 'small-g' grounding relation. Consider the following potential conversation between two fictitious philosophers:

Ted: The property of *being red* supervenes on the set of all possible shades of red.

Amy: I see, but why is it that this supervenience relation holds?

Ted: Well, that is because the property of *being red* is Grounded in each of the possible shades of red. Whenever the property of *being red* is instantiated, this is *because* one of the possible shades of red is instantiated. In other words, in each particular case, *being red* is instantiated *in virtue of* one of the shades, like *being crimson* or *being scarlet*, being instantiated.

Amy: So there is a metaphysical dependency between these properties. But why is it that *being red* is instantiated *in virtue of* any one of the shades being instantiated? Why is it that the Grounding relation holds?

> *Ted:* I do not understand what you are asking for. I already told you that *being red* is Grounded in each of its possible shades. What else is there to say?

This seems to be somewhat unsatisfying.[143] Wilson puts the point in the following way (2014: 549):

> [I]nvestigations into metaphysical dependence, conducted without any reference to specific metaphysical details, *cannot be carried out*. Consider the perversely uninterested metaphysician who aims only to determine which entities are metaphysically dependent, and which are not. Such a metaphysician will find themselves hopelessly stymied, for given the associated underdetermination, we cannot assess a given claim about what is or is not metaphysically dependent, either relative to a domain or in general, until we know which specific grounding relations are at issue[.]

I agree to Wilson's point. It seems to me that Amy's question is indeed sensible to ask. What would an appropriate answer look like? I think that at least one way to answer the question would be to appeal to one of the 'small-g' grounding relations and say something like this:

> *Ted:* The property of *being red* is Grounded in the possible shades of red, or is instantiated in virtue of one of the shades being instantiated, because there is a determinable-determinate relationship between *being red* and each of its shades. This illuminates the modal relation and accounts for nothing-over-and-above-ness. After all, *being a particular shade of red* is *being red* in a specific way.

This seems to be the kind of answer that Wilson has in mind as well, although she thinks that, all things considered, the intermediate step that introduces Grounding is illegitimate. I agree with her that Grounding alone leaves open certain questions that we can answer by appealing to the more fine-grained 'small-g' grounding relations, but I do not think that we should give up on Grounding.

Even Jonathan Schaffer, one of the main advocates of Grounding, grants that bare Grounding claims do not provide us with everything we want to know with regard to how exactly the entities in question are linked. He draws

---

[143] If you do not find this unsatisfying, try to consider an analogous conversation in which the properties in question are not *being red* and its shades, but a mental property and some physical properties. In such a case, the purely Grounding-based answer seems even more obviously unsatisfying.

an analogy between Grounding and causation, and compares the claims of two fictitious metaphysicians Natalie and Sigmund. Natalie claims that the natural grounds the normative, whereas Sigmund claims that smoking causes lung cancer. In both cases, Schaffer insists that they say something informative, but admits that in both cases, not all has been said that needs to be said about the case in question (2016: 151):

> I agree with Wilson that Natalie's bare grounding claim leaves open how the grounding pattern works, and think that there is an important lesson to be drawn from this. But I think that the lesson is not to discard the notion of grounding but to develop it further, in ways that allow one to go beyond bare grounding claims and add even more information about the underlying pattern.

Suppose that referring to one of the 'small-g' relations adds such information about the underlying pattern, and that we grant that the 'small-g' relations cannot be replaced by Grounding. Then, somebody more skeptical about Grounding than Schaffer may still ask what work can be done by Grounding that cannot be done by the 'small-g' grounding relations alone. Since our fictitious philosopher Ted could have provided the alternative answer at the end of the conversation directly to Amy's initial question why the supervenience relation holds, we still need a good reason to introduce the intermediate step in the first place, especially if the aim is postulate a generic Grounding relation, rather than merely a generic concept of Grounding.

5.3.2 Full Grounding, partial Grounding, and the strong emergentist view

We have seen earlier that the distinction between necessitation dualism and physicalism cannot be made by appeal to supervenience alone, because supervenience is compatible with cases of nothing-over-and-above-ness as well as cases of something-over-and-above-ness. We have also seen that some have interpreted the strong emergentist view along such lines. One reason to adopt Grounding in addition to the 'small-g' relations might be that it allows us to properly draw the distinction between physicalism and strong emergentism understood as a variant of necessitation dualism – something I have argued in section 4.4.6 to be what the notion of metaphysical dependence has to account for. Grounding seems to be able to do that. After all, Grounding is incompatible with cases of something-over-and-above-ness, if only stipulatively.

Wilson grants that the ability of Grounding to make such a distinction might be a motivation for accepting the notion as useful. However, she immediately raises a concern (2014: 543–544):

Consider again the case of robustly emergent mental states. Since these are over and above physical states, they are not Grounded in physical states. But according to the robust emergentist, emergent mental states are nonetheless dependent on physical states. Exactly how is a matter of further commitments, but there is nothing to prevent this dependence from being of the metaphysical variety, even if robustly emergent states do not *completely* metaphysically depend on physical goings-on.

This is somewhat puzzling. I take the general dialectical situation with regard to Grounding to be such that everybody in the debate grants that the expressions 'metaphysically depends on' and 'is nothing over and above', can almost[144] be used interchangeably. Based on this, friends and foes of Grounding debate whether we can understand these notions in terms of Grounding. This understanding also seems to be suggested by several passages in Wilson's own paper.[145] But here, she suddenly claims that the emergentist might argue that mental states are metaphysically dependent on physical states even though the former are something over and above the latter states.

What Wilson has in mind is apparently a weaker notion of *partial* metaphysical dependence that is indeed compatible with something-over-and-above-ness. Friends of Grounding likewise distinguish (full) Grounding, which they associate with (full) metaphysical dependence, from a weaker notion of partial metaphysical dependence, which they call 'partial Grounding' (Fine 2012: 50):

> Another familiar distinction is between full and partial ground. [...] A is a partial [...] ground for C if A, on its own or with some other truths, is a ground of C (i.e. A, Γ < B, where Γ is a possibly empty set of "other truths"). Thus given that A, B is a full ground for A ∧ B, each of A and B will be a partial ground for A ∧ B. Each will be relevant to the grounding of A ∧ B, even though neither may be sufficient on its own.

---

[144] I say 'almost' because cases of identity are clearly cases of nothing-over-and-above-ness, but it is debatable whether they are cases of metaphysical dependence. Wilson claims they are, whereas I agree to most friends of Grounding that they are not. The point at hand does not hang on whether or not cases of identity count, because nobody thinks that emergent properties are identical to physical ones.

[145] Wilson starts her crusade against Grounding with the claim that "[i]t has recently been suggested that a distinctive relation – call it ('big-G') 'Grounding' – is at issue in contexts in which some entities, propositions or facts are claimed to 'metaphysically depend on' (in a constitutive rather than causal sense), 'hold in virtue of', be 'nothing over and above', or be 'grounded in' some others" (2014: 535). Later on, she says that "investigations [into 'small-g' grounding relations] take the idioms of metaphysical dependence ('in virtue of', 'nothing over and above', 'grounded in') to be schematic placeholders for specific metaphysical relations [...] which serve [...] to characterize diverse forms of metaphysical dependence in a genuinely explanatory and illuminating way" (2014: 539).

5.3 No work for Grounding? — 189

Wilson indeed acknowledges the distinction between full and partial Grounding in a footnote, but denies that it can help solving the problem (2014: 544 [fn27]):

> Per usual, Fine's work anticipates this concern, in explicitly allowing for partial Grounding. I cannot enter into the more subtle details of Fine's investigations here; suffice to say that a relation of partial Grounding is not up to the task of making sense of the usual ('in virtue of'; 'nothing over and above') idioms of metaphysical dependence that proponents of Grounding take as implicitly defining their posit. It is especially unclear how a relation of partial Grounding is supposed to comport with Schaffer's and Rosen's supposition that Grounding is primitive. Is the basic primitive Partial Grounding, and if so, how does this comport with Complete Grounding? Note that one cannot define Complete Grounding in terms of Partial Grounding, along lines of defining parthood in terms of primitive proper parthood and identity. Rather, to handle the case of robust emergentism, primitivists about Grounding will require, it seems, at least two primitively related primitive relations.

With regard to Wilson's first point, that partial Grounding does not make sense of the usual idioms of metaphysical dependence, I think she is correct at least with regard to the 'nothing over and above' idiom. However, friends of Grounding do not claim that if *B* is a partial Ground of *A*, then *A* is nothing over and above *B* in the first place. With regard to the 'in virtue of' idiom, as long as we properly distinguish between 'wholly in virtue of'- and 'partly in virtue of'-claims, I also do not see the problem. Entities which have the property of *being red and round* have it partly in virtue of *being red*, and partly in virtue of *being round*, and nobody would claim in the first place that partial Grounding has to account for 'wholly in virtue of'-claims. In general, I fail to see why it should be a problem for the friend of Grounding that partial Grounding cannot account for nothing-over-and-above-ness. It is full Grounding, not partial Grounding, that is thought to account for nothing-over-and-above-ness.

Wilson's second point, that a relation of partial Grounding, in order not to undermine the supposition that full Grounding is primitive, must be included as a further primitive, is somewhat more difficult to assess. She first claims that full Grounding cannot be defined in terms of partial Grounding. In order to show this, she tries to draw an analogy between the two notions of Grounding and the notions of proper and improper parthood. Improper parthood can be defined using proper parthood as a primitive, and then using the notion of identity in addition to the notion of proper parthood to define the notion of improper parthood: "*P* is a[n improper] part of *Q* just in case *P* is a proper part of *Q* or *P* is identical with *Q*" (2018: 506). So far, this sounds fine. But then she moves on to say that "this strategy won't work for Grounding, since proponents of Grounding maintain that fully Grounded goings-on are not identical with Grounding goings-on (and in any case full metaphysical dependence is compatible with non-identity)" (2018: 506). This is correct, but I have to admit that I do not understand how this shows what Wilson takes it to show, i.e. that "there's no hope of taking partial Grounding to be primitive, and then defining full Grounding in terms of it" (2018: 506). I certainly agree that we cannot say that P is fully Grounded in Q just in case P is partially Grounded in Q or P is identical with Q. But how do we get from there to the claim that there is no way to define full Grounding in terms of partial Grounding? Wilson unfortunately does not tell us.

That said, I do not want to argue that we should define full Grounding in terms of partial Grounding. I just do not understand how Wilson's argument is supposed to work. To be sure, Kit Fine, one of the main advocates of Grounding, agrees to Wilson that full Grounding cannot be defined in terms of partial Grounding. Fine explicitly argues for this claim in a passage that immediately follows the one I quoted above in which he introduces the notion of partial Grounding. However, he provides an argument that is more illuminating than Wilson's (Fine 2012: 50):

> Partial ground has been defined in terms of full ground, but it would not appear to be possible to define full ground in terms of partial ground. For the partial grounds of A ∨ B and A ∧ B are the same, i.e. A and B when A and B are the case. But each of A and B is a full ground of A ∨ B though not, in general, of A ∧ B. And so how are we to distinguish between the full grounds of A ∨ B and A ∧ B if appeal is only made to their partial grounds? It is for this reason that pride of place should be given to the full notion in developing an account of ground.

Let me explain how Fine's argument works using an example: Suppose that A is the fact that object o is red, and B is the fact that object o is round, where o is the name of a particular object, say, the ball in my shed. Now, the conjunctive fact that object o is red and round is fully Grounded in the set of facts consisting of A (the fact that o is red) and B (the fact that o is round), but neither A nor B is sufficient on its own to fully Ground the conjunctive fact. A and B partially Ground the conjunctive fact, but neither fully Grounds it. Things are different with regard to the disjunctive fact that object o is red or round. While this fact is also Grounded in the set of facts consisting of both A and B, each of these facts on its own is sufficient to fully Ground the disjunctive fact. What we want to say is that again, each A and B partially Grounds the disjunctive fact, but nevertheless, each of them also fully Grounds it. So, even though there is a difference between the two cases when it comes to full Grounds, there is no difference when it comes to partial Grounds. Thus, it is hard to see how we could understand the difference with regard to the full Grounds by looking only at the partial Grounds, which are the same in both cases. So after all, it turns out that Wilson's original claim that the prospects of defining full Grounding in terms of partial Grounding are dim is correct, but not for the reason she provides (or, rather, does not provide).

According to Fine, partial Grounding is to be defined in terms of full Grounding, rather than *vice versa*, instead: *B* partially grounds *A* if *B*, either alone or together with some further facts, fully Grounds *A*. However, as Wilson (2018: 506–507) correctly points out, this turns out to be problematic if we look at the case of the emergentist, because even though the emergentist might want to claim that mental facts are partially Grounded in physical facts, there is no full Ground for mental facts to be found. Mental facts, though partially Grounded, are fundamental. But unless there is a full Ground for every fact for which we want to claim that it is partially Grounded, we cannot define partial Grounding in the way Fine suggests. So we would either need to deny that emergent mental facts, though not fully Grounded, can still be partially Grounded, or take partial Grounding to be a further primitive notion in addition to primitive Grounding. Furthermore, in order to account for the relation between full and partial Grounding, a third primitive posit might become necessary. Since primitive posits are metaphysically costly, this is certainly an issue.

Once we properly distinguish full and partial Grounding, even if it turns out to be metaphysically costly, it seems that Wilson's concern that the emergentist might claim that mental states, though something over and above physical states, can still metaphysically depend on physical states, can be accounted for. The emergentist can claim that emergent mentality partially, but not fully, metaphysically depends on the physical. Wilson thus cannot claim that "Grounding – at least as presented as the proper target of 'in virtue of' idioms and the like – conflates over and above-ness with absence of metaphysical dependence" (Wilson 2014: 544). There is no conflation here: If (full) metaphysical dependence is absent, then something-over-and-above-ness is indeed present (unless we have a case of identity, in which case we neither have metaphysical dependence nor something-over-and-above-ness). Wilson seems to agree: "[T]o be sure strongly emergent goings-on can't be *entirely* metaphysically dependent on lower-level physical goings-on, on pain of being, contra the intended contrast, nothing over and above the physical base phenomena" (2018: 506). Hence, it seems that Wilson just insists that the expression 'metaphysical dependence' is to be used more broadly to also capture the cases of partial dependence. But in this case, the quarrel turns out mainly terminological, and we might just grant her usage of the expression and add a 'full' in front of 'metaphysical dependence' to make clear that we have been talking about full metaphysical dependence all along.

In any case, a notion of metaphysical dependence that takes the emergentist view to allow for such dependence, even if it is a form of dualism, cannot be what we aim for in our search for the metaphysical dependence relation required for defining physicalism. Hence, if the notion of (full) Grounding is incompatible with the kind of metaphysical dependence the strong emergentist may allow can only be in favor of Grounding, rather than against it. Whether we further need a notion of partial Grounding in order to account for the view of the strong emergentism is another issue that does not seem to pose an immediate problem to the definition of physicalism in terms of (full) Grounding. Since the strong emergentist claims that the mental is neither identical to nor fully Grounded in the physical, it is properly distinguished from physicalism using the notion of full Ground only. Whether or not we may need a further notion of partial dependence to fully flesh out the emergentist position to distinguish it from other views within the dualist camp is certainly an interesting question, but does not seem to concern us too much here given that we aim at understanding physicalism rather than emergentism.

Nevertheless, I want to make a suggestion in this regard. Maybe, we can even account for strong emergentism with the notion of full Grounding in conjunction with some of the tools that the 'small-g' grounding relations provide us with. In fact, this suggestion does not seem to be too far from what Wilson herself has in mind to frame the strong emergentist position. In her (2015), she takes strongly emergent properties to bestow their bearer with some causal powers not bestowed by any of the physical properties. Nevertheless, some of their other causal powers are indeed shared with physical properties. This latter point seems to account for the idea that there is a partial dependence of mental on physical properties. The idea that emergent properties are still fundamental, if not already accounted for by reference to the additional causal powers, can be framed in terms of those properties not being (fully) Grounded – something that is frequently claimed by advocators of Grounding, such as Schaffer: "x is fundamental $=_{df}$ nothing grounds x" (2009: 373). Of course, Wilson does not agree to the last step, because she thinks that the notion of fundamentality must not be defined in terms of Grounding, but has rather to be taken as a primitive notion (2018: 497; see also her 2014: 560):[146]

> [W]hat is fundamental is metaphysically basic (both intensionally and extensionally), if anything is: to be fundamental, as I see it, is effectively to be metaphysically axiomatic. As such, it is metaphysically inapropos to characterize the fundamental in terms adverting to (an absence of) dependence, or in any other terms.

---

146 Note that this view is actually shared at least by Kit Fine (2001), who thinks that both Grounding and fundamentality are to be taken as primitive.

Aside from these intuitions, she worries that "a characterization of the fundamental as that which is not dependent rules out various live accounts of what fundamental goings-on there might be, including self-dependent Gods, mutually dependent monads, and [...] partially-dependent strongly emergent features" (2018: 498). The latter concern is unwarranted, given the way I just suggested to account for such features. With regard to the other two 'live accounts', I am prepared to bite the bullet, and claim that if these notions of dependence are coherent in the first place, the relations they pick out are not metaphysical dependence relations as understood here.

5.3.3 The priority argument: Grounding as a priority-fixing relation

A further argument Wilson considers (2014: 563–566; 2018: 497–500) that friends of Grounding might put forward is that a Grounding relation is required to fix the order of priority between the entities standing in 'small-g' grounding relations, insofar as at least some of the relations are unable to accomplish that on their own. Wilson's favorite example of a dependence relation that plausibly does not fix the order of priority on its own is the mereological part-whole relation. If it would, then priority monists (PM), who think that wholes are more fundamental than their parts, and priority pluralists (PP), who think that parts are more fundamental than wholes, would talk past each other, because they would not talk about *the* part-whole relation, but about two different relations we might call the part-whole$_{PM}$ relation and the part-whole$_{PP}$ relation.

In this case, the idea is that if a 'small-g' grounding relation does not fix the direction of priority between its relata, then Grounding might come to the rescue and do the fixing for it. Importantly, in this case, it does not suffice to postulate a concept of Grounding without postulating a relation of Grounding. After all, if we need something to fix the priority of the relata of 'small-g' grounding relations, what we need is a metaphysical posit. However, Wilson thinks that even though Grounding would be apt to fix the order of priority, we do not need Grounding for that purpose. What we need instead, on her view, is a primitive notion of fundamentality (2018: 497):

> [T]here are two cases where the direction of priority associated with the holding of a given small-g relation might be at issue: first, cases where the relation connects fundamental to non-fundamental goings-on; second, cases where the relata are each non-fundamental. Neither, I argue, requires appeal to Grounding.
> For the first sort of case, I argue that, as is standard in contexts where metaphysical dependence is at issue, what more is needed is specification of what is presumed [...] to be fundamental. [...] [G]iven that the whole is fundamental, then proper parts of the whole are

non-fundamental; given that atoms are fundamental, fusions of the atoms are non-fundamental. Similarly for cases of physicalist dependence. For example, given that the fundamental goings-on are maximally determinate (as physicalists sometimes assume), then determinables of these goings-on are non-fundamental; and so on. So in order for the small-g relations to fix the direction of priority between fundamental and non-fundamental goings-on, no appeal to Grounding is required.

On Wilson's view, priority is fixed by the fundamental entities' *being fundamental*, together with (a) the links between these entities and non-fundamental entities established by the 'small-g' grounding relations, and (b) the 'small-g' grounding links between non-fundamental entities. In the case where a fundamental entity is linked to a non-fundamental entity, the priority is fixed immediately by the one entity's *being fundamental*. In the case where two non-fundamental entities are linked, the priority is fixed by the way these entities are linked via further 'small-g' grounding relations to fundamental entities. A friend of Grounding might allow all that, and add the claim that we can understand the notion of fundamentality in terms of Grounding, as discussed at the end of the previous section. Wilson tries to resist this claim to avoid that her view collapses into a variant of the Grounding view after all.

I do not think that Wilson's reasons are very convincing. I have already mentioned above that she has two concerns about an analysis of fundamentality in terms of Grounding. One is that such a Grounding-based account rules out cases of fundamental entities that are either self- or mutually dependent, and I have already said what I think about these examples. The other concern is that analyzing the notion of fundamentality in other terms conflicts with the intuition that "[t]he fundamental is, well, *fundamental:* entities in a fundamental base play a role analogous to axioms in a theory – they are basic, they are 'all God had to do, or create'" (2014: 560).

Several authors have objected that Wilson conflates different things here. Cameron argues that once we properly distinguish between the real definition of fundamental features and the definition of the term 'fundamental', which fixes which concept we associate with the term, we may resolve the difficulty in favor of a Grounding-based account of our concept of fundamentality (2016: 389 [fn7]):

> The fundamental *features* of reality should not admit of real definition – for they are, well, fundamental. But that doesn't mean that the ideology of fundamentality itself does not admit of definition. The fundamental is fundamental, but 'The fundamental' might not be.

I agree with Cameron that we need to properly distinguish between the definition of the term 'fundamental' and the real definition of fundamental features of reality. But Cameron's concession that fundamental features of reality do not admit of real definition somewhat misses the mark. After all, Wilson's concern is not whether there is a real definition of some fundamental feature of reality (e. g. *what it is* for a particle to have a certain spin, or what the particle's *having a certain spin* consists in, if that is a fundamental feature of reality) – this might indeed be incoherent with their *being fundamental*. Cameron's attempt only seems to work if we take fundamentality itself to be a fundamental feature of reality. Raven's criticism of Wilson's concern challenges exactly this assumption (2017: 637):

> Even if certain concepts are primitive in that they have no non-circular analysis, it does not follow that the property *being primitive* is primitive. Maybe the property can be analyzed roughly as: x is *primitive* iff there is no non-circular analysis of x. If so, the triviality that a primitive concept is primitive does not entail that the property *being primitive* is primitive. Analogously, the triviality that a fundamental entity is fundamental does not entail that the property *fundamentality* is fundamental.

Wilson answers to Raven, as well as to another similar criticism raised by Berker[147] that Wilson conflates two distinct issues: providing a metaphysical characterization of those things that are fundamental, on the one hand, and of the fact that those things are fundamental, on the other, that she is not guilty of any such confusion, and tries to spell out in some more detail what exactly she has in mind when she says that the fundamental should not be defined in other terms (2018: 499–500):

> What I need for purposes of implementing my account of priority-fixing is that Grounding isn't needed to *metaphysically determine* (as the un-Grounded) which goings-on are fundamental. My concern about metaphysically characterizing the fundamental as the un-Grounded is not that it would render fundamental goings-on non-fundamental (*pace* Raven) or such as to hold in virtue of something (*pace* Berker). On the contrary: part of my argument against characterizing the fundamental as the un-Grounded is that fundamental goings-on *themselves* may 'hold in virtue of something' – e. g., may metaphysically depend on each other, and so be relationally metaphysically characterized. My concern is rather that it doesn't make sense to take what is fundamental at a world (by which I mean: the overall extension of what is fundamental at a world) to be *metaphysically determined* by non-basic facts or goings-on concerning the overall extension of what is not dependent at that world. If anything is appropriately seen as *not* determined by *other* facts or goings-on at a world, it is, I claim, the overall extension of what is fundamental. This is the concep-

---

147 Wilson (2018: 499) quotes a passage from a footnote in a draft version of Berker (2017). In the final paper, the footnote does not appear anymore. I do not know whether Wilson's answer has convinced Berker that his point was mistaken, or whether he had other reasons to remove the point from his paper.

tion, to my mind, that is suggested by the all God had to do' heuristic, with God playing the role of the primitive positive basic determiner[.]

Wilson seems to make multiple claims here that we need to have a look at individually. *First*, she takes Raven's reading of her original concern to be that once we understand *being fundamental* as *being un-Grounded*, we need to admit that fundamental goings-on turn out to be non-fundamental. She then claims that on her view, since she wants to allow for fundamental goings-on to mutually metaphysically depend on each other, we should not understand the fundamental in terms of the un-Grounded. I think this is mistaken, and in any case a dialectically rather weak point, for reasons we have already discussed earlier when focusing on Wilson's concerns regarding a Grounding-based understanding of strong emergentism. If we take what is fundamental to be understood in terms of what is un-Grounded, the notion of Grounding is the notion of full Grounding. However, cases of mutual dependence are inconsistent with such notion. The simplest way out for the friend of Grounding is to deny that there are cases of mutual dependence between fundamental goings-on. One way to explain away the intuition of mutual dependence between fundamental goings-on is that there are rather mutual causal dependencies, or some other kind of mutual dependence that is not of the metaphysical kind. Similarly, the notion of full Grounding is not the one in question when it comes to understanding strong emergentism. There may be a problem with a Grounding-based attempt of understanding fundamentality if the claim were that the fundamental is not even partially Grounded in anything. But this is not the claim of friends of Grounding in the first place.

Second, it seems that Wilson is worried that by understanding the fundamental as the un-Grounded, we buy into the claim that which entities are fundamental in a world is determined by what is non-fundamental in the world. In terms of the creationist metaphor, her concern seems to be that on the conception of the fundamental as the un-Grounded, God needs not only fix the fundamental facts, but also needs to fix further facts in order to somehow afterwards sort out which ones are the fundamental facts. I do not quite understand how any of this follows from taking the fundamental to be the un-Grounded. If the claim were that the fundamental is that which is part of the minimal set required to Ground everything else, or something along these lines, I could see how such a worry might arise. But taking the fundamental to be the un-Grounded does not make any assumptions about what might be Grounded in the fundamental, and so I do not see how Wilson's concern is appropriate.

Let me set aside the question whether the fundamental can be understood as the un-Grounded for a moment, and address some different concerns regarding Wilson's fundamentality-based account of fixing the direction of priority. In order to see the importance of such considerations with regard to our main topic, the metaphysical dependence relation for physicalism, consider the following: On Wilson's account, the tools we have in our metaphysics toolkit are the 'small-g' relations and absolute fundamentality. From that, we need to construct our account of metaphysical dependence. At least some of the 'small-g' relations alone are supposedly unable to fix the order of priority between the relata of the 'small-g' relations. Suppose, for the sake of argument, that mental and physical properties are linked via a 'small-g' relation that does not by itself fix the direction of priority. So in order to make sure that it is the mental that depends on the physical, rather than *vice versa* (or that there is no priority at all), we need to know which one is more fundamental – something that, according to Wilson, requires her notion of absolute fundamentality.

I have to admit that since we are focusing on metaphysical dependence of properties on other properties, I am not fully convinced that the relevant 'small-g' grounding relations in these cases do not fix the order of priority by themselves. The part-whole relation, which serves as Wilson's prime example for which the priority-fixing issue seems quite plausible, arguably does not have the right kind of relata to be central to our case. What about the 'small-g' relations we considered above? At least as far as I know, nobody has yet argued for the claim that higher-order functional properties might be more fundamental than their realizers. With regard to the set-subset account of realization, could it be that a property *A* has a subset of the causal powers of another property *B*, and *A* is prior to *B*? I am less sure than in the higher-order property case, but it is at least not obvious that it can. What about the determinable-determinate relation? As we have seen, it has been appealed to by some as a candidate relation to link mental to physical properties. Moreover, it has been considered to be a relation that needs to be supplemented in order to fix the order of priority (e. g. Cameron 2016: 387; Wilson 2012). So at least some think that in some of the cases relevant to us, we need a further metaphysical posit to fix the order of priority. So let me pretend that I am convinced (which I am not) that for some of the 'small-g' relations relevant for our case, we need something that fixes the order of priority, and see whether this would provide us with some work to do for a Grounding relation.

Schaffer (2016: 158–159) raises the concern that a fundamentality-based account is unable to handle cases in which no fundamental level exists, at least if the notion of fundamentality is an absolute rather than a relative one. More specifically, much of what Schaffer and Wilson say suggests that both have in mind a mereologically fundamental level. For example, Schaffer says that "[i]f parts are always more fundamental than wholes, and if 'gunky' structures with limitless descending chains of parthood are possible, then one seems to get scenarios with no fundamental entities at all" (2016: 158 [fn11]).

I have already pointed out in chapter 2 that mereological levels are not the main focus in the case of physicalism, because it suffices that non-physical properties are linked via relations of dependence to physical properties, independent of the mereological level on which we find instances of the physical properties. Nevertheless, physicalism should be compatible with an infinite descent of mereological levels, so if Wilson's account requires that there is a fundamental mereological level, then we have one more reason to reject it. Wilson replies to Schaffer's worry that she does not need to make such an assumption (2018: 499):

> I argue, first, that if the supposedly infinitely descending levels converge on a limit level, then the (non-existent) limit can serve as a fundamental level; second, that if the archeology of levels below a certain level L makes no difference to all higher-level goings-on, then L can play the same role as a fundamental level in fixing priority between goings-on at or above L; and third, that in the absence of convergence or a level below which archeology doesn't matter, then (modulo small-g relations whose holding alone fixes the direction of priority) there will be no directions of priority, and this is as it should be, as per the 'all God had to do' metaphor (God would in such cases have to bring into existence *all* the goings-on).

Let me discuss Wilson's three lines of argument one after the other. Her first response is to say that even if there is no fundamental level, the infinite descent might still converge to a limit level. Here, she takes up an analogy from Montero (2006: 179):

> [E]ven successive decompositions can still bottom out into something fundamental. For example, just as the infinite decreasing sequence of numbers 1/2, 1/3, 1/4, ... is still bounded below by zero, there could be infinite descending sequences of decompositions, with fundamental entities below them all.

Wilson even claims that we do not need any goings-on in the limit at all in order to fix the order of priority *via* her notion of fundamentality (2016: 197):

> I furthermore add (or take away) from Montero's line of thought is that even if the goings-on in the limit do not exist, the valence of priority may still be established by reference to goings-on in this limit, much as the thermodynamic properties and behavior of a gas are properly modeled as non-fundamental features of statistical mechanical collections in the "thermodynamic limit", as the number of particles and the volume each approach infinity. In other words, goings-on in the limit may act as a fundamental level.

I have a hard time making sense of the analogy with the case of the sequence of numbers. If we are talking about mereological levels, then the consideration might make *some* sense, insofar as the idea might be that parts of wholes become smaller and smaller, while still having strictly positive sizes, with zero being what the sizes converge to even though this limit is strictly speaking never reached. But once we talk about more or less fundamental properties, and take into account that a fundamental property is not just any old property of a mereologically fundamental particular, I do not see how the analogy is supposed to work at all. However, since what I have quoted above is all that Wilson says about the case, it is hard to formulate a clear argument against her point. Thus, instead of guessing what she might have in mind, and then arguing against such a straw person, I would rather like to invite her to say more about how the analogy is supposed to work, and how exactly the priority is fixed in case the goings-on in the limit do not exist at all.

What about Wilson's second suggestion, that some intermediate level can serve as a fundamental level with respect to the levels above? Here, she claims the following (2016: 197–198):

> [P]riority might be fixed in the absence of a fundamental level if there is a level at which the archeology of further dependence relations ceases to be relevant to priority relations at or "above" that level. Such a level acts as a fundamental base for what lies above; hence, for example, the physical level might operate as a fundamental level for purposes of understanding priority relations among broadly scientific phenomena, even if the physical entities are non-fundamental relative to some deeper level of reality.

So far, the notion of a level Wilson talks about seemed to be tied to mereology. Now, she talks about 'the physical level'. I am not quite sure what exactly she means by 'the physical level'. However, what she says in the earlier article in which she defines her notion of the physical (see section 3.3.2) suggests that she still roughly focuses on a roughly mereological understanding. I draw this conclusion from her claim that the distinction between physics and the special sciences tracks what she calls 'constitutional complexity', which sounds very much like a mereological notion, and that she takes both molecular physics and astrophysics not to count as physics (2006: 92–93 [fn4]):

> [W]hat entities a science treats corresponds roughly to the divisions in subject matter associated with the various fundamental and special sciences (which divisions track, among other things, constitutional complexity). [...] I will stick with the intuitive notion, which in the case of physics primarily tracks relative fundamentality. Two points of clarification are in order. First, the notion of constitutional complexity at issue in designations of relative fundamentality is not intended to rule out there being fields among the relatively fundamental entities, which serve as a constitutional basis for molecules, proteins, plants, and so on. It is, however, intended to rule out galaxies and the like as being relatively fundamental, so that astrophysics (like molecular physics) is a special science, to be distinguish-

ed from (fundamental) physics. Second, the qualifier 'relatively' in the expression 'relatively fundamental' is intended as compatible with physical entities' not being fundamental, for two reasons. First, many entities treated by physics are not themselves fundamental – e.g., protons. Second, notwithstanding physicalism's foundationalist aspirations, satisfying these aspirations does not entail commitment to there being a fundamental level

I have several concerns with regard to a notion of the 'physical level' construed along these lines. *First*, I take it that such an account of 'physical level' begs the question against views that try to combine physicalism with priority monism (Schaffer 2010). *Second*, once one considers physical properties, it is hard to see how one can tie them to a particular mereological level (or set of mereological levels). After all, properties like *having mass*, which seem to be prototypical physical properties if anything is, are instantiated by entities at all levels of the mereological hierarchy. Thus, we cannot tie the notion of a physical level to the mereological levels at which physical properties are instantiated. *Third*, Wilson's claim that the physical entities might be non-fundamental relative to some 'deeper level of reality' (whatever she means by that exactly), combined with her understanding of physicalism as the claim that all broadly scientific goings-on are nothing over and above physical goings-on, might be taken to suggest that physicalism, on her account, might be true in a case in which physical properties, although fundamental relative to the properties of the special sciences, are based on something else themselves. In contrast to this reading of Wilson's claim, I take physicalism to be false in such a case. Generally, I would again like to hear more about Wilson's notion of a 'physical level' in order to better understand what she has in mind.

Moreover, I have a more general concern that does not focus on whether the mereological hierarchy, the hierarchy of sciences or some other hierarchy is involved. Since the order of priority is not fixed by the 'small-g' grounding relations, but rather by the location of the fundamental level, how do we know which side is up and which side is down the hierarchy if the relatively fundamental level is set somewhere in the middle of the hierarchy? In other words, how do we know that what Wilson describes as the 'deeper level of reality' is not actually up, rather than down the hierarchy? In such a case, it seems that we need a notion of relative fundamentality after all, which, as she notes with regard to an argument by Cameron (2016), is closer to a notion of Grounding than Wilson wants to allow for (2018: 498 [fn8]):

> Indeed, Grounding is often characterized as a primitive relation or notion of relative fundamentality; hence Cameron's argument presupposes that I endorse Grounding or a close cousin thereof, which I don't.

This does not yet mean that by introducing a notion of relative fundamentality, we introduce a notion of full Grounding. Rather, I take relative fundamentality to be more closely related to a notion of partial Grounding. To see this, take the case of a conjunctive property (or fact) and its conjuncts again. The property of *being red* is certainly more fundamental than the property of *being red and round*, and but the latter is something over and above the former property, and thus *being red* does not fully Ground *being red and round*, even though it arguably partially Grounds it. Once there is a need for a notion of relative fundamentality, or partial Grounding, for her account as well, Wilson's claim that her view is more economical with regard to the number of primitives breaks down. Whether we add a primitive notion of (absolute) fundamentality or a primitive notion of full Grounding does not seem to make a difference.

Given such a situation, a Grounding-based account might be better off than a fundamentality-based one. As Schaffer points out, while fundamentality is easily defined in terms of Grounding, the reverse is at least not obviously possible (2016: 158):

> Wilson's framework is impoverished compared to the grounding framework. It seems to me that absolute fundamentality can easily be defined in terms of grounding (the fundamental is that which has no deeper grounds), and so a framework using grounding as a primitive can easily be used to say everything one wants to say via absolute fundamentality. But there is no obvious definition to be found in the other direction, and so it is not at all obvious that using absolute fundamentality as a primitive will allow one to say everything one wants to say in terms of relative fundamentality, or in the even stronger linking terms of the grounding connection.

Note also that a notion of relative fundamentality (or partial Grounding) does not help to define full Grounding, as we have seen earlier. Thus, while a combination of full and partial Grounding provides us with notions of fundamentality for free, the reverse does not seem to work.

Wilson's final claim is basically that if neither of the first two options turns out to be viable, then there is no order of priority after all (2016: 198):

> But what if there is no fundamental level, no convergence on a fundamental level, and no level at which deeper archeology ceases to matter? In that case, one may reasonably deny that it makes sense to posit any priority relations between non-fundamenta (besides those fixed just by the relation alone, as might be the case with the set membership relation).

It seems to me that this just begs the question against those who claim that the order of priority is fixed via Grounding rather than via absolute fundamentality. Why think that in the absence of a fundamental level or something similar, there is no priority between parts and wholes, determinables and determinates, etc., on the assumption that these relations do not fix the priority of their relata on their own? If the priority is fixed via relations of Grounding, or maybe relative fundamentality, we can still distinguish between worlds without a fundamental level in which there is a priority between the relata of the 'small-g' relations, and worlds in which there is no such priority.

Aside from these concerns regarding Wilson's notion of fundamentality and its requirements with regard to a fundamental level, Schaffer raises a further concern, which – at least to some extent – is also reflected in some of the considerations above. Do fundamentality claims not raise similar questions as the ones Wilson worries about with regard to Grounding? In particular, one question is indeed important: how much more plausible is it in the case of fundamentality that there is just one unified notion that can capture all cases, as opposed to different notions of fundamentality that capture different cases, than it is for Grounding (2016: 161):

> Could the metaphysician rest with bare claims of the form "this is fundamental" (/"this is not fundamental")? Of course not. With the posit of fundamentality will come the need to settle certain framework questions (e.g., does fundamentality entail existence?), and to integrate the machinery of fundamentality into the machinery of Wilson's "small-'g'" relations (e.g., Can entities related by proper parthood both be fundamental? Can entities related by set formation both be fundamental?) And – perhaps most relevantly given the current dialectic – there will be the question (one which Wilson especially should face) as to whether there is a single unif[i]ed notion of fundamentality, as opposed to a merely schematic notion standing in for some yet-to-be-specified "small-'f'" status, such as *being mereologically atomic* and *being set theoretically elemental*.

I think Wilson indeed says enough in her writings to answer at least Schaffer's exemplary framework questions. But friends of Grounding can of course say, and have said, similar things. In any case, the intuition that there must be proper distinctions between different notions of fundamentality – and I think there are quite a few that need to be distinguished (see also section 2.2.2) – as well as the question if, and if so, how, such notions are unified by a generic notion, is something that needs to be accounted for by somebody like Wilson, whose metaphysical framework so heavily relies on such a posit.

In summary, I take these considerations to at least show that a fundamentality-based account is more problematic than Wilson expects, and that a Grounding-based account of fixing the direction of priority is, *mutatis mutandis*, still tenable. However, this presumes that priority-fixing is needed also in the restricted sense at issue where we are only concerned with dependence relations between properties. I am not fully convinced that we do need a priority-fixing relation in these cases, because I am not convinced that the relevant 'small-g' relations cannot fix the order of priority on their own. But since I have no watertight argument that all of them are able to do so, I want to remain officially neutral on this issue, and have a look at a final line of argument in favor of adding Grounding to the metaphysician's toolkit in addition to the 'small-g' grounding relations.

5.3.4 The unity argument: Grounding as a unifier of 'small-g' grounding relations

Once we grant that the 'small-g' relations cannot be replaced by Grounding, and set aside the question whether or not we need the relation of Grounding to fix the order of priority between the relata of the 'small-g' grounding relations, what other work might Grounding do that is reason enough to add the notion to our toolkit? Consider a point that Wilson makes in arguing against a purely Grounding-based view of metaphysical dependence. Wilson (2014: 549) worries that the claim that the mental is Grounded in the physical is compatible with too many variants of physicalism about the mental:

> [S]uppose someone claims that the mental is Grounded in the physical. Am I in position to know whether I should agree with them? Not at all. [...] [T]he bare assertion of Grounding is compatible with both reductive and non-reductive versions of physicalism – indeed, perhaps even with anti-realist eliminativism about the mental [...]. Absent further information about the specific grounding relation(s) supposed to be at issue, I am stuck: I am not in position to assess, much less endorse, the claim that the mental is Grounded in – is metaphysically dependent on, nothing over and above – the physical.

Wilson's main concern seems to be that in case we just have Grounding and none of the 'small-g' relations, in agreeing with the claim that the mental is Grounded in the physical, we are forced to agree to the specific variant of physicalism about the mental the person who makes the claim endorses.[148] But in order to distinguish between different variants of physicalism, and to sort out the extent to which one agrees with the person that makes the Grounding claim, we need more in our repertoire of metaphysical relations than Grounding.

---

[148] This would be a problem indeed, but I do not think that by endorsing the claim, one would agree to the particular variant in question. Consider an analogous situation in which somebody says "Ice cream is very tasty!", but prefers strawberry ice cream over all other kinds. By agreeing with the person on the claim that ice cream is very tasty, I do not yet agree to their particular preference of the strawberry kind.

I do not take the claim that the mental is Grounded in the physical to be compatible with either reductive versions of physicalism, at least if reduction amounts to type identity between mental and physical properties, because Grounding is asymmetric and irreflexive, nor do I take it to be compatible with anti-realist eliminativism, because the eliminativist denies the existence of mental properties,[149] but Grounding is factive. However, there are still several variants of non-reductive physicalism that are compatible with Grounding but in addition appeal to different more fine-grained notions of metaphysical dependence. For example, there are different variants of realization-based accounts, as well as accounts that appeal to the determinable-determinate relation.

Once one takes the more fine-grained notions of metaphysical dependence on board as well, *pace* Wilson, I think it is a feature rather than a bug that Grounding is compatible with many variants of (non-reductive) physicalism. It can thereby serve as a unifier of these more fine-grained relations. A friend of Grounding might say that the Grounding *relation* holds in addition to the fine-grained relations, which are different species of Grounding. But even if there is no such further relation, it still seems to be useful to have a unifying *concept* of Grounding. So the unity argument for Grounding, other than the priority argument, can be put forward both for the stronger claim that there is a relation of Grounding (as well as the corresponding concept), and for the weaker claim that there is only a unifying concept. If there is independent reason to think that we need the relation as well, like the advocator of the priority argument thinks, this concept will rigidly pick out the Grounding relation. Otherwise, the concept will non-rigidly pick out whatever 'small-g' relation obtains in the case under consideration.

Relatedly, Ted Sider suggests (in personal communication with Wilson) that "when generally formulated, such doctrines are neutral on how things are grounded, and just say that things are grounded in a certain way. The various forms of physicalism are, as he says, 'all forms of physicalism'; it is important to recognize them as such, and the posit of Grounding provides a basis for doing so" (Wilson 2014: 556). This is a very important observation. As we have seen earlier, each of the different 'small-g' grounding relations considered earlier is arguably sufficient, but not necessary for metaphysical dependence. So the hope is that a more general notion of Grounding that has an intermediate level of

---

[149] While I take the anti-realist eliminativist view to be a variant of physicalism (given that other properties that are neither mental nor physical are properly accounted for), strictly speaking, it is not a *domain-specific* physicalist view about the mental. Since the advocate of such a view denies that there are mental properties, mental properties on such a view are neither identical to physical properties nor metaphysically dependent on physical properties.

grain in between supervenience and the 'small-g' relations can help us to unify the different versions of physicalism that appeal to different 'small-g' relations.

Wilson is of course again skeptical and claims the following (2014: 556–557):

> From the fact that we may formulate or recognize certain general theses as expressing that, for example, all broadly scientific goings-on are 'Grounded in' or stand in 'a grounding relation' to – or are 'nothing over and above', 'hold in virtue of', etc. – some other goings-on, it does not follow that such formulations or recognitional abilities are tracking a distinctive aspect of metaphysical reality. For there is a natural and more parsimonious view according to which references to 'Grounding', 'a grounding relation', or 'nothing over and above-ness' are schematically and neutrally ranging over specific 'small-g' grounding relations.

If the claim is that we need as a unifier a generic *relation* of Grounding, as opposed to merely a generic *concept* of Grounding, then Wilson has a point. The mere observation that there are certain commonalities between the 'small-g' relation does indeed not by itself justify the posit of an additional relation. Thus, I take it that the unity argument, other than the priority argument, is primarily suitable to establish the usefulness of a unifying concept of Grounding. Most friends of Grounding indeed want to establish the stronger claim, but for our purposes, a unifying concept of Grounding is all we need.

Indeed, as Schaffer points out, Wilson seems to require a generic notion of Grounding as well in order to make sense of the idea that the 'small-g' relations she lists are indeed 'small-g' grounding relations (2016: 155):

> My second answer as to why genus notions may still be helpful is that without the genus notion one may be unable to *enumerate the species*. For instance, a theorist who refused the general notion of causation would have no clear way to enumerate her own "small-'c'" causal relations. To illustrate, let us imagine that she starts off by invoking some more specific causative notions like "baking, making, waking ..." How can she continue? She cannot say "... and all other species of causation" because that would be cheating (explicitly invoking the very notion of causation that she has foresworn). And she cannot just say "... and so on" because what could that mean for her (besides serving as a device to implicitly invoke the very concept of causation that she has foresworn)? Likewise, the theorist who refused the general notion of grounding would have no clear way to enumerate her own preferred menu of "small-'g'" grounding relations. Wilson herself (2014: 535) resorts to "and so on" when listing her own open-ended plurality of "small-'g'" grounding relations, and so one must wonder how she understands her own list to continue, if not in terms of listing further species of the very genus notion that she has foresworn, namely *grounding*.

I interpret Schaffer's concern to be a point in favor of at least a generic concept of Grounding, even if he wants it to do more. Given that Wilson does consider the 'small-g' relations she lists to be relations of metaphysical dependence, *amongst others*, it is hard to see how she can do without at least a generic concept of

Grounding even if she denies the existence of a corresponding relation. After all, without such a concept, how should we pick out all and only the relations that can serve as relations of metaphysical dependence?

Wilson replies to Schaffer by putting forth the following considerations (2016: 181–182):

> [The following] remarks apply to [...] [the claim] that a general notion or relation provides a basis for speaking open-endedly about the species-level notions or relations. Here again, attention to the standard treatments of determinables and special science entities is informative, for the formal treatments of these entities also provide a basis for useful generalizations, pertaining to predictions, counterfactual reasoning, and explanation, and for speaking open-endedly about determinates or lower-level natural phenomena. But the standard accommodation of these features is again in deflationary terms, according to which the availability of explanatory generalizations and use of general concepts/terms is taken to reflect not distinctively general features of reality but rather inexact resemblances between determinate or lower-level physical goings-on, which resemblances track certain patterns in lower-level phenomena that, were we better epistemically, perceptually, or theoretically situated, could be omitted without loss of metaphysical generality. And here again the methodology is immediately and in the first instance driven by parsimony considerations.

In Wilson's analogy to determinables and determinates, she claims that determinates inexactly resemble each other, and that these resemblances track a pattern we associate with determinables that could in principle be omitted if we were better situated, and thus there would not be a need to appeal to determinables. Similarly, if we would know exactly which 'small-g' relations obtain in which particular actual (or even possible) case, there would be no need to appeal to Grounding or some other generic notion of metaphysical dependence to make sense of what the world is like (at least if we do not need a relation of Grounding to do some other work, like fixing the priority between the relata of the 'small-g' relations), and considerations of parsimony tell us to not postulate any entities we don't require.

To me, this again sounds very much like a criticism of postulating a generic Grounding relation, and less like a criticism of appeal to a generic concept of Grounding or metaphysical dependence. Once we allow that there are similarities between the 'small-g' relations, appeal to a generic concept that tracks the 'small-g' relations via these similarities does not seem to be influenced by considerations of parsimony. After all, as Wilson herself says, the principle of parsimony says that "thou shalt not posit entities beyond necessity" (2016: 181), and I take that not to entail that thou shalt not posit concepts beyond necessity, and I don't think that in the case of formulating physicalism, we can do without such a generic concept anyway.

To get back to my interpretation of Schaffer's original concern as being in favor of a generic concept of Grounding, nothing Wilson says seems to strictly controvert the claim that she herself requires appeal to a generic concept of Grounding to fix which relations belong to the set of 'small-g' relations. As we will see, however, Wilson is less confident when it comes to robust similarities between 'small-g' relations, and thus also with regard to a robust generic concept of metaphysical dependence, than I am. If there is no robust such concept, the question remains how the members of the set of all and only the 'small-g' relations are fixed, or what makes a relation apt to be considered a 'small-g' relation. How weak the similarities of 'small-g' relations are, according to Wilson, can be seen in her discussion of some related considerations regarding the idea that Grounding might act as a unifier of the 'small-g' grounding relations.

As I see it, even the postulate of a generic concept of Grounding requires that the 'small-g' relations share certain commonalities that are typically associated with Grounding. Basically, what is needed is that they share those criteria that advocates of what I called the 'orthodox' view of Grounding associate with their generic Grounding relation. They need to be asymmetric (and thus irreflexive), as well as transitive, which makes them strict partial ordering relations. Furthermore, they need to be necessitating relations, at least in the weak sense discussed in chapter 3. Moreover, they must, in one way or the other, account for the idea that one of the relata (the dependent one) is nothing over and above the other relatum.

This is similar to the criteria Karen Bennett (2017: 32) claims to unify what she calls 'building relations', although there are some differences. Bennett requires her building relations to be *directed*, i.e. antisymmetric and irreflexive (which is equivalent to the asymmetry requirement), but she does not require them to be transitive. She also requires necessitation, but does not require that the builders necessitate the built entities. Rather, the built entities are necessitated by their builders in conjunction with further background conditions that neither include nor by themselves build the built entities (2017: 52). This is very similar to what I claim as well. Finally, Bennett requires that building relations are generative – they license talk using "generative locutions like 'in virtue of'" (2017: 58). Whether or not generativity requires the postulate of a generic Grounding (or in her case: 'Big-B' Building) relation is something she wants to be neutral on. Again, this is very similar to how I see things, although I think more needs to be said about the metaphysical background picture to illuminate how the 'in virtue of' talk can be licensed, and I will do so in section 5.4.2.

Do the 'small-g' relations indeed have the requested features in common? Wilson (2014: 569–570) is again skeptical. With regard to the requirement of being strict partial ordering relations, she starts by claiming that some cases in which metaphysical dependence is claimed fail to be transitive. As an example, she provides the case of set membership, where some take impure sets to metaphysically depend on their members, but the relation is not transitive.[150] Similarly, as I have pointed out earlier, Schaffer, even though he assumed transitivity in his early work on Grounding (2009), has become skeptical of transitivity at least in certain cases of Grounding (Schaffer 2013).

Let me discuss her point regarding Schaffer's examples first. As Wilson correctly points out (2014: 570 [fn85]), the cases Schaffer discusses are what she calls 'mixed' cases: the 'small-g' relations that underlie Grounding in the first and second step are different to each other. Take his example of the dented sphere. First, Schaffer claims that "[t]he fact that the thing has a dent grounds the fact that the thing has shape S" (2012: 126). Note that this is a case of partial, rather than full Grounding. Moreover, what underlies the Grounding claim, at least according to Wilson, is a relation of partial mereological constitution between the dent and shape S. Second, Schaffer claims that "[t]he fact that the thing has shape S grounds the fact that it is more-or-less spherical" (2012: 126). Here, we arguably have a case of full Grounding, where the relevant 'small-g' relation is the determinable-determinate relation. The particular shape S is a determinate of more-or-less sphericality. Finally, Schaffer denies that "[t]he fact that the thing has a dent grounds the fact that it is more-or-less spherical", since "the thing is more-or-less spherical *despite* the minor dent, not because of it" (2012: 127), and thus he claims that transitivity fails.

The other two examples Schaffer discusses are similar with regard to being 'mixed cases', in two ways. They all involve a mixture of full and partial Grounding, and the underlying 'small-g' relations are different for each case. Raven (2013) and Litland (2013) both agree that the Grounding statement Schaffer denies to be true is true after all, contrary to the first intuition, so that the examples do not turn out to be counterexamples against transitivity after all. I find their arguments plausible, but I want to focus on a different point. If Schaffer's example cases are counterexamples to transitivity, they are counterexamples to the transitivity of partial Grounding, not of full Grounding, and the latter is the relation we are primarily interested in, if we want to focus on a generic relation at all. Second, *pace* Wilson, Schaffer's cases do not tell against the transitivity of any of the 'small-g' relations. After all, as she herself points out, all cases are such that different relations underlie the two different steps in each case. Still, she seems to overlook that to be a counterexample against transitivity, it is required that the relation in question is the same in both steps.

---

150 Impure sets are sets that do not contain sets as members.

This is different in the set membership case Wilson puts forward. Here, we indeed have a set membership relation in both cases, and it is pretty obvious that transitivity fails. Suppose Carol is a member of the set of females, and this set is a member of the set of impure sets. If transitivity would hold, then Carol would be a member of the set of impure sets. But since Carol is not an impure set, transitivity does not hold. It clearly would require a very strange metaphysical background view to claim that transitivity holds in this case, and that Carol is indeed an impure set. It is slightly more plausible to claim that the two steps involve two different set membership relations: one only takes two sets as its relata, whereas the other one takes a non-set and a set as its relata, so that we again do not have a case where the same 'small-g' relation is involved. But for our purposes, the most plausible claim seems to be to just deny that the example bears much relevance for our purposes,[151] since it is again a case of partial, rather than full Grounding. Moreover, the metaphysical dependence relations we are interested in are those that relate properties, and if there is unity with regard to the features of the metaphysical dependence relations between properties, that is all we need to allow for a unified concept of Grounding (of properties). Nothing rules out of course that these relations may belong to an even broader family of relations that take different relata, and might be less formally unified.

Against asymmetry, Wilson (2014: 570) points out that some have claimed that there are cases of symmetric metaphysical dependence. We have already seen some allegedly symmetric cases in section 4.4.2, but they turned out to be implausible. Naomi Thompson (2016: 46–47) proposes two more potential cases. Consider the case of two true propositions: A proposition *P*, the proposition *that the proposition Q is true*, and the proposition *Q*, the proposition *that the proposition P is true*. She further suggests that propositions are Grounded in their constituents. Hence, *P* is Grounded in *Q* and the property of *being true*, and likewise, *Q* is grounded in *P* and the property of *being true*. The upshot is that *P* is Grounded in *Q*, and *vice versa*.

This is certainly an interesting case, but only because it shows that one's theory has become so general that it allows for abstract cases that do not tell us anything about what the world under consideration is like. Note also that again, the relevant Grounding relation is partial Grounding, rather than full Grounding. So at most, it is a counterexample against the strict asymmetry of partial Grounding. But more generally, I am somewhat inclined to just bluntly

---

151 Notably, Bennett (2017: 56–57) denies (without further argument) that *set membership* is a building relation. However, she thinks that *set formation* is.

deny the possibility of such pairs of propositions without any more argument than a question to the advocate of such an argument: Can you tell me some more details about the facts that make those propositions true?

Thompson (2016: 47) discusses another example that needs a little more attention. Take the mass m, the volume V and the density ρ of a homogenous fluid, or more generally, the property of *having mass m*, the property of *having volume V* and the property of *having density ρ*. With regard to the three quantities, the equation $\rho = m/V$ holds, but this can likewise be transformed to $\rho V = m$ or $V = m/\rho$. Thompson argues that there is no principled way to say which two of the three quantities are metaphysically prior to the third. So Thompson suggests that the best move is to claim that each pair of quantities Grounds the third one, in effect leading to a case of symmetric Grounding. Note that this position, in conjunction with transitivity, also entails that the dependency is reflexive, so that the density depends on the density, the volume on the volume, and the mass on the mass.

Hofweber (2009: 269 – 270) considers the case of the three quantities as well. However, he claims that our concept of density is derived from our concept of mass and our concept of volume. On his view, we should give up on searching for a metaphysical priority between the three quantities, and stick with the conceptual priority of our concepts of mass and volume with respect to our concept of density. Let me set aside the generally skeptical part of Hofweber's consideration here, and suppose that Hofweber is right about the priority relations between our concepts. This is in line with how the typical units of measurement we use today relate to each other. In the SI system, we measure mass in $[kg]$, and volume in $[m^3]$ (which is based on the SI unit for length, $[m]$), and density in $[kg/m^3]$. There is not even an established alternative name for this unit of measurement, like in the case of the SI unit for force, which is $[N]$ ("Newton"), and corresponds to $[kg \cdot m/s^2]$. Does the conceptual priority of the concepts of mass and volume with respect to the concept of density work as an indicator of how the metaphysical priority of the corresponding properties looks like? I think that conceptual priority and metaphysical priority may come apart in some cases,[152] but at least, I take it that conceptual priority is a *prima facie* guide to metaphysical priority. But even if this is a case in which our conceptual

---

152 It is also interesting to note a further observation that Hofweber (2009: 270 [fn6]) mentions in a footnote and attributes to Marc Lange: In Newton's *Principia*, mass is introduced as derived from density and volume: "Quantity of matter is a measure of matter that arises from its density and volume jointly. [...] I mean this quantity whenever I use the term 'body' or 'mass'" (Newton 1999 [1687]: 403 – 404). For further discussion of this definition and its problems, see Cohen 1999: 86 – 92).

priority does not correspond to the metaphysical priority, it still remains plausible to claim that there is a relation of metaphysical priority between the three quantities – we just may not know for sure which ones are prior to which. But this is an epistemic rather than a metaphysical problem. So it remains at least an option to deny symmetric Grounding in this case, and I think it is quite plausible to do so.

None of the cases put forward so far against a unified notion of metaphysical dependence that appeals to certain formal features all fine-grained relations of metaphysical dependence relevant for our purposes share were very convincing. The formal features we have considered are asymmetry and transitivity. But Wilson does not leave it at that. She also claims that there are reflexive cases of metaphysical dependence, so that the last formal feature, irreflexivity, breaks down as well, and in turn also provides more reason to think that the asymmetry claim is false, since reflexive cases are by definition symmetric cases as well.

I have already mentioned Wilson's reason for thinking that metaphysical dependence relations need not be irreflexive earlier. On her view, both token and type identity count as 'small-g' grounding relations (2014: 571):

> [I]n investigating grounding, we aim to make sense of the usual idioms of metaphysical dependence, and identity claims are paradigmatic of claims taken to establish that certain goings-on are nothing over and above certain other goings-on.

So far, I have nothing to object to what Wilson literally says here. And I also agree that the "nothing over and above" idiom typically tracks metaphysical dependence – that is, in those cases where the underlying relation is not identity. As I already said earlier, it is a theoretical virtue of an asymmetric and irreflexive notion of metaphysical dependence that it tracks metaphysical priority, or relative fundamentality, so that if A is Grounded by B, B is more fundamental than A. Note also that without such a link, it is hard to see in the first place how a relation of Grounding might help to fix the order of priority among the relata of the 'small-g' grounding relations. Moreover, such features fit rather well with the pre-theoretic intuition that it sounds odd to say that something depends on itself, which is most likely based on pre-theoretic intuitions about a close connection between dependence and priority, or relative fundamentality.

Wilson further tries to establish her more inclusive understanding of metaphysical dependence by arguing that if we take metaphysical dependence relations to be strictly asymmetric and irreflexive, this rules out certain views as incoherent (2014: 571–572):

> [W]hy not allow that fundamental goings-on can ground themselves, along lines of the self-justificatory status of basic beliefs on a foundationalist epistemology, or the self-sustaining status of God on many theologies? Given such possibilities, it seems better to suppose that grounding is non-reflexive, with some cases of grounding being reflexive and others not.

In principle, I agree with Wilson's general aims of being as liberal as possible. However, in the particular cases she mentions, it is not even clear what is gained by saying that fundamental goings-on can Ground themselves. For the sake of argument, let us suppose that we grant cases of self-Grounding, and then ask the further question which 'small-g' relation accounts for the self-Grounding of the fundamental goings-on. Now suppose that, in line with Wilson's claim that identity is a 'small-g' grounding relation, somebody claims that the self-Grounding of the fundamental goings-on is due the fact that an identity relation holds between those goings-on and themselves. I take it to be obvious that this does not add anything the friend of asymmetric Grounding would not allow for anyway. After all, nobody would deny that everything is self-identical. Moreover, if the relation in question is identity, I do not see how this helps us making a distinction between cases in which dependence holds and cases in which it does not – since everything whatsoever is self-identical no matter what, no useful distinctions can be made on the basis of such a claim.

A similar story can be told with regard to a version of the realization relation according to which improper subsethood of associated causal powers is sufficient for realization. Of course we could in principle say that every property realizes itself because the causal powers bestowed by a property are an improper subset of the causal powers that very property bestows, and so even fundamental properties can metaphysically depend on themselves in this sense, but again, nothing seems to be gained that a friend of asymmetric dependence cannot claim as well, without taking such a relation to be among the 'small-g' grounding relations.

I do not know which other reflexive relations Wilson has in mind, but unless she tells us and makes a convincing point that shows what is gained from allowing such reflexive cases, I suggest that we stick with an understanding of metaphysical dependence that is less inclusive, but has clear theoretical virtues and fits to our pre-theoretic intuitions. Aside from that, it is worth noting that Wilson does not seem to live up to her own general aim of being as liberal as possible in other respects. Remember the discussion of her view regarding the notion of a physical property. There, she has no scruples to rule out *a priori* certain live panpsychist views, according to which fundamental physical properties are identical to mental properties.

With these considerations, I would like to finish the discussion of Wilson's concerns regarding the formal features that different 'small-g' grounding relations have in common, and that help substantiating the claim that there is at least a generic concept of Grounding, or metaphysical dependence, that unifies the 'small-g' grounding relations. Our investigations have shown that Wilson's claim that the relevant metaphysical dependence relations are neither conjoined by the formal feature of transitivity, nor asymmetry, nor irreflexivity, and thus are not strict partial ordering relations, can be resisted. We have also seen that there is nothing wrong in principle with Wilsons view that "there is a natural and [...] parsimonious view according to which references to 'Grounding', 'a grounding relation', or 'nothing over and above-ness' are schematically and neutrally ranging over specific 'small-g' grounding relations" (2014: 557). This is indeed very close to my claim that if there is no generic relation of Grounding, then there is at least a generic concept of Grounding that non-rigidly picks out the 'small-g' grounding relation depending on the relevant context. The difference between Wilson's view and mine with regard to this point is that she thinks that this can be established even if none of the features typically associated with Grounding are shared among the 'small-g' grounding relations, whereas I think that under the circumstances Wilson envisages, it becomes difficult to track which relations count as 'small-g' grounding relations. Once one has given up most of the potential candidate features that may help distinguishing relations of metaphysical dependence from other relations, there is no basis for a robust generic concept of Grounding.

5.4 Grounding Grounding

In the Grounding literature, a further concern has been discussed by a number of authors (e.g. Sider 2011; Dasgupta 2014; Wilson 2018) that potentially raises problems for a Grounding-based physicalist view. Given the abstract nature of Grounding, the question arises what, if anything, Grounds facts about Grounding. I will address these issues in the following sections, and argue that while some of these issues do not arise if we frame physicalism as I do, we can still learn some important lessons from the answers advocates of Grounding have provided.

5.4.1 What Grounds Grounding?

Shamik Dasgupta (SD) discusses a problem for Grounding-based physicalist accounts, which he attributes to Sider (2011). Others (e.g. Bennett 2011; deRosset 2013; Litland 2017) have likewise discussed the general problem of what Grounds Grounding, but since Dasgupta explicitly discusses the impact of the problem on physicalism, I draw on his particular exposition of the problem.

Suppose you have a Grounding claim of the following form (2014: 560):

(C) The fact that SDs brain is in physical state P grounds the fact that SD is conscious.

Now, according to Dasgupta, the question arises what, if anything, Grounds (C), a fact about Grounding. Since (C) is not a physical fact, because it is in part a fact about consciousness,[153] one might think that physicalism requires that (C) is Grounded in physical facts. However, Dasgupta thinks that it is more plausible that (C) is Grounded in facts about consciousness, and thus in non-physical facts. Thus, if physicalism indeed requires (C) to be Grounded in physical facts, then physicalism turns out to be false. What makes physicalism false in this case does not have anything to do with the particular nature of the properties the facts in question are about, aside from the point that they are non-physical. Rather, what allegedly makes trouble for physicalism is the nature of the Grounding relation. But this is strange. So, the upshot of the argument should not be that physicalism is false, but that the formulation in terms of Grounding is inadequate.

In more structured form, the argument can be put in the form of a *reductio* (2014: 561):

(1) Physicalism is true only if all nonphysical facts "arise out of" physical facts.
(2) Y "arises out of" the Xs if and only if Y is grounded in the Xs.
(3) General considerations about the nature of ground suggest that some nonphysical facts, for example (C), are not grounded in physical facts.
(4) If physicalism is false, this will be revealed – if at all – by first-order considerations about the nature of consciousness or value or what have you, but not by general considerations about the nature of ground itself.

(1), (2) and (3) together are incompatible with (4). Thus, if one wants to maintain (4), one needs to reject at least one of the three other claims. Since (2) is ba-

---

153 On my view of the physical, facts about consciousness might turn out to be physical facts after all if the nature of physical properties turns out to be phenomenal, as the Russellian identity theorist claims. But it is at least not obviously a physical fact, and described here in phenomenal terms, so I will set this option aside for the moment.

sically a version of the claim that metaphysical dependence is to be understood in terms of Grounding, or what I called $MD_{Grounding}$ earlier in this chapter, friends of Grounding cannot deny (2). So what remains is to deny either (1) or (3). Dasgupta suggests that (3) is true, and that we should thus deny (1). I likewise deny (1), but for somewhat different reasons than Dasgupta, and I also cast some doubt on some of the considerations of Dasgupta that support (3).

5.4.2 Grounding Grounding in the natures of the relata

Let me start by discussing Dasgupta's line of reasoning that leads him to accept (3) and deny (1). In order to get a better grip on what might Ground facts like (C), he considers an analogous case that is less controversial than (C). Suppose you have a particular event *e*, a conference. The people at the conference are engaged in certain activities, like giving and listening to talks, asking questions, and so forth. Let us call all the activities typical for conferences the C-activities. Now, Dasgupta considers the following Grounding claim (2014: 566):

> (F) The fact that *e* contains people engaged in C-activities grounds the fact that *e* is a conference.

He then asks what grounds (F), and provides the following answer (2014: 567):

> Why did those activities make the event a *conference* (rather than a football match)? A very natural answer has to do with the kind of thing that conferences are, in general. A conference is the kind of thing that you get when people engage in those activities; that is why, when those particular people in *e* engaged in them, the result was a conference.

According to this view, which Dasgupta calls 'brute connectivism', what Grounds the Grounding facts is something about the Grounded fact, or something about the constituent properties of the Grounded fact. This view comes in several varieties. Some might take it to be a conceptual truth that there is a conference just in case there are people engaged in C-activities. Others might want to frame it in terms of real definition – it is due to the nature, or essence, of conferences, or the nature of the property of *being a conference*, that whenever there are people engaged in C-activities, there is a conference because of that. I will focus on the brute essentialist variant of brute connectivism. This is because it is more broadly applicable than the brute conceptualist variant. After all, in the interesting cases of Grounding, like the mental-physical case, arguably there is no such conceptual connection to be found.

Dasgupta also allows for variants of brute connectivism according to which the Grounding relation obtains due to the nature of the Grounded fact, conjoined with the Ground. On such a view, (F) is Grounded in the conjunction of two facts (2014: 568):

(F.i) Event *e* contains people engaged in C-activities.
(F.ii) It is essential to being a conference that if an event contains people engaged in C-activities then it is a conference.

Dasgupta further contrasts brute connectivism with what he calls 'reductionism', a variant of which is defended by Bennett (2011) and deRosset (2013). According to the reductionist, Grounding facts are Grounded in the Grounds alone, rather than (also) in the nature of the Grounded facts. If this is so, then, given that the Grounds are ultimately physical, no problem arises for the physicalist. But Dasgupta thinks that this view is mistaken, on the basis of the idea that making reference to the nature of the Grounded facts provides a better explanation for the Grounding fact than making reference to the nature of the Grounds (2014: 572):

> For one thing, the proposed explanations sound bad. To see this let us consider one in the flesh. Question 1: Why is this event a conference (rather than, say, a football match)? Answer: Because it contains people engaged in C-activities. So far, so good. Question 2: Why is it that those activities make the event count as a conference (rather than a football match)? The simple reductionist says: Because those people [are] engaged in C-activities. This is not a good explanation. Compare this to brute connectivism. To Question 2, the brute essentialist (for example) answers: Because it lies in the nature of what a conference is that you have a conference whenever people engage in C-activities. It is clear which is the better explanation.

In the case at hand, this seems rather plausible. However, I am not convinced that the line of reasoning can be generalized to all cases. Let us take our beloved case of *being red* and *being crimson* again, and ask: Why is the book on my desk red? Answer: Because it is crimson. But why is it that (the book's) *being red* is Grounded in (the book's) *being crimson?* The reductionist says: Because it is crimson. Again, this is not a very good explanation. However, there is a better explanation in the vicinity that appeals not to the Ground directly, as the reductionist claims, but to the nature of the property that is a constituent of the Ground: Because it lies in the nature of *being crimson* that it is *being red*, not *simpliciter*, but in a specific way. This seems to be a rather plausible answer. What does the brute essentialist say instead? Probably something along the following lines: Because it lies in the nature of what it is for something to be red that it is red whenever it is crimson. That seems much less illuminating, at least to me. Thus, I think that it is more plausible to think that while in some cases, Grounding relations are Grounded in the nature of what is Grounded, there are other cases in which it is the nature of the Grounds that Ground the Grounding relations (or maybe even both).

On the basis of the idea that a Grounding fact like (F) is Grounded in (F.i) and (F.ii), Dasgupta returns to the original Grounding fact (C). What Grounds (C), on his view, is the conjunction of the following facts (2014: 580):

(C.i) SD's brain is in physical state P, and
(C.ii) It is essential to being conscious that if something's brain is in physical state P then it is conscious.

Now, (C.ii) is a fact about consciousness, and thus (most probably) not a physical fact. Thus, (C.ii) is again in tension with premise (1) of the *reductio* argument in the previous section, unless it has itself a physical Ground – or so it might seem, according to Dasgupta. He distinguishes between two different kinds of facts: *autonomous* facts and *substantive* facts (2014: 575–576):

> I suggest that we introduce a distinction between substantive and autonomous facts. Roughly, a fact is *substantive* if it is apt for being grounded, and *autonomous* if not. The idea will be that the general mind-body connections are autonomous, and that physicalism does not require autonomous facts to have a physical ground. [...] I said that a substantive fact is apt for being grounded. By this I mean that the question of what grounds it can legitimately be raised and given a sensible answer, an answer that either states its ground or else states that it has none. In contrast, an autonomous fact is not apt for being grounded in the first place, by which I mean that the question of what grounds it does not legitimately arise.

On the basis of this distinction, Dasgupta claims that (C.ii) is an autonomous fact for which it does not make sense to ask what Grounds it, very much like some have claimed that it does not make sense to ask why it is that an identity relation holds, given that it holds[154] (2014: 579; see also Papineau 1993). This move is important, because it allows Dasgupta to claim that even though (C.ii) is not Grounded in anything, it is not – strictly speaking – a fundamental fact, understood as one that is unGrounded.

Dasgupta thus denies (1), and provides a revised requirement for physicalism. First, he distinguishes between what he calls 'strong physicalism' (SP) and 'weak physicalism' (WP), which he defines as follows (2014: 581):

---

[154] Note that we need to distinguish this indeed nonsensical question from the question why we should think in the first place that the properties picked out by different unrelated concepts are identical, which is perfectly legitimate.

(SP) All nonphysical facts are grounded in physical facts.
(WP) All *substantive* nonphysical facts are grounded in facts that are either physical *or autonomous*.

The first variant, (SP), is obviously too strong and leads to the problem that physicalism, so construed, is false once some facts are Grounded in facts like (C.ii), which are not Grounded in physical facts. This is not the case with the second variant, (WP). Since (C.ii) is an autonomous fact, according to Dasgupta, it does not matter for the truth of physicalism if some fact is Grounded in (C.ii).

However, Dasgupta thinks that (WP) is too weak, because autonomous facts like (C.ii) receive a special role. The problem he sees is not with (C.ii) in particular, but with autonomous facts that are in a particular way unlike (C.ii). And it is this difference that allegedly clashes with physicalist intuitions. The difference Dasgupta has in mind is the following (2014: 583):

> The existence of a Christian God does not fit with the physicalist picture regardless of whether its existence is autonomous; and yet its existence is consistent with WP if its existence is autonomous. [...] What, then, is the difference between (C.ii), on the one hand; and facts about the existence of a Christian God [...] on the other? [...] Well, (C.ii) states a physical sufficient condition for my being conscious, and (according to brute essentialism) underwrites a physical explanation of my being conscious. But the existence of God [...] does neither.

He thus moves on to define a third variant, 'moderate physicalism' (MP), which is based upon (WP) (2014: 584):

(MP) (i) WP is true, and (ii) all autonomous facts help underwrite the kind of grounding explanations required by WP.

Philip Goff argues that Dasgupta's moderate physicalism is too strong (2017: 54):

> The physicalist can surely accept that there are non-physical properties and individuals in other possible worlds, which would seem to require that there are autonomous facts concerning unactualized non-physical natures. And surely such autonomous facts have little to do with grounding explanations in a purely physical world.

As far as I understand it, Goff's problem is that if it is part of the essence of being conscious that if something is in physical state P then it is conscious, as (C.ii) claims, and we also accept that ectoplasmic creatures can be conscious, then it is probably also part of the essence of being conscious that if something is in ectoplasmic state E then it is conscious. Again, this is an autonomous fact,

5.4 Grounding Grounding — 219

but it does not help underwrite Grounding explanations in a physicalist world. This is indeed a problem.

Goff instead suggests a modified version of moderate physicalism, 'reasonably moderate physicalism' (RMP) (2017: 54):

> (RMP) Physicalism is the thesis that all facts that are not narrowly physical facts and that are substantive (i.e., apt to be grounded) are wholly constitutively grounded either in narrowly physical facts alone, or in facts that are autonomous *and* in narrowly physical facts.

In Goff's version, it is not required that all autonomous facts help underwrite Grounding explanations. All that is required is that all substantive facts have some narrowly physical facts as parts of their Grounds, and any non-physical facts that are also part of their Grounds are autonomous facts. Whether or not there are further autonomous facts is irrelevant.

Here, Goff uses the notion of constitutive Grounding. He does not tell us exactly what constitutive Grounding amounts to. He instead offers us an account of a particular form of constitutive Grounding: *Grounding by analysis* (2017: 45):

> Fact X is grounded by analysis in fact Y iff:
> – X is grounded in Y, and
> – Y logically entails what is essentially required for the entities contained in X (including property and kind instances) to be part of reality.

Since the expression 'grounded' appears on both sides of the definition, this is not a reductive analysis of Grounding – Grounding remains a primitive notion on his account. What is specific to the variant of Grounding is the second clause. What this amounts to can be more easily seen using an example. Goff uses the example very much like Dasgupta's conference example. Take the fact F_1 that there is a party, and the fact F_2 that Rod, Jane and Freddy are reveling. Now, the idea is that the fact that there is a party (F_1) is grounded in the fact that Rod, Jane and Freddy are reveling (F_2). Moreover, Goff claims that the fact that Rod, Jane and Freddy are reveling logically entails what is essentially required for there to be a party. What is essentially required for there to be a party? Well, that there are people reveling. Since the fact that Rod, Jane and Freddy are reveling plausibly logically entails that there are people reveling, this establishes that F_1 is grounded by analysis in F_2. This is very similar to how Dasgupta frames things.

Finally, as I have suggested in section 5.2.2, Melnyk's account of physical realization he puts forth in his 2018 very much resembles the accounts of Grounding just discussed, and Goff explicitly points out that his account "is very similar to (and influenced by) Melnyk's view", and that he has "disagreement with him only in details" (2017: 58). This is surprising at first sight, given that Melnyk (2016) argues that Grounding-based accounts of physicalism are to be rejected. The reason is however that he has an understanding of Grounding that is different to how Goff and Dasgupta understand it, which becomes obvious in the following claim (2016: 255):

> "Grounding" [...] is stipulated to refer to a relation that is primitive: when it holds between two items, it doesn't do so in virtue of anything else – it just holds.

What is primitive is the notion of Grounding, not the relation itself. Otherwise, it would not make sense to ask what Grounds Grounding in the first place. Moreover, he does not understand Grounding in the way we have framed things earlier, so when he uses the expression 'Grounding', he is talking about something else than I do (2016: 250):

> The putative grounding relation that my question concerns is not meant to be a generic relation under which such familiar relations as supervenience, realization, and composition fall as species. Rather, it is supposed to be a relation on a par with such relations; and it might be posited either in addition to, or as a replacement for, such relations and their kin.

Given that, it is no wonder that Melnyk thinks that his account is very different to a Grounding-based account. But once we consider Grounding along the lines of the previous sections, the differences become rather minor. So let us have a look at Melnyk's latest account of physical realization (2018: 483–484):

> p physically realizes m [...] [if and][155] only if
> (i) m is a token of a mental state-type M with a certain *higher-order essence:* for a token of M to exist just is for there to exist a token of some or other (lower-order) state-type such that tokens of that (lower-order) state-type play role R_M, the role distinctive of M.
> (ii) p is a token of a physical state-type P such that, (logically) necessarily, given the physical laws and (perhaps) physical circumstances C, tokens of P play role R_M; and
> (iii) the laws of physics hold and physical circumstances C obtain.
> (iv) [T]he token of mental state-type M whose existence is entailed by claims (i) through (iii) = m.

---

155 This inclusion may look suspicious, but it is just due to the way Melnyk introduces his notion by first stating clauses (i) to (iii) as necessary conditions for The physical realization of m by p, and then adding (iv) as a fourth condition separately. Directly afterwards, he states that "p physically realizes m [...] if and only if claims (i) through (iv) are true" (2018: 484).

Much of what Melnyk says here is very similar to what he says in his earlier version discussed in section 5.2.2, but what is important for us here is what he says in clause (i). There, he claims that *M* has what he calls a *higher-order essence*. It is due to the nature of property *M* that it is instantiated if there is an instance of some type or other that plays a certain role. This is pretty close to what Dasgupta and Goff argue for. So Melnyk's account of realization is similar to these Grounding-based accounts, and whether we talk about Grounding or realization in this case becomes mainly a terminological issue. As I said earlier, I tend to think that we should not use the term 'realization' due to the fact that Melnyk's notion of a role is more liberal than many other advocates of realization-based accounts have in mind, as becomes clear in the following statement (2018: 484):

> [C]laim (i) speaks of *playing a role* only for the sake of role-playing's familiarity, and not because realization actually requires role-playing. To capture the full generality of realization, it would be better to speak, more broadly, of *meeting a condition*, where meeting a condition could indeed be playing a causal role, but could also be, e. g., standing in a certain spatio-temporal relation to something, or exhibiting a certain internal structure, or having a certain history, or having a certain bio-function[.]

The way the term 'Grounding' is used in the debate more closely resembles what I have in mind when I talk about a generic relation of metaphysical dependence, but since I explicitly restrict myself to dependence relations between properties, it may be better to altogether avoid talking about either 'Grounding' or 'realization', and to stick with 'metaphysical dependence' instead.

5.4.3 Lessons from the debate about Grounding Grounding

After having primarily looked at the accounts of others in the previous section, in this section, I want to focus on how I see things with regard to the issue of Grounding Grounding, and what lessons we can draw from the points discussed. Let me start with some considerations with regard to an observation made by Wilson (2018: 508):

> That the question 'What Grounds Grounding?' is a spandrel question generated by Grounding's overly abstract 'nature' is supported by the fact that no comparable question arises when the operative understanding of physical dependence is instantiated with one or other small-g relation. [...] If someone tells you that mental states are determinables of physical determinates, there's no temptation to ask, 'But in virtue of what do they stand in the determinable-determinate relation? And so on. In the twenty-four years since Yablo [...] suggested that the physical acceptability, multiple realizability, and distinctive efficacy of mental states is accommodated by taking mental states to be determinables of

physical states, there have been many critical discussions of this view [...]; but not one has raised these sorts of meta-level dependence questions.

Again, there is something right about what Wilson says. However, unlike her, I do not find the question in virtue of what properties stand in a determinable-determinate relation to be unintelligible.[156] Take the red-crimson example again. Of course, if somebody says that the property of *being red* is a determinable of *being crimson*, we have no temptation to ask why this is so. However, this is not because the question is not intelligible. Rather, it is because it is part of the nature of *being crimson* that it is a specific way of *being red*, and we understand that it is due to the nature of these properties that they stand in the determinable-determinate relation. Given that we understand how this works in principle, based on examples like the red-crimson case, we generalize to other cases. For example, once one buys into the claim that mental properties are determinables of more determinate physical properties, one understands that this must be analogous to the red-crimson case, and it is due to the nature of the properties in question that they stand in a determinable-determinate relationship. Given that it might not be fully transparent to us what the nature of certain properties amounts to, we might have a hard time buying into the claim in the first place, and maybe for good reason, but once we do, this is what we should say.

Likewise, we can ask such questions about the other 'small-g' relations. Take the set-subset account of realization, and combine it with the powers-based view of property individuation. We can ask again: Given that two properties stand in a set-subset-realization relation to each other, why is it that the one property stands in this relation to the other? Well, because it is the very nature of the one property to bestow its bearer with a certain set of causal powers, and the very nature of the other property to bestow its bearer with another set of causal powers, and as it turns out, the one is a subset of the other.

Finally, let us have a look at the higher order realization relation. Here again, it is part of the nature of the realized functional property to be instantiated whenever there is an instance of a property that plays a certain role *C*, and it is part of the nature of the realizer property to play role *C*, and it is due to the nature of these properties that they stand in the corresponding realization relation. In all these cases, there is nothing strange with either the question or the answer to it.

---

156 What I would find strange however are questions that more closely resemble the question of Grounding Grounding: "If *A* is a determinable of *B*, what is *A is a determinable of B* a determinable of?" or "If *A* is realized by *B*, what is *A is realized by B* realized by?" – such questions do not seem to make much sense.

Given these considerations, it is very reasonable to think that it is due to the nature of the properties in question that they stand in the 'small-g' relations at hand. Given that we buy into the claim that it is part of the nature of the properties in question to have the features they need to be so related, it does indeed not make much sense to ask why it is that they have that nature. To have that nature is just what it is to be the property in question. Furthermore, as we have seen earlier in this chapter when looking at the dialogue between our fictitious philosophers Amy and Ted, we can understand why a Grounding relation holds, or at least why the concept of Grounding (or metaphysical dependence) is applicable in a particular case, by pointing at a particular 'small-g' grounding relation.

We can see which lesson we can learn from the discussion in the previous section by putting these pieces together. Properties stand in various fine-grained metaphysical dependence relations to each other – those I followed Wilson to call 'small-g' relations even though she had a broader spectrum of relations in mind than I have, since I restrict myself to relations between property types. These relations have certain commonalities that make them fall under a common concept of metaphysical dependence, or even make them species of a common generic and less fine-grained relation of metaphysical dependence. What makes them stand in these metaphysical dependence relations is ultimately the very nature of the properties in question, and it does not make any sense to ask why it is that this is the nature they have, once we buy into the claim that it is the very nature of the properties in question. This final step is what we have learned from the accounts of Dasgupta, Goff, and Melnyk, with the difference pointed to earlier that I do not think that it is always the nature of the dependent property that saves the day.

Given this broader picture, what is the influence on the thesis of physicalism? Like Dasgupta and Goff, I think that even in those cases in which the metaphysical dependence relationship holds (partly) due to the nature of the dependent property, no harm is done to the thesis of physicalism. But since my definition of physicalism is different from theirs, the problem they pose does not arise in the first place. Dasgupta, like Goff, follows most friends of Grounding and takes the relata of Grounding to be facts, and starts out with a definition of physicalism in which he quantifies without further restrictions over all facts. On this basis, all the nasty problems discussed in the previous section arise.

In contrast, according to my definition of physicalism, the relata of the metaphysical dependence relation(s) are property types rather than facts. Moreover, while physicalism is a thesis about properties and relations, it is not a thesis about all properties and relations whatsoever. Rather, it is a thesis about the properties of contingent or causal individuals, as well as relations between such entities. Since property types are not individuals, the relations among these entities need not be physical relations, or metaphysically depend on physical properties and relations, in order for physicalism to be true. Thus, if we understand metaphysical dependence in terms of a relation along the lines of Grounding that takes properties as relata, the issue just does not arise. We do not need to make sure that the metaphysical dependence relations in question are themselves physical, or metaphysically dependent on physical properties and relations. This is not what physicalism is about.

5.5 Summary

In this chapter, I have argued that we should understand the notion of metaphysical dependence required for physicalism along the lines of the orthodox view of Grounding, although with some caveats. Most importantly, I argued that we should restrict ourselves to a notion of dependence that applies to property types, and leave aside broadly metaphysical dependence relations that take objects (such as the mereological parthood relation), sets (such as the set membership relation), or entities from other categories as relata. I have then argued that a generic relation of metaphysical dependence along the lines of Grounding cannot replace what Wilson calls 'small-g' relations, such as different variants of realization and the determinable-determinate relation, but may nevertheless do some useful work if the 'small-g' relations in question are unable to fix the order of priority between their relata. With regard to this, I have pointed out that Wilson's alternative fundamentality-based account turns out to be more problematic than she thinks, which suggests that we are better off with a Grounding-based account. Moreover, I have argued that even if there is no generic *relation* of Grounding, we can still make sense of a generic *concept* of Grounding, or metaphysical dependence, that helps us unifying the 'small-g' grounding relations based on some of their features and enables us to define physicalism. These relations are strict partial ordering relations, they come with the appropriate modal constraints to account for the modal requirements of physicalism, and are such that the natures of the related properties illuminate why the relation holds, and why it is that the dependent property is instantiated in virtue of the dependence base property (or properties) being instantiated. Such a generic concept is all we need to frame minimal physicalism. Finally, I have argued that the problems some have raised for Grounding-based accounts of physicalism with regard to Grounding Grounding relations do not arise if we understand physicalism in the way I do.

6 Conclusion

In this book, I have provided an account of what I call *minimal physicalism*, that is, an account of physicalism that frames the minimal commitments that come with any proper physicalist view. I have argued that we should understand the thesis of physicalism as follows:

(P) Physicalism is true of world *w iff*
  (a) every positive qualitative property had by any individual at *w* that exists contingently or is causal either
    (i) is a narrowly physical property instantiated at *w* or
    (ii) metaphysically depends on narrowly physical properties and relations instantiated at *w* or
    (iii) is a property that is necessarily had by every individual, and
  (b) every positive qualitative relation had by any plurality at *w* that exists contingently or is causal either
    (i) is a narrowly physical relation instantiated at *w* or
    (ii) metaphysically depends on narrowly physical properties and relations instantiated at *w* or
    (iii) is a relation that is necessarily had by every plurality formed of the same number of individuals.

While physicalism so construed attributes being physical only to properties of individuals, it also captures the idea that entities from other categories, such as events and facts, are physical as well, because they inherit their being physical from the properties' being physical. This provides us with an answer to the question what it means that *everything* is physical.

I have further argued that the notion of a narrowly physical property should not be understood directly in terms of a particular physics, or in purely negative terms. Rather, we should fix the reference of the predicate '... is a (narrowly) physical property' by pointing to prototypical example properties from current physics. Any property that is of the same kind as, or shares a particular part of its nature with, these prototype properties is to be considered a narrowly physical property:

F is a physical property *iff* (i) the instantiated properties posited by current physics all have in common a certain non-empty part of their nature *P*, and (ii) *P* is part of the nature of *F*, and (iii) *F* does not have *P* as a part of its nature solely due to being a conjunctive property that has as a conjunct a property that satisfies (ii).

On this account, we do not need to know what the nature of physical properties is in order to fix the reference appropriately. Rather, whether or not a property is physical depends on objective similarity relations between properties. This makes the view very liberal, as it is in principle compatible with a wide variety of views regarding what the nature of physical properties might be. Moreover, the account nicely captures the idea that physicalism is a form of metaphysical monism. This provides us with an answer to the question what it means that everything is *physical*.

Finally, I have argued that the notion of metaphysical dependence that features in the thesis of physicalism cannot be understood in purely modal terms. Likewise, physicalism entails, but is not entailed by, the purely modal statements familiar from the literature based on the notions of supervenience or necessitation that allow advocates of rival views to argue against physicalism using conceivability arguments and the like. These arguments are based on the premise that physicalism entails such modal commitments. The notion of metaphysical dependence that features in the definition of physicalism is more fine-grained than purely modal notions. However, most of the more fine-grained notions discussed in the literature, such as variants of higher-order property realization, set-subset realization, and the determinable-determinate relation, are too fine-grained to serve as the metaphysical dependence relation in question. A notion of metaphysical dependence along the lines of the notion of Grounding, which has gained much attention in the recent years, is able to serve as a unifier of the more fine-grained relations. Whether or not appeal to such a generic notion, or *concept*, of metaphysical dependence goes along with the posit of a generic *relation* of metaphysical dependence of which the other relations are species depends on whether there is work to do for such a relation. If the relevant fine-grained dependence relations cannot fix the order of priority between their relata on their own, there is reason to believe that there is such a generic relation, but I officially want to remain neutral in this regard. If there is a generic relation, the generic concept rigidly picks out this generic relation. If there is no such relation, then the generic concept non-rigidly picks out the more fine-grained relation that obtains in each particular case. In order to frame what relations fall under the generic concept, we can use certain features that the relevant relations have in common. They are strict partial ordering relations, they entail the relevant modal constraints, and are such that the natures of the relata illuminate why the relation in question holds, and why it is that the dependent entity is instantiated in virtue of the instantiation of the base properties. This provides us with an answer to the question what it means that there is *nothing over and above* the physical.

Given these considerations, we now have a better understanding of what minimal physicalism is, and what the commitments are that come with the thesis. Nevertheless, this does not mean that there is no further work to do. For example, it was not an aim of this project to investigate whether minimal physicalism is true or false of the actual world. Moreover, we would of course like to have a more detailed picture of what the nature of physical properties amounts to, even though we do not need to know in order to formulate physicalism properly. Moreover, advocates of particular physicalist theses still need to make plausible which of the particular 'small-g' grounding relations link which domain of properties to the domain of physical properties, and thus make plausible which particular variant of physicalism is the most acceptable with regard to our world. Thus, there is still plenty of work to do. What I have provided here is a general framework these accounts can be based upon, which provides us with an understanding of what it is that these views all have in common and makes them variants of physicalism.

Bibliography

Adams, R. M. (1974): Theories of Actuality. *Noûs* 8 (3), 211–231.
Almotohari, M. and Rochford, D. (2012): Is Direct Reference Theory Incompatible with Physicalism? *The Journal of Philosophy* 108 (5), 255–268.
Alter, T. and Nagasawa, Y. (2012): What Is Russellian Monism? *Journal of Consciousness Studies* 19 (9–10), 67–95.
Armstrong, D. M. (1997): *A World of States of Affairs*. Cambridge: Cambridge University Press.
Bailey, A. M. and Rasmussen, J. (2016): How Valuable Could a Material Object Be? *Journal of the American Philosophical Association* 2 (2), 332–343.
Baysan, U. (2015): Realization Relations in Metaphysics. *Minds & Machines* 25, 247–260.
Bennett, K. (2004): Global Supervenience and Dependence. *Philosophy and Phenomenological Research* 68 (3), 501–529.
Bennett, K. (2011): By Our Bootstraps. *Philosophical Perspectives* 25 (1), 27–41.
Bennett, K. (2017): *Making Things Up*. Oxford: Oxford University Press.
Bickle, J. (2013): Multiple Realizability. In: Zalta, E. N. (ed.): *The Stanford Encyclopedia of Philosophy*, URL: https://plato.stanford.edu/entries/multiple-realizability/.
Black, M. (1952): The Identity of Indiscernibles. *Mind* 61 (242), 153–164.
Bliss, R. (2014): Viciousness and Circles of Ground. *Metaphilosophy* 45 (2), 245–256.
Block, N. (1990): Inverted Earth. *Philosophical Perspectives* 4, 53–79.
Bourget, D. and Chalmers, D. J. (2014): What Do Philosophers Believe? *Philosophical Studies* 170 (3), 465–500.
Braddon-Mitchell, D. and Jackson, F. (2007): *The Philosophy of Mind and Cognition*. Second Edition. Malden, MA: Blackwell.
Broad, C. D. (1925): *Mind and Its Place in Nature*. London: Kegan Paul.
Cameron, R. P. (2016): Do We Need Grounding? *Inquiry* 59 (4), 382–397.
Campbell, K. (1997): Review of: Physicalism. The Philosophical Foundations. *Philosophy and Phenomenological Research* 57 (1), 223–226.
Carnap, R. (1931): Die physikalische Sprache als Universalsprache der Wissenschaft. *Erkenntnis* 2 (1), 432–465.
Carnap, R. (1932): Psychologie in physikalischer Sprache. *Erkenntnis* 3 (1), 107–142.
Chalmers, D. J. (1996): *The Conscious Mind. In Search for a Fundamental Theory*. Oxford: Oxford University Press.
Chalmers, D. J. (2010): *The Character of Consciousness*. Oxford: Oxford University Press.
Chalmers, D. J. (2017 [2015]): Panpsychism and Panprotopsychism. In: Brüntrup, G. and Jaskolla, L. (eds.): *Panpsychism. Contemporary Perspectives*. Oxford: Oxford University Press, 19–47. [Previously published in: Alter, T. and Nagasawa, Y. (eds.) (2015): *Consciousness in the Physical World*. Oxford: Oxford University Press, 246–276]
Chomsky, N. (2005): *Language and Mind*. Third Edition. Cambridge: Cambridge University Press.
Churchland, P. M. (1981): Eliminative Materialism and the Propositional Attitudes. *The Journal of Philosophy* 78 (2), 67–90.
Clapp, L. (2001): Disjunctive Properties: Multiple Realizations. *The Journal of Philosophy* 98 (3), 111–136.

Cohen, I. B. (1999): A Guide to Newton's Principia. In: Newton, I. (1999 [1687]): *The Principia: Mathematical Principles of Natural Philosophy.* Translated and edited by I. B. Cohen and A. Whitman. Berkeley: University of California Press.
Cornman, J. (1971): *Materialism and Sensations.* New Haven, CT: Yale University Press.
Correia, F. (2005): *Existential Dependence and Cognate Notions.* Munich: Philosophia.
Correia, F. (2013): Metaphysical Grounds and Essence. In: Hoeltje, M., Schnieder, B., and Steinberg, A. (eds.): *Varieties of Dependence. Ontological Dependence, Grounding, Supervenience, Response Dependence.* Munich: Philosophia, 271–296.
Correia, F. and Schnieder, B. (2012): Grounding: An Opinionated Introduction. In: Correia, F. and Schnieder, B. (eds.): *Metaphysical Grounding. Understanding the Structure of Reality.* Cambridge: Cambridge University Press, 1–36.
Cowling, S. (2015): Non-qualitative Properties. *Erkenntnis* 80 (2), 275–301.
Cowling, S. (2016): Haecceitism. In: Zalta, E. N. (ed.): *The Stanford Encyclopedia of Philosophy,* URL: https://plato.stanford.edu/entries/haecceitism/.
Crane, T. and Mellor, D. H. (1990): There Is No Question of Physicalism. *Mind* 99 (394), 185–206.
Crook, S. and Gillett, C. (2001): Why Physics Alone Cannot Define the 'Physical': Materialism, and the Formulation of Physicalism. *Canadian Journal of Philosophy* 31 (3), 333–359.
Daly, C. (1998): What Are Physical Properties? *Pacific Philosophical Quarterly* 79, 196–217.
Daly, C. and Liggins, D. (2010): Do Object-Dependent Properties Threaten Physicalism? *The Journal of Philosophy* 107 (11), 610–614.
Dasgupta, S. (2014): The Possibility of Physicalism. *The Journal of Philosophy* 111 (9–10), 557–592.
Davidson, D. (1993): Thinking Causes. In: Heil, J. and Mele, A. (eds.): *Mental Causation.* Oxford: Clarendon Press, 3–17.
Davidson, D. (2001a [1967]): The Logical Form of Action Sentences. In: Davidson, D.: *Essays on Actions and Events.* Oxford: Oxford University Press, 105–122. [Previously published in: Rescher, N. (ed.) (1967): *The Logic of Decision and Action.* Pittsburgh: University of Pittsburgh Press, 81–95]
Davidson, D. (2001b [1969]): The Individuation of Events. In: Davidson, D.: *Essays on Actions and Events.* Oxford: Oxford University Press, 163–180. [Previously published in: Rescher, N. (ed.) (1969): *Essays in Honor of Carl G. Hempel.* Dordrecht: D. Reidel, 216–234]
Davidson, D. (2001c [1970]): Events as Particulars. In: Davidson, D.: *Essays on Actions and Events.* Oxford: Oxford University Press, 181–188. [Previously published in: *Noûs* 4 (1) (1970), 25–32]
Davidson, D. (2001d [1970]): Mental Events. In: Davidson, D.: *Essays on Actions and Events.* Oxford: Oxford University Press, 207–224. [Previously published in: Foster, L. and Swanson, J. W. (eds.) (1970): *Experience and Theory.* Amherst: University of Massachusetts Press, 79–101]
deRosset, L. (2013): Grounding Explanations. *Philosophers' Imprint* 13 (7), 1–26.
Descartes, R. (1982 [1644]): *Principles of Philosophy.* Translated and edited by V. R. Miller and R. P. Miller. Dordrecht: D. Reidel.
Descartes, R. (2008 [1641]): *Meditations on First Philosophy.* Translated and edited by M. Moriarty. Oxford: Oxford University Press.

Díaz-León, E. (2008): We Are Living in a Material World (and I Am a Material Girl). *Teorema* 27 (3), 85–101.
Dorr, C. and Hawthorne, J. (2013): Naturalness. In: Bennett, K. and Zimmerman, D. W. (eds.): *Oxford Studies in Metaphysics Vol. 8*. Oxford: Oxford University Press, 3–77.
Dowell, J. L. (2006a): Formulating the Thesis of Physicalism: An Introduction. *Philosophical Studies* 131 (1), 1–23.
Dowell, J. L. (2006b): The Physical: Empirical, Not Metaphysical. *Philosophical Studies* 131 (1), 25–60.
Ehring, D. (1996): Mental Causation, Determinables and Property Instances. *Noûs* 30 (4), 461–480.
Fine, K. (1994): Essence and Modality. *Philosophical Perspectives* 8, 1–16.
Fine, K. (2001): The Question of Realism. *Philosophers' Imprint* 1 (1), 1–30.
Fine, K. (2010): Some Puzzles of Ground. *Notre Dame Journal of Formal Logic* 51 (1), 97–118.
Fine, K. (2012): Guide to Ground. In: Correia, F. and Schnieder, B. (eds.): *Metaphysical Grounding. Understanding the Structure of Reality*. Cambridge: Cambridge University Press, 37–80.
Fiorese, R. (2016): Stoljar's Dilemma and Three Conceptions of the Physical: A Defence of the Via Negativa. *Erkenntnis* 81 (2), 201–229.
Fodor, J. A. (1974): Special Sciences (Or: The Disunity of Science as a Working Hypothesis). *Synthese* 28, 97–115.
Francescotti, R. (2014): The Problem of Extras and the Contingency of Physicalism. *Philosophical Explorations* 17 (2), 241–254.
Funkhouser, E. (2006): The Determinable-Determinate Relation. *Noûs* 40 (3), 548–569.
Gettier, E. L. (1963): Is Justified True Belief Knowledge? *Analysis* 23 (6), 121–123.
Gillett, C. and Loewer, B. (2001): Preface. In: Gillett, C. and Loewer, B. (eds.): *Physicalism and Its Discontents*. Cambridge: Cambridge University Press, ix–x.
Gillett, C. (2003): The Metaphysics of Realization, Multiple Realizability, and the Special Sciences. *The Journal of Philosophy* 100 (11), 591–603.
Gillett, C. and Witmer, D. G. (2001): A 'Physical' Need: Physicalism and the Via Negativa. *Analysis* 61 (4), 302–309.
Goff, P. (2017): *Consciousness and Fundamental Reality*. Oxford: Oxford University Press.
Goff, P., Seager, W., and Allen-Hermanson, S. (2017): Panpsychism. In: Zalta, E. N. (ed.): *The Stanford Encyclopedia of Philosophy*, URL: https://plato.stanford.edu/entries/panpsychism/.
Haugeland, J. (1982): Weak Supervenience. *American Philosophical Quarterly* 19 (1), 93–103.
Hawthorne, J. P. (2002): Blocking Definitions of Materialism. *Philosophical Studies* 110 (2), 103–113.
Heil, J. (2003): *From an Ontological Point of View*. Oxford: Oxford University Press.
Heil, J. (2011): Powers and the Realization Relation. *The Monist* 94 (1), 34–53.
Hellman, G. (1985): Determination and Logical Truth. *The Journal of Philosophy* 82 (11), 607–616.
Hempel, C. G. (1949): The Logical Analysis of Psychology. In: Feigl, H. and Sellars, W. (eds.): *Readings in Philosophical Analysis*. New York: Appleton Century Crofts, 373–384.
Hempel, C. G. (1969): Reduction: Ontological and Linguistic Facets. In: Morgenbesser, S., Suppes, P., and White, M. (eds.): *Philosophy, Science, and Method: Essays in Honor of Ernest Nagel*. New York: St. Martin's Press, 179–199.

Hempel, C. G. (1980): Comments on Goodman's 'Ways of Worldmaking'. *Synthese* 45 (2), 193–199.
Hobbes, T. (1998 [1651]): *Leviathan*. Edited by J. C. A. Gaskin. Oxford: Oxford University Press.
Hoffmann, V. and Newen, A. (2007): Supervenience of Extrinsic Properties. *Erkenntnis* 67 (2), 305–319.
Hofweber, T. (2005): Supervenience and Object-Dependent Properties. *The Journal of Philosophy* 102 (1), 5–32.
Hofweber, T. (2009): Ambitious, Yet Modest, Metaphysics. In: Chalmers, D. J., Manley, D., and Wasserman, R. (eds.): *Metametaphysics: New Essays on the Foundations of Ontology*. Oxford: Oxford University Press, 260–289.
Horgan, T. (1982): Supervenience and Microphysics. *Pacific Philosophical Quarterly* 63, 29–43.
Horgan, T. (1993): From Supervenience to Superdupervenience: Meeting the Demands of a Material World. *Mind* 102 (408), 555–586.
Howell, R. J. (2013): *Consciousness and the Limits of Objectivity: The Case for Subjective Physicalism*. Oxford: Oxford University Press.
Hüttemann, A. (2004): *What's Wrong with Microphysicalism?* London and New York: Routledge.
Hüttemann, A. and Papineau, D. (2005): Physicalism Decomposed. *Analysis* 65 (1), 33–39.
Jackson, F. (1982): Epiphenomenal Qualia. *The Philosophical Quarterly* 32 (127), 127–136.
Jackson, F. (1994): Armchair Metaphysics. In: Michael, M. and O'Leary-Hawthorne, J. (eds.): *Philosophy in Mind: The Place of Philosophy in the Study of Mind*. Dordrecht: Kluwer, 23–42.
Jackson, F. (1998). *From Metaphysics to Ethics: A Defence of Conceptual Analysis*. Oxford: Oxford University Press.
Jenkins, C. S. (2011): Is Metaphysical Dependence Irreflexive? *The Monist* 94 (2), 267–276.
Johansson, I. (2000): Determinables as Universals. *The Monist* 83 (1), 101–121.
Kim, J. (1966): On the Psycho-Physical Identity Theory. *American Philosophical Quarterly* 3 (3), 227–235.
Kim, J. (1978): Supervenience and Nomological Incommensurables. *American Philosophical Quarterly* 15 (2), 149–156.
Kim, J. (1993a): *Supervenience and Mind. Selected Philosophical Essays*. Cambridge: Cambridge University Press.
Kim, J. (1993b [1973]): Causation, Nomic Subsumption and the Concept of Event. In: Kim, J.: *Supervenience and Mind. Selected Philosophical Essays*. Cambridge: Cambridge University Press, 3–21. [Previously published in: *Journal of Philosophy* 70 (1973), 217–236]
Kim, J. (1993c [1976]): Events as Property Exemplifications. In: Kim, J.: *Supervenience and Mind. Selected Philosophical Essays*. Cambridge: Cambridge University Press, 33–52. [Previously published in: Brand, M. and Walton, D. (eds.) (1976): *Action Theory*. Dordrecht: D. Reidel, 159–177]
Kim, J. (1993d [1984]): Concepts of Supervenience. In: Kim, J.: *Supervenience and Mind. Selected Philosophical Essays*. Cambridge: Cambridge University Press, 53–78. [Previously published in: *Philosophy and Phenomenological Research* 45 (1984), 153–176]

Kim, J. (1993e [1987]): 'Strong' and 'Global' Supervenience Revisited. In: Kim, J.: *Supervenience and Mind. Selected Philosophical Essays.* Cambridge: Cambridge University Press, 79–91. [Previously published in: *Philosophy and Phenomenological Research* 48 (1987), 315–326]

Kim, J. (1993f [1988]): Supervenience for Multiple Domains. In: Kim, J.: *Supervenience and Mind. Selected Philosophical Essays.* Cambridge: Cambridge University Press, 109–130. [Previously published in: *Philosophical Topics* 16 (1988), 129–150]

Kim, J. (1993g [1990]): Supervenience as a Philosophical Concept. In: Kim, J.: *Supervenience and Mind. Selected Philosophical Essays.* Cambridge: Cambridge University Press, 131–160. [Previously published in: *Metaphilosophy* 21 (1990), 1–27]

Kim, J. (1996): *Philosophy of Mind.* Boulder, CO: Westview Press.

Kim, J. (1997): Does the Problem of Mental Causation Generalize? *Proceedings of the Aristotelian Society* 97, 281–297.

Kim, J. (1998): *Mind in a Physical World: An Essay on the Mind-Body Problem and Mental Causation.* Cambridge, MA: MIT Press.

Kim, J. (1999): Making Sense of Emergence. *Philosophical Studies* 95, 3–36.

Kim, J. (2005): *Physicalism, or Something Near Enough.* Princeton, NJ: Princeton University Press.

Kirk, R. (1974): Sentience and Behaviour. *Mind* 83 (329), 43–60.

Kripke, S. A. (1980): *Naming and Necessity.* Cambridge, MA: Harvard University Press.

Leibniz, G. W. (2014 [1714]): Monadology. Translated and edited by L. Strickland. In: Strickland, L.: *Leibniz's Monadology. A New Translation and Guide.* Edinburgh: Edinburgh University Press, 14–33.

Leuenberger, S. (2008): Ceteris Absentibus Physicalism. In: Zimmerman, D. W. (ed.): *Oxford Studies in Metaphysics Vol. 4.* Oxford: Oxford University Press, 145–170.

Leuenberger, S. (2013): Supervenience Among Classes of Relations. In: Hoeltje, M., Schnieder, B., and Steinberg, A. (eds.): *Varieties of Dependence. Ontological Dependence, Grounding, Supervenience, Response Dependence.* Munich: Philosophia, 325–346.

Leuenberger, S. (2014a): Grounding and Necessity. *Inquiry* 57 (2), 151–174.

Leuenberger, S. (2014b): From Grounding to Supervenience? *Erkenntnis* 79 (1), 227–240.

Levine, J. (2001): *Purple Haze. The Puzzle of Consciousness.* Oxford: Oxford University Press.

Levine, J. and Trogdon, K. (2009): The Modal Status of Materialism. *Philosophical Studies* 145, 351–362.

Lewis, D. K. (1983): New Work for a Theory of Universals. *Australasian Journal of Philosophy* 61 (4), 343–377.

Lewis, D. K. (1986): *On the Plurality of Worlds.* Oxford: Blackwell.

Lewis, D. K. (1991): *Parts of Classes.* Oxford: Blackwell.

Litland, J. E. (2013): On Some Counterexamples to the Transitivity of Grounding. *Essays in Philosophy* 14 (1), 19–32.

Litland, J. E. (2018): Could the Grounds's Grounding the Grounded Ground the Grounded? *Analysis* 78 (1), 56–65.

Locke, J. (1975 [1690]): *An Essay Concerning Human Understanding.* Edited by P. H. Nidditch. Oxford: Clarendon Press.

Loewer, B. (2001): From Physics to Physicalism. In: Gillett, C. and Loewer, C. (eds.): *Physicalism and its Discontents.* Cambridge: Cambridge University Press, 37–56.

Loux, M. J. (2006): *Metaphysics. A Contemporary Introduction*. Third Edition. New York and London: Routledge.
Malebranche, N. (2014 [1674–75]): *The Search After Truth*. Translated and edited by T. M. Lennon and P. J. Olscamp. Cambridge: Cambridge University Press.
Markosian, N. (2000): What Are Physical Objects? *Philosophy and Phenomenological Research* 61 (2), 375–395.
Maurin, A. (2013): Tropes. In: Zalta, E. N. (ed.): *The Stanford Encyclopedia of Philosophy*, URL: https://plato.stanford.edu/entries/tropes/.
McLaughlin, B. P. (1992): The Rise and Fall of British Emergentism. In: Beckermann, A., Flohr, H., and Kim, J. (eds.): *Emergence or Reduction? Prospects for Nonreductive Physicalism*. Berlin: De Gruyter, 49–93.
McLaughlin, B. P. (1995): Varieties of Supervenience. In: Savellos, E. E. and Yalçin, Ü. D. (eds.): *Supervenience: New Essays*. Cambridge: Cambridge University Press, 16–59.
McLaughlin, B. P. (1997): Supervenience, Vagueness, and Determination. *Philosophical Perspectives* 11, 209–230.
McLaughlin, B. P. (2007a): On the Limits of A Priori Physicalism. In: McLaughlin, B. P. and Cohen, J. (eds.): *Contemporary Debates in Philosophy of Mind*. Malden, MA: Blackwell, 200–223.
McLaughlin, B. P. (2007b): Mental Causation and Shoemaker-Realization. *Erkenntnis* 67 (2), 149–172.
McLaughlin, B. P. (2009): Review of Sydney Shoemaker's "Physical Realization", *Notre Dame Philosophical Reviews*, URL: https://ndpr.nd.edu/news/physical-realization/ (Accessed: February 14, 2020).
McLaughlin, B. P. and Bennett, K. (2018): Supervenience. In: Zalta, E. N. (ed.): *The Stanford Encyclopedia of Philosophy*, URL: https://plato.stanford.edu/entries/supervenience/.
Melnyk, A. (1997): How to Keep the 'Physical' in Physicalism. *The Journal of Philosophy* 94 (12), 622–637.
Melnyk, A. (2003): *A Physicalist Manifesto. Thoroughly Modern Materialism*. Cambridge: Cambridge University Press.
Melnyk, A. (2006): Realization and the Formulation of Physicalism. *Philosophical Studies* 131 (1), 127–155.
Melnyk, A. (2016): Grounding and the Formulation of Physicalism. In: Aizawa, K. and Gillett, C. (eds.): *Scientific Composition and Metaphysical Ground*. London: Palgrave Macmillan, 249–269.
Melnyk, A. (2018): In Defense of a Realization Formulation of Physicalism. *Topoi* 37 (2), 483–493.
Merricks, T. (2015): *Propositions*. Oxford: Clarendon Press.
Montero, B. (1999): The Body Problem. *Noûs* 33 (2), 183–200.
Montero, B. (2001): Post-Physicalism. *Journal of Consciousness Studies* 8 (2), 61–80.
Montero, B. (2006): Physicalism in an Infinitely Decomposable World. *Erkenntnis* 64, 177–191.
Montero, B. (2013): Must Physicalism Imply the Supervenience of the Mental on the Physical? *The Journal of Philosophy* 110 (2), 93–110.
Montero, B. (2015): Russellian Physicalism. In: Alter, T. and Nagasawa, Y. (eds.): *Consciousness in the Physical World*. Oxford: Oxford University Press, 209–223.

Montero, B. and Papineau, D. (2005): A Defense of the Via Negativa Argument for Physicalism. *Analysis* 65 (3), 233–237.

Moore, G. E. (1942): A Reply to My Critics. In: Schilpp, P. A. (ed.): *The Philosophy of G. E. Moore.* Evanston, IL: Northwestern University, 535–677.

Morgan, C. L. (1923): *Emergent Evolution.* London: Williams and Norgate.

Nagel, T. (1974): What Is It Like to Be a Bat? *The Philosophical Review* 83 (4), 435–450.

Neurath, O. (1931): Physicalism: The Philosophy of the Viennese Circle. *The Monist* 41 (4), 618–623.

Newton, I. (1999 [1687]): *The Principia: Mathematical Principles of Natural Philosophy.* Translated and edited by I. B. Cohen and A. Whitman. Berkeley: University of California Press.

Ney, A. (2008a): Defining Physicalism. *Philosophy Compass* 3 (5), 1033–1048.

Ney, A. (2008b): Physicalism as an Attitude. *Philosophical Studies* 138 (1), 1–15.

Nimtz, C. (2009): 'Physisches' und Multi-Realisierbarkeit, oder: zwei Probleme für den Physikalismus gelöst. In: Michel, J. (ed.): *Physikalismus – Willensfreiheit – Künstliche Intelligenz.* Paderborn: Mentis, 23–42.

Nimtz, C. and Schütte, M. (2003): On Physicalism, Physical Properties, and Panpsychism. *Dialectica* 57 (4), 413–422.

Papineau, D. (1993): Physicalism, Consciousness and the Antipathetic Fallacy. *Australasian Journal of Philosophy* 71 (2), 169–183.

Papineau, D. (2002): *Thinking about Consciousness.* Oxford: Oxford University Press.

Papineau, D. (2008): Must a Physicalist Be a Microphysicalist? In: Hohwy, J. and Kallestrup, J. (eds.): *Being Reduced. New Essays in Reduction, Explanation, and Causation.* Oxford: Oxford University Press, 126–148.

Paull, R. C. and Sider, T. (1992): In Defense of Global Supervenience. *Philosophy and Phenomenological Research* 52 (4), 833–854.

Place, U. T. (1956): Is Consciousness a Brain Process? *British Journal of Psychology* 47 (1), 44–50.

Platinga, A. (1974): *The Nature of Necessity.* Oxford: Oxford University Press.

Platinga, A. (1976): Actualism and Possible Worlds. *Theoria* 42 (1–3), 139–160.

Poland, J. (1994): *Physicalism. The Philosophical Foundations.* Oxford: Clarendon Press.

Polger, T. W. (2004): *Natural Minds.* Cambridge, MA: MIT Press.

Post, J. F. (1987): *The Faces of Existence. An Essay in Nonreductive Metaphysics.* New York: Cornell University Press.

Prelević, D. (2018): Physicalism as a Research Programme. *Grazer Philosophische Studien* 95 (1), 15–33.

Putnam, H. (1975a): The Meaning of 'Meaning'. In: Gunderson, K. (ed.): *Language, Mind, and Knowledge* (Minnesota Studies in the Philosophy of Science 7). Minneapolis, MN: University of Minnesota Press, 131–193.

Putnam, H. (1975b [1967]): The Nature of Mental States. In: Putnam, H.: *Mind, Language and Reality. Philosophical Papers Vol. 2.* Cambridge: Cambridge University Press, 429–440. [Previously published as "Psychological Predicates" in: Capitan, W. H. and Merrill, D. D. (eds.) (1967): *Art, Mind, and Religion.* Pittsburgh: University of Pittsburgh Press, 37–48]

Quine, W. V. (1953 [1948]): On What There Is. In: Quine, W. V.: *From a Logical Point of View.* Cambridge, MA: Harvard University Press, 1–19. [Previously published in: *The Review of Metaphysics* 2 (5) (1948), 21–38.]

Raven, M. J. (2013): Is Ground a Strict Partial Order? *American Philosophical Quarterly* 50 (2), 193–201.
Raven, M. J. (2017): New Work for a Theory of Ground. *Inquiry* 60 (6), 625–655.
Rayo, A. and Uzquiano, G. (2006): Introduction. In: Rayo, A. and Uzquiano, G. (eds.): *Absolute Generality*. Oxford: Oxford University Press, 1–19.
Rosen, G. (2010): Metaphysical Dependence: Grounding and Reduction. In: Hale, B. and Hoffmann, A. (eds.): *Modality. Metaphysics, Logic, and Epistemology*. Oxford: Oxford University Press, 109–136.
Rosen, G. (2015): Real Definition. *Analytic Philosophy* 56 (3), 189–209.
Russell, B. (1927): *The Analysis of Matter*. London: Kegan Paul.
Schaffer, J. (2003): Is There a Fundamental Level? *Noûs* 37 (3), 498–517.
Schaffer, J. (2009): On What Grounds What. In: Chalmers, D. J., Manley, D., and Wasserman, R. (eds.): *Metametaphysics: New Essays on the Foundations of Ontology*. Oxford: Oxford University Press, 347–383.
Schaffer, J. (2010): Monism: The Priority of the Whole. *Philosophical Review* 119 (1), 31–76.
Schaffer, J. (2012): Grounding, Transitivity and Contrastivity. In: Correia, F. and Schnieder, B. (eds.): *Metaphysical Grounding. Understanding the Structure of Reality*. Cambridge: Cambridge University Press, 122–138.
Schaffer, J. (2016): Ground Rules: Lessons from Wilson. In: Aizawa, K. and Gillett, C. (eds.): *Scientific Composition and Metaphysical Ground*. London: Palgrave Macmillan, 143–169.
Seager, W. (2010): Concessionary Dualism and Physicalism. *Royal Institute of Philosophy Supplement* 67, 217–237.
Shagrir, O. (2002): Global Supervenience, Coincident Entities, and Anti-Individualism. *Philosophical Studies* 109 (2), 171–196.
Shoemaker, S. (1980): Causality and Properties. In: van Inwagen, P. (ed.): *Time and Cause*. Dordrecht: D. Reidel, 109–135.
Shoemaker, S. (1982): The Inverted Spectrum. *The Journal of Philosophy* 79 (7), 357–381.
Shoemaker, S. (1998): Causal and Metaphysical Necessity. *Pacific Philosophical Quarterly* 79, 59–77.
Shoemaker, S. (2001): Realization and Mental Causation. In: Gillett, C. and Loewer, B. (eds.): *Physicalism and its Discontents*. Cambridge: Cambridge University Press, 74–98.
Shoemaker, S. (2007): *Physical Realization*. Oxford: Oxford University Press.
Shoemaker, S., (2011): Realization, Powers, and Property Identity. *The Monist* 94 (1), 3–18.
Sider, T. (1999): Global Supervenience and Identity Across Times and Worlds. *Philosophy and Phenomenological Research* 59 (4), 913–937.
Sider, T. (2011): *Writing the Book of the World*. Oxford: Oxford University Press.
Skiles, A. (2015). Against Grounding Necessitarianism. *Erkenntnis* 80 (4), 717–751.
Smart, J. J. C. (1959): Sensations and Brain Processes. *Philosophical Review* 68, 141–156.
Smith, A. D. (1993): Non-reductive Physicalism? In: Robinson, H. (ed.): *Objections to Physicalism*. Oxford: Clarendon Press, 225–250.
Spurrett, D. and Papineau, D. (1999): A Note on the Completeness of 'Physics'. *Analysis* 59 (1), 25–29.
Stalnaker, R. (1996): Varieties of Supervenience. *Philosophical Perspectives* 10, 221–242.
Stephan, A. (1999): *Emergenz: Von der Unvorhersagbarkeit zur Selbstorganisation*. Paderborn: Mentis.

Stoljar, D. (2008): Distinctions in Distinction. In: Hohwy, J. and Kallestrup, J. (eds.): *Being Reduced. New Essays in Reduction, Explanation, and Causation.* Oxford: Oxford University Press, 263–279.
Stoljar, D. (2010): *Physicalism.* London and New York: Routledge.
Stoljar, D. (2015): Physicalism. In: Zalta, E. N. (ed.): *The Stanford Encyclopedia of Philosophy*, URL: https://plato.stanford.edu/entries/physicalism/.
Strawson, G. (2006): Realistic Monism: Why Physicalism Entails Panpsychism. In: Freeman, A. (ed.): *Consciousness and Its Place in Nature.* Exeter: Imprint Academic, 3–31.
Strawson, G. (2008 [2003]): Real Materialism. In: Strawson, G.: *Real Materialism and other Essays.* Oxford: Oxford University Press, 19–51. [Previously published in: Antony, L. and Hornstein, N. (eds.) (2003): *Chomsky and His Critics.* Oxford: Blackwell, 49–88]
Thompson, N. (2016): Metaphysical Interdependence. In: Jago, M. (ed.): *Reality Making.* Oxford: Oxford University Press, 38–56.
Tiehen, J. (2016): Physicalism Requires Functionalism: A New Formulation and Defense of the Via Negativa. *Philosophy and Phenomenological Research* 93 (1), 3–24.
van Cleve, J. (1990): Mind-Dust or Magic? Panpsychism Versus Emergence. *Philosophical Perspectives* 4, 215–226.
van Fraassen, B. (2002): *The Empirical Stance.* New Haven, CT: Yale University Press.
Vicente, A. (2011): Current Physics and 'the Physical'. *British Journal for the Philosophy of Science* 62 (2), 393–416.
Walter, S. (2006): Determinables, Determinates, and Causal Relevance. *Canadian Journal of Philosophy* 37 (2), 217–243.
Walter, S. (2011): Zombies, Dualismus und Physikalismus. *Zeitschrift für philosophische Forschung* 65 (2), 241–254.
Wilkes, K. V. (1978): *Physicalism.* London and New York: Routledge.
Williamson, T. (2003): Everything. *Philosophical Perspectives* 17 (1), 415–465.
Wilson, J. M. (1999): How Superduper Does a Physicalist Supervenience Need to Be? *Philosophical Quarterly* 49 (194), 33–52.
Wilson, J. M. (2002): Causal Powers, Forces, and Superdupervenience. *Grazer Philosophische Studien* 63 (1), 53–78.
Wilson, J. M. (2005): Supervenience-based Formulations of Physicalism. *Noûs* 39 (3), 426–459.
Wilson, J. M. (2006): On Characterizing the Physical. *Philosophical Studies* 131 (1), 61–99.
Wilson, J. M. (2009): Determination, Realization and Mental Causation. *Philosophical Studies* 145 (1), 149–169.
Wilson, J. M. (2010a): What is Hume's Dictum, and Why Believe It? *Philosophy and Phenomenological Research* 80 (3), 595–637.
Wilson, J. M. (2010b): Non-reductive Physicalism and Degrees of Freedom. *British Journal of Philosophy of Science* 61, 279–311.
Wilson, J. M. (2012): Fundamental Determinables. *Philosophers' Imprint* 12 (4), 1–17.
Wilson, J. M. (2013): A Determinable-Based Account of Metaphysical Indeterminacy. *Inquiry* 56 (4), 359–385.
Wilson, J. M. (2014): No Work for a Theory of Grounding. *Inquiry* 57 (5–6), 535–579.
Wilson, J. M. (2015): Metaphysical Emergence: Weak and Strong. In: Bigaj, T. and Wüthrich, C. (eds.): *Metaphysics in Contemporary Physics.* Leiden: Brill, 345–402.

Wilson, J. M. (2016): The Unity and Priority Arguments for Grounding. In: Aizawa, K. and Gillett, C. (eds.): *Scientific Composition and Metaphysical Ground*. London: Palgrave Macmillan, 171–204.

Wilson, J. M. (2017): Determinables and Determinates. In: Zalta, E. N. (ed.): *The Stanford Encyclopedia of Philosophy*, URL: https://plato.stanford.edu/entries/ determinate-determinables/.

Wilson, J. M. (2018): Grounding-Based Formulations of Physicalism. *Topoi* 37 (2), 495–512.

Witmer, D. G. (1999): Supervenience Physicalism and the Problem of Extras. *Southern Journal of Philosophy* 37 (2), 315–331.

Yablo, S. (1992): Mental Causation. *Philosophical Review* 101 (2), 245–280.

Index of names

Adams, Robert Merrihew 40
Almotohari, Mahrad 37
Alter, Torin 50
Armstrong, David M. 183

Bailey, Andrew 23
Baysan, Umut 148, 172
Bennett, Karen 8, 25, 116, 123–125, 135, 144f., 147, 165, 207, 209, 214, 216
Berker, Selim 195
Bickle, John 24
Black, Max 34, 93
Bliss, Ricki 145, 169
Block, Ned 111
Bolzano, Bernard 170
Bourget, David 1
Braddon-Mitchell, David 102
Broad, Charlie Dunbar 149f., 154

Cameron, Ross P. 194f., 197, 200
Campbell, Keith 89
Carnap, Rudolf 2, 9–11, 49, 82, 101, 170
Chalmers, David J. 1, 4, 6, 21f., 29, 35f., 38–40, 47f., 50, 68, 71f., 75, 85f., 89f., 93, 110f., 117f., 131, 133, 139–141, 148, 162
Chomsky, Noam 5, 66
Churchland, Paul M. 23
Clapp, Lenny 184
Cohen, Bernard 210
Cornman, James W. 75
Correia, Fabrice 7, 163, 165f., 168, 170
Cowling, Sam 33–36
Crane, Tim 55
Crook, Seth 5, 51, 53, 61f., 68, 72

Daly, Chris 37, 50, 55
Dasgupta, Shamik 7f., 13, 163, 213–221, 223
Davidson, Donald 15–17, 115f.
deRosset, Louis 214, 216
Descartes, René 2, 10–13, 45, 66, 71f., 92
Díaz-León, Esa 6, 102, 104
Dorr, Cian 135
Dowell, Janice 5, 46f., 54f., 64, 68–73, 87

Ehring, Douglas 184

Fine, Kit 7, 25, 95, 146, 158, 166–170, 188–192
Fiorese, Raphaël 78f., 81, 84
Fodor, Jerry 24
Francescotti, Robert 129
Funkhouser, Eric 184

Gettier, Edmund 44
Gillett, Carl 1, 5, 24, 51, 53, 61f., 68, 72, 74, 78
Goff, Philip 8, 50, 86, 164, 218–221, 223
Goodman, Nelson 51

Haugeland, John 119
Hawthorne, John 135, 138f., 141–143
Heil, John 93, 153
Hellman, Geoffrey 46, 51
Hempel, Carl Gustav 4, 11, 46, 51
Hobbes, Thomas 2, 9–12
Hoffmann(-Kolss), Vera 119
Hofweber, Thomas 4, 36–38, 169, 210
Horgan, Terence 7, 111, 119, 121, 130, 142, 152, 154
Howell, Robert 5, 91–98, 100f., 105f.
Hüttemann, Andreas 28

Jackson, Frank 4–6, 47, 99f., 102, 118, 128, 131, 133–140, 162
Jenkins, Carrie S. 169
Johansson, Ingvar 183

Kim, Jaegwon 6, 16, 18f., 28, 89, 116f., 119–122, 124f., 136f., 143, 145f., 149f., 153, 184
Kirk, Robert 110
Kripke, Saul 6, 23, 33, 65, 75, 103, 112f., 150

Leibniz, Gottfried Wilhelm 71
Leuenberger, Stephan 111, 121, 125, 130, 141, 163, 169

Index of names

Levine, Joseph   111, 163
Lewis, David K.   5f., 29, 40, 49, 68, 84f., 88, 111, 130f., 134–140, 162
Liggins, David   37
Litland, Jon Erling   169, 208, 214
Locke, John   13f.
Loewer, Barry   1, 163
Loux, Michael J.   16f.

Malebranche, Nicolas   71
Markosian, Ned   15
Maurin, Anna-Sofia   16
McLaughlin, Brian P.   6, 36, 114, 116f., 122f., 125, 147, 149, 176f.
Mellor, David Hugh   55
Melnyk, Andrew   3f., 7f., 14, 19–21, 23, 46, 52, 56–63, 149, 152, 163f., 169, 173–177, 179, 219–221, 223
Merricks, Trenton   19
Montero, Barbara   5, 22, 30, 57, 59, 61, 73–75, 78–81, 84, 86, 89f., 111, 198
Moore, George Edward   57
Morgan, C. Lloyd   149

Nagasawa, Yujin   50
Nagel, Thomas   110
Neurath, Otto   2, 9–11, 49, 51, 83, 101
Newen, Albert   119
Newton, Isaac   210
Ney, Alyssa   46, 57
Nimtz, Christian   6, 85, 91, 102f.

Papineau, David   5, 28f., 73f., 217
Paull, Cranston   137
Place, Ullin T.   6, 74
Platinga, Alvin   40
Poland, Jeffrey   5, 46, 49, 56, 64–68, 70–73, 89
Polger, Thomas W.   24, 174
Post, John F.   56
Prelević, Duško   57
Putnam, Hilary   6, 24, 103, 118

Quine, Willard van Orman   16, 170

Rasmussen, Joshua   23
Raven, Michael J.   168f., 195f., 208

Rayo, Agustín   10
Rochford, Damien   37
Rosen, Gideon   25, 168, 189
Russell, Bertrand   50, 85

Schaffer, Jonathan   4, 6f., 25–27, 29, 50, 79, 163, 166–170, 186f., 189, 192, 197f., 200–202, 205–208
Schnieder, Benjamin   163, 165f., 168, 170
Schütte, Michael   6, 85, 91, 102f.
Seager, William   86, 111
Shagrir, Oron   123f.
Shoemaker, Sydney   8, 111, 143, 151, 154, 163, 176–178, 184
Sider, Ted   6, 123, 137, 204, 213f.
Skiles, Alexander   169
Smart, John Jamieson Carswell   6
Smith, Arthur David   74–78, 83
Spurrett, David   5, 73
Stalnaker, Robert   119, 123, 137
Stephan, Achim   149
Stoljar, Daniel   5, 7, 10f., 15, 22, 24–27, 29, 39f., 52, 54f., 75f., 84f., 87f., 91, 100, 113f., 130, 137, 141, 148f., 152–159, 161f., 164
Strawson, Galen   6, 50, 103

Thompson, Naomi   209f.
Tiehen, Justin   78
Trogdon, Kelly   111

Uzquiano, Gabriel   10

van Cleve, James   150f.
van Fraassen, Bas   57
Vicente, Agustín   56

Walter, Sven   111, 184
Wilkes, Kathleen Vaughan   45f., 51
Williamson, Timothy   10
Wilson, Jessica   4f., 7f., 19, 25, 52, 62f., 68, 76, 79, 86–90, 143f., 149–151, 155, 157, 159, 163f., 169–171, 176, 179f., 183–209, 211–213, 221–224
Witmer, D. Gene   74, 78, 128f., 132f.

Yablo, Stephen   8, 142, 148, 181, 183f., 221

Index of subjects

absolute fundamentality 26–29, 47, 197, 201
abstract entity 20, 40f.
actual physical theory 5
actual world physics 5, 49, 87
alien physical property 5, 49f., 63, 72, 88, 98, 105
a posteriori accounts of the physical 51, 68, 86
a posteriori physicalism 36, 51, 110
a priori accounts of the physical 51, 73
a priori physicalism 110
attitude 46, 57f.
attitudinal view 57
autonomous fact 217–219

'Big-G' Grounding relation 163, 171, 188
blocker 130, 138–141
broadly physical property 22f., 31
building relation 8, 144, 207, 209

Cartesian soul 13, 15, 47, 98
categorical base 22, 50, 92–94, 96, 104
categoricalism 92f., 96
causal argument 73
causal exclusion problem 184
causal power 8, 135, 143, 149, 151, 159, 173, 176–179, 192, 197, 212, 222
causal relation 16, 21, 165, 205
causation 21, 89, 166, 168, 187, 205
ceteris absentibus physicalism 111, 141
chain of necessitation 81f.
chain of dependence 81
coarse-grained 7, 168, 185
complete physics 54, 70
conceivability argument 4, 47f., 110, 114, 117, 139, 141, 226
conjunctive property 31, 79–81, 104f., 109, 148, 176, 182, 201, 226
constitutive property 13, 18f.
co-variation 7
currentism 51f., 56, 63, 72, 83, 87
current physics 4, 6, 46f., 51–55, 60–63, 87f., 102–107, 225

deity 20f., 33, 64
dependence base 4, 8, 35, 42, 120, 126, 145, 168, 224
determinable-determinate relation 8, 28f., 171, 180–184, 197, 204, 208, 221f., 224, 226
direction of priority 50, 100, 107, 193f., 197f., 202
direct reference theory 36
disposition 22, 50, 85f., 92–99, 104, 165
dispositionalism 92
distinctness 7, 100, 148, 155–161
distinctness in essence 157, 159
domain-specific physicalism 5, 83, 96, 110, 115
downward incorporation 5, 67f., 70–73
duplicate *simpliciter* 84, 128, 131, 136f.

early modern materialism 2, 10–14, 43, 49, 73
ectoplasm 13, 15, 38f., 47, 127, 134, 140f.
ectoplasmic property 48f., 82, 105, 118f., 129f., 133f.
ectoplasmism 48, 82, 86
eliminativism 23f., 203f.
emergentism 7, 149f., 152f., 187, 189, 192, 196
epiphenomenal ectoplasm problem 130
epiphenomenalism 180
essence 9, 12, 33, 39, 95, 146, 157–160, 165, 173, 176, 178, 215, 218, 220f.
event 3, 10, 15–19, 21, 43, 69, 71, 78, 115, 123, 149, 215f., 225
explanatory 7, 62, 69f., 152–154, 168f., 171, 188, 206
extendedness 13f., 16, 51, 73f., 102
externalism about mental content 119
extrinsic property 119f., 130

final physics 54
fine-grained 7f., 162f., 184–186, 204, 211, 223, 226
first-order property 14, 22

Index of subjects

fixing the reference   5, 65, 99f., 102, 106f., 225f.
folk psychology   23, 58, 60
formal features of Grounding   167
full dependence   27, 30f.
full Grounding   187, 189–192, 196, 201, 208f.
functionalism   14, 143
functional property   24, 27f., 93, 118, 159f., 173–176, 197, 222
fundamental individual   27
fundamentality   4, 8, 22, 24–29, 79–81, 84, 135, 192–198, 201f., 224
fundamental level   4, 25–27, 79, 197–202
fundamental particle   34, 48, 53, 66
future physics   4, 6, 46, 49, 51f., 54f., 73, 86f.
futurism   51, 54, 63f., 69, 83, 87, 106

global necessitation   114, 124
global supervenience   121–129, 132, 134, 136, 138, 147
Grounding   7–10, 25, 125, 144, 153, 163–172, 184–197, 200–224, 226f.

haecceities   33–35, 38f.
haecceitism   36, 93
haecceitistic property   4, 33–36, 38, 128
Hempel's dilemma   5f., 46, 51, 55f., 64, 99
higher-order essence   220f.
higher-order property   8, 14, 143, 159f., 173f., 197
higher-order property realization   172–174, 226
historical ancestors of physicalism   43, 51
Hume's Dictum   7, 155–161

idealism   2, 48, 60, 62, 89–91, 96f., 161
ideal physics   54, 70, 88
identity relation   42, 77, 83, 91, 112f., 121, 144f., 154, 172, 181, 212, 217
identity theory   5, 16, 74, 78, 100, 154
immaterial soul   5, 45, 53, 55–57, 66, 71, 129f.
indiscernibility   122, 124, 129, 136
individual necessitation   114, 126, 181
individual supervenience   116, 119–121, 126

infinite descent   29f., 198
intentional property   74, 92
intermediate global property supervenience   123f.
intrinsic property   119

knowledge argument   4, 47

Laplace's demon   54
law   10, 45, 50, 52, 55, 60, 70–72, 94–96, 98, 117f., 131, 135, 141, 148, 151f., 154f., 176
law of nature   50, 70f., 92–95, 97, 117, 148
law of physics   117, 148, 220
lone ammonium molecule problem   137

material substance   12f., 73
matter   13f., 85, 210
mental domain   2, 8, 61, 118, 142
mental predicate   5, 64, 67f., 70–72, 87
mental substance   12
merely physical property   75–77
merely physical state of affairs   75–77
mereological distinctness   157
mereological hierarchy   14, 26f., 29, 50, 79, 84, 100, 107, 200
mereological level   26, 28f., 84, 198, 200
mereologically fundamental   27, 84, 88, 90, 197, 199
mereological supervenience   121
mereology   26, 199
metaphysical necessity   93, 117–119, 148–151, 154f.
metaphysical priority   50, 61, 166, 210f.
metaphysical structure   7
method of cases   45
micro-level   50
microphysicalism   28f., 37, 50
minimal physical duplicate   131f., 136, 138
minimal physicalism   2, 9, 37, 48, 50, 97, 149f., 224f., 227
modal co-variation   7
modal distinctness   156f., 161
monism   15, 48, 89–91, 95–98, 105f., 115, 152, 226
multiple domain supervenience   120f., 150
multiple Groundability   167f.

multiple realizability   6, 24, 93, 118, 129, 160, 167, 178, 184, 221

narrowly physical property   22–24, 27, 30–32, 35, 39–42, 44, 102, 108, 114, 225
naturalistic dualism   71
natural-kind term   6, 103
natural property   134–136, 138 f.
necessitation dualism   148 f., 151 f., 154–161, 187
negative predicate   56
negative property   38 f., 133, 140
neo-Cartesian   5, 91 f., 106
neutral monism   89, 91
NFM constraint   91
nominalism   11
nomological necessity   117 f., 150
non-mental   5, 67, 74 f., 77–79, 81 f.
non-rigid designator   112, 167, 204, 213, 226
normative property   21
number   3, 19–22, 33, 164, 198
numerical distinctness   155 f., 160

oath   46, 57
object-based reference-fixing account   99, 102
object-dependent property   36 f.
Occam's razor   62, 159
order of priority   8, 50, 107, 146, 193, 197 f., 200 f., 203, 211, 224, 226
ordinary object   13–16, 99

panpsychism   5, 48, 68, 77, 84–86, 88, 90 f., 97, 100–102, 212
panpsychist identity theory   85
partial dependence   27, 30 f., 191 f.
partial Grounding   187–192, 201, 208 f.
part-whole relation   26, 119, 121, 171 f., 193, 197, 224
phenomenal property   21, 50, 66, 74–78, 86, 89 f., 93–98, 106 f., 109 f., 130, 162, 174, 180, 214
physical duplicate world   118, 130, 134, 138, 141, 162
physical entity   3, 5, 14, 20, 23, 60, 71, 199 f.

physicalism$_{Chalmers}$ 140, 162
physicalism$_{Jackson}$ 136–138
physicalism$_{Lewis}$ 136–138
physicalism *simpliciter*   2, 49, 83, 110
physical law   71, 117 f., 131, 175, 179, 220
physical level   37, 199 f.
physical object   5, 14 f., 18, 36 f., 52, 73, 84, 99, 102
physical predicate   17, 56, 67 f., 70 f., 73
physical theory   5, 14, 45 f., 51–55, 60–62, 66 f., 69 f., 72, 87, 102
physics   2, 4, 6, 11, 14 f., 23, 46–57, 60–69, 71–73, 83, 85–88, 99–101, 104–106, 179, 199 f., 225
pluralism   3, 7, 26 f., 31, 48, 61, 70, 97, 103, 106, 110 f., 118, 128, 193
plurality   40–42, 44, 108 f., 114 f., 121, 140, 160, 172, 183, 205, 225
positive predicate   56
positive property   38 f., 130, 132 f., 139–142
powers-based realization   176
predicate of physics   4, 14, 52, 54, 56
primitive   7, 25, 34, 40, 79, 135, 149, 159, 161, 165, 169–171, 184, 189–193, 195 f., 200 f., 219 f.
priority argument   193, 204 f.
priority monism   26, 28 f., 50, 193, 200
problem of blockers   138, 140
problem of extras   129, 138
progress of physics   48, 53, 63, 72, 105
property-based reference fixing account   101, 103, 106 f.
property dualism   3, 21, 90, 93, 106, 115, 128
property-preserving isomorphism   122 f., 129, 132, 134
proposition   10, 17, 19, 40, 56 f., 76, 111–113, 139, 166, 175, 179, 188, 209 f.
purely physical property   75–78
purely physical state of affairs   75–77

qualitatively   34 f., 93, 128
qualitative property   34–38, 40, 42, 44, 108, 111, 127, 225
quantum field theory   52 f., 62

radical eliminativist physicalism   23 f.
realism   3, 11, 13, 40, 57, 59, 203 f.
realization   8, 24, 149, 163 f., 171–180, 183 f., 197, 204, 212, 219–222, 224, 226
realization physicalism   58–60, 62
regularity   71
relative fundamentality   26–30, 69, 144, 146, 199–202, 211
rigid designator   112, 167, 204, 226
Russellian identity theory   85 f., 89, 96, 106
Russellian monism   50, 89 f.

sameness-in-kind   6, 102, 105
same-subject necessitation   76
second-order property   14 f.
semantic physicalism   11, 49, 51, 101
set-subset relation   8, 159, 176, 178
'small-g' grounding relation   8 f., 163, 170–172, 185–188, 192–194, 197 f., 200, 202–209, 211–213, 221–224, 227
solidity   13 f., 16, 51, 73 f.
space-time   37, 64–66, 69, 114, 121
spatio-temporal distinctness   157
spatio-temporal power   96, 98
special science   11, 24, 49, 73, 199, 206
special science property   23, 49, 72, 83 f., 86, 88, 96, 100, 106, 200
spirit of physicalism   60 f., 89
SR attitude   58–60, 63
stipulative definition   44
strict partial ordering relation   8, 167, 182, 207, 213, 224, 226
strong global property supervenience   123
strong individual supervenience   116 f., 120–122, 125
strongly emergent property   159, 192

substance   10–14, 18, 71, 73, 106, 115, 165
substance dualism   3, 21, 55, 71, 115
substantive fact   217, 219
superdupervenience   7, 142, 152–154

theoretical integration   68, 70
theory of general relativity   52 f.
thick property   95
thin property   94–96, 98
token identity   171 f.
token physicalism   14 f., 21, 26
topic-neutral term   49, 56
trans-world disposition set (TDS)   94–96, 98
trans-world identity   39 f.
trope   10, 16, 20, 135, 165
truth-aptness   46, 57, 107
type identity   23, 74, 142, 156, 174, 177, 204, 211
type identity physicalism   23 f.
type identity theory   6, 74, 119
type physicalism   21 f., 149

unity argument   203–205
universal   15 f., 135

via negativa   5, 73–75, 77–79, 81–83, 85–88, 91, 97

weak global property supervenience   123
weak individual supervenience   116 f.
weakly emergent property   159
(w→w*)-property-preserving isomorphism   132

zombie   48, 110, 117, 123, 137–139, 141
zombie argument   4, 89, 110

www.ingramcontent.com/pod-product-compliance
Lightning Source LLC
Chambersburg PA
CBHW031425150426
43191CB00006B/395